Ex Libris

Elizabeth Eineigl

ALL THE WORLD'S ANIMALS
INSECTS

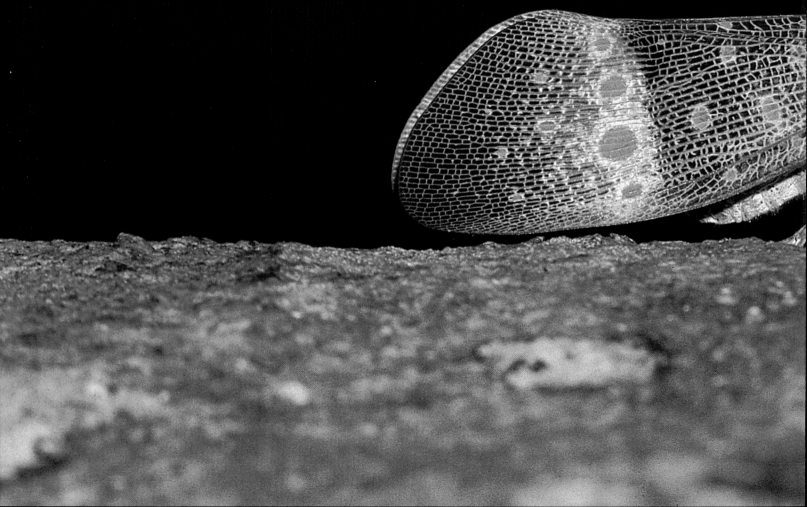

ALL THE WORLD'S ANIMALS
INSECTS

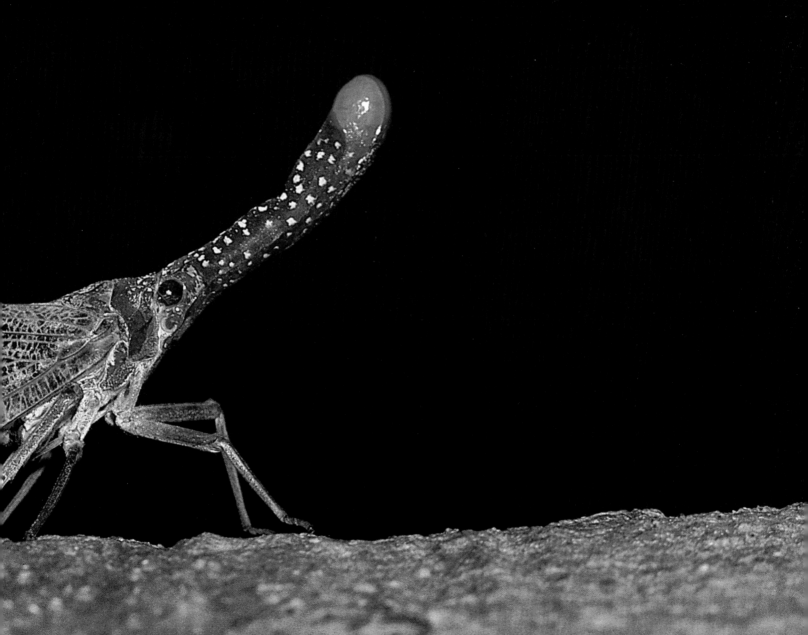

TORSTAR BOOKS
New York · Toronto

CONTRIBUTORS

ABa Anne Baker BSc
British Museum (Natural History)
London, England

MCB Martin C. Birch MA DPhil
Department of Zoology
University of Oxford
England

NMC N. Mark Collins MA DIC PhD
IUCN Monitoring Centre
Cambridge
England

WRD W. R. Dolling BSc ARCS
British Museum (Natural History)
London, England

PDH Paul D. Hillyard BSc
British Museum (Natural History)
London, England

MAJ Mark A. Jervis BSc PhD
Department of Zoology
University of Cardiff
Wales

CHCL Christopher H. C. Lyal BSc PhD
British Museum (Natural History)
London, England

LJL Linda J. Losito BSc
Oxford
England

AWRM Angus W. R. McCrae PhD
Oxford
England

GCM George C. McGavin BSc DIC PhD
Hope Entomological Collections
University of Oxford
England

PLM Peter L. Miller PhD
Department of Zoology
University of Oxford
England

LAM Laurence A. Mound DSc
British Museum (Natural History)
London, England

CO'T Christopher O'Toole FRES
Hope Entomological Collections
University of Oxford
England

AJP A. John Pantin MA DPhil
Royal Holloway College
University of London
Surrey, England

JMP Jennifer M. Palmer
British Museum (Natural History)
London, England

KP Keith Porter BSc DPhil
Oxford Polytechnic
England

MJS Malcolm J. Scoble BSc PhD
British Museum (Natural History)
London, England

SSi Stephen Simpson BSc PhD
Department of Zoology
University of Oxford
England

BWi Bernice Williams BSc DPhil FRES MIBiol
Medical Entomology Centre
University of Cambridge
England

PGW Patricia G. Willmer BA MA PhD
Department of Zoology
University of Oxford
England

MRW M. R. Wilson BSc PhD
Commonwealth Institute of Entomology
c/o British Museum (Natural History)
London, England

ALL THE WORLD'S ANIMALS
INSECTS

TORSTAR BOOKS
300 E. 42nd Street,
New York, NY 10017

Project Editor: Graham Bateman
Editor: Bill MacKeith
Art Editor: Chris Munday
Art Assistant: Wayne Ford
Picture Research: Alison Renney
Production: Clive Sparling
Design: Niki Overy
Index: Philip Gardner

Originally planned and produced by:
Equinox (Oxford) Ltd
Littlegate House
St Ebbe's Street
Oxford OX1 1SQ

Editor
Christopher O'Toole
Hope Entomological Collections
University of Oxford
England

Advisory Editors
Professor Tom Eisner
Cornell University
Ithaca, New York
USA

Dr Borge Petersen
University of Copenhagen
Denmark

Artwork Panels
Richard Lewington

On the cover: Katydid nymph
Page 1: Flower mantis
Pages 2–3: Lantern fly
Pages 4–5: Monarch butterflies
Pages 6–7: Micropteryx calthella
Pages 8–9: Moth caterpillar

Library of Congress Cataloging in Publication Data

Main entry under title:

Insects.

 (All the world's animals)
 Bibliography: p.
 Includes index.
 I. Insects. I. Series.
QL467.I57 1987 595.7 86-11331

ISBN 0-920269-72-9 (Series: All the World's Animals)
ISBN 0-920269-82-6 (Insects)

In conjunction with *All the World's Animals* Torstar Books offers a 12-inch raised relief world globe.
 For more information write to:
 Torstar Books
 300 E. 42nd Street
 New York, NY 10017

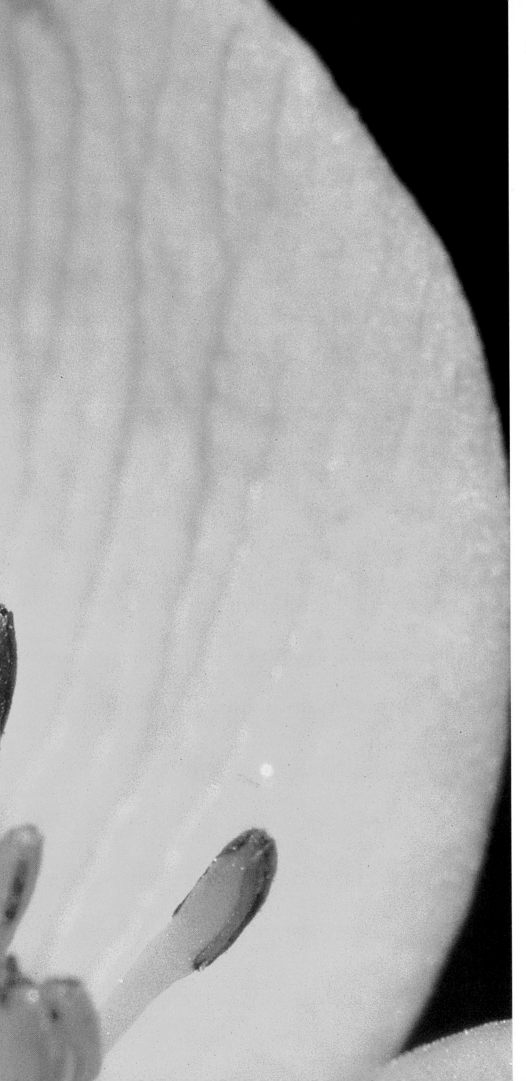

CONTENTS

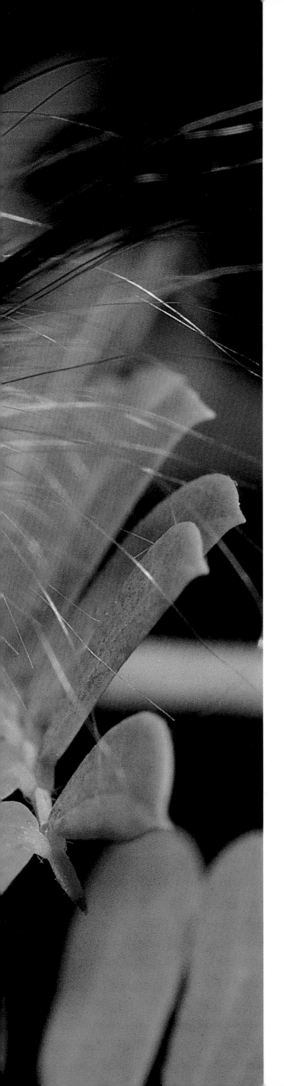

FOREWORD

Zoology's highest accolade must surely be awarded to the insects for their remarkable efficiency, dexterity, tenacity, strength and ingenuity. Together with their close relatives, the arachnids and the myriapods, insects have colonized every habitat on our planet, often with extraordinary survival techniques, such as the weaver ant's nest-building.

Phenomenal statistics are a testament to the truth of their success. More than eight out of ten animal species belong to the insect world; two fifths of these are beetles. Insects are so numerous that for every living person there are an estimated 200 million: in the temperate climes of rural southern England, for example, there are around 12.5 million spiders per acre. Perhaps even more startling are the results of recent tropical forest surveys which suggest there may be at least another 25 million species yet to be discovered.

Insects reveals, in dramatic color and narrative, a rich cross-section of the lives, metamorphoses and habits of these ubiquitous creatures: from the superbly camouflaged phasmids that mimic sticks and leaves to the migratory Monarch butterfly whose striking colors warn predators of its poison; from the singing and jumping crickets and grasshoppers to the mites that have turned hitch-hiking into an art; and from the highly social termites in their air-conditioned nests to the garden ants which cultivate aphids for their sweet honeydew.

Vital to the complex operations of the living world, insects play a multitude of roles in maintaining our planet's ecosystems. But their effects on human ecology are double-edged. Flies, for example, are undisputed carriers of diseases, but are also indispensable pollinators of flowers and recyclers of organic waste. And while some insects, such as parasitic wasps, are helpful in the biological control of other arthropod pests, others such as locusts are major herbivores and can devastate economically important crops and trees. These and many other arthropod stories have been assembled in *Insects* where the fascinating work of some of the finest entomologists and experts in arthropod behavior has been brought together to provide a rare insight into the extraordinary lives of the world's most numerous creatures.

How this book is organized

This volume is structured at a number of levels. First, there is a general essay highlighting common features and main variations of the biology (particularly the body plan), ecology and behavior of the arthropods and their evolution. Second, essays on each family highlight topics of particular interest, but invariably include a summary of species or species groupings, description of anatomy and unusual features of representative species and, in many cases, color artwork that enhances the text by illustrating representative species engaged in characteristic activities.

The main text of *Insects*, which describes individual species or groups of species, covers details of physical features, distribution, evolutionary history, diet and feeding behavior, as well as their social dynamics and spatial organization, classification and their relationship with man.

Our survey brings together a wealth of new information, hitherto buried in specialist journals and texts. Opening with an account of what it is to be an arthropod, how these miracles of miniaturization work, develop and grow, we follow with accounts of all the major taxonomic groups, starting with the two superclasses of the phylum Uniramia, the myriapods (millipedes and centipedes) and the hexapods (mainly insects). Within the insects, each of the 28 different orders is treated separately, with a summary panel of salient facts, accompanied by a wider-ranging text outlining the major aspects of the group's natural history. An introduction to that other main group of terrestrial arthropods, the arachnids (class Arachnida of the phylum Chelicerata) is followed by sections on the ticks and mites, the spiders, and the scorpions and remaining sub-classes. Throughout the book, boxed features and double-page features focus on topics of special interest in behavior, morphology, ecology or economic or medical importance.

The illustrations do more than record the stunning variety of color, form and life style in terrestrial arthropods. Almost all the photographs were taken in the wild, in locations all over the world. Here are revealed, in the subjects' natural habitat, details of their life cycles and behavior, from egg, through larval stages and molting to adulthood, courtship, mating, feeding and defence, flight and death. Extensive captions expand the scope of the text and identify species by family as well as by scientific name (if not given in the accompanying text or summary panel), and any common name.

WHAT IS AN ARTHROPOD?

Uniramians
Phylum Uniramia
About 1 million species described in two major groupings, the many-legged **myriapods** (superclass Myriapoda), comprising the **centipedes** (class Chilopoda), **millipedes** (class Diplopoda) and classes Pauropoda and Symphyla, and the 6-legged **hexapods** superclass Hexapoda), comprising the **insects** (class Insecta), **springtails** (class Collembola), and classes Protura and Diplura.

Chelicerates
Phylum Chelicerata
About 70,000 species, comprising the terrestrial **spiders, scorpions, ticks and mites** (class Arachnida, the **arachnids**), and also the aquatic horseshoe or king crabs (class Merostomata), sea spiders (class Pycnogonida) and probably the extinct trilobites (class Trilobita).

Velvet worms
Phylum Onychophora
About 120 species.

Crustaceans
Phylum Crustacea
Some 30,000 species, mostly aquatic (crabs, shrimps etc, with some terrestrial, eg woodlice, land crabs not covered here).

Tongue worms
Phylum Pentastomida
About 90 aquatic species (not covered here).

Water bears
Phylum Tardigrada
About 180 species, mostly aquatic (not covered here).

ARTHROPODS are by far the most successful animals ever to have evolved on this planet. In seas, freshwaters and on land, they easily outnumber all other animal groups. Only man, by virtue of greater individual size, manipulative skill, and intelligence, can rival them; but still the arthropods eat his foodstuffs, materials and buildings, parasitize and weaken his livestock, and spread disease. Nevertheless arthropods are essential to man's survival: crustaceans are major food sources for the fish we eat, while terrestrial arthropods assist in nutrient recycling, produce silk, waxes, dyes and honey, and pollinate many of our crops. The balance between arthropods and ourselves is finely tuned, for the arthropods constitute the vital backbone of most ecosystems.

Why are the arthropods so successful? The answer is probably quite simple—they have an external skeleton (exoskeleton) or "cuticle." This is their single most important diagnostic feature. Most of the special adaptations and devices of the group stem from this basic characteristic.

One Origin or Several?
Arthropods probably evolved in the Cambrian period 600–500 million years ago, from some form of worm not unlike modern marine annelids, which also have segments but are soft-bodied, with simple lobe-like appendages. Annelids and arthropods share some developmental features as well, and have very similar nervous systems. But there is a long-standing debate about whether arthropods branched just once from proto-annelid stock, diversifying thereafter, or whether there were several separate independent evolutionary lines. The former view (monophyletic origin of arthropods) holds "Arthropoda" to be a true phylum; but the latter implies polyphyly, with the argument that arthropods are a heterogenous and unreal assemblage, and most commonly recognizes three principal modern phyla. These are the Crustacea (crabs, shrimps etc), the Chelicerata (the arachnids—spiders, scorpions, mites and horseshoe crabs) and the Uniramia (insects, and centipedes and millipedes)—with the extinct trilobites perhaps closest to the chelicerates.

This controversy persists partly because the early arthropod fossil record is poor and cannot give final answers. There can be little doubt that arthropods do all look similar, at first glance making a satisfying grouping. They do also share many design features, besides external resemblance: similar guts, eyes, musculature, gonads and sperm, and an "open-plan" blood system. Monophyletic theory suggests all these likenesses must unite the groups, and cannot have arisen independently.

However, anatomical studies of the supposedly similar features have revealed important discrepancies. Arachnids have their mouth one segment further forward than crustaceans and insects, and they have piercing chelicerae as jaws, rather than

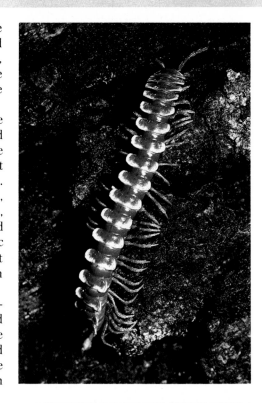

Velvet Worms—A Missing Link?

The velvet worms or "walking worms" (phylum Onychophora) are an ancient group of tropical and south temperate terrestrial animals seemingly intermediate between annelid worms and "proper" arthropods: some biologists view them as a "missing link."

Velvet worms live in moist, damp places, such as leaf litter on the forest floor, preying on worms and insects. If attacked they exude a sticky gum, squirted from the papillae placed either side of the mouth. The sexes are separate and many of the 120 or so species give birth to live young.

The cylindrical body, with a length ranging between 0.4–6in (1–15cm), bears stumpy legs and its whole surface is covered with periodically molted chitinous cuticle, perforated by many respiratory tracheae. There is one pair of antennae, and the stout, claw-like mandibles are suited to the carnivorous diet. Internally blood bathes the tissues directly, without blood vessels except for a dorsal heart. All these features are

shared with arthropods. However, the antennae are fleshy and ringed (annulated), the body wall is thin, flexible and permeable, not a hard exoskeleton, and the animal moves by contracting sheets of muscles to affect its shape and length, in a very worm-like fashion, with only limited assistance from the 14–43 pairs of short, soft, unjointed legs. Because of these distinctions, therefore, despite sharing many features, including common ancestors, with arthropods such as insects and myriapods, the velvet worms are placed in their own phylum. Onychophorans are named for the two claws on the tip of each leg (Onycho-phora = claw bearers). The best known genus is *Peripatus*.

▲ **Guarding her egg clutch,** a Harlequin bug, *Tectocoris diopthalmus* (Scutelleridae), in New South Wales, Australia. Unlike the sea-dwelling crustaceans, terrestrial arthropods lay fertilized eggs with a protective shell of cuticle.

◀ **Many-legged myriapod** ABOVE, six-legged insect and eight-legged arachnid all progress by wave-like movements of jointed limbs, as in this blue keeled, or flat-backed, millipede (*Polydesmus* species) in Mexico.

◀ **A velvet worm** BELOW, *Macroperipatus insularis*, in Jamaica, gives birth to live young.

chewing mandibles. Even the mandibles of crustaceans and insects are dissimilar, formed with a whole limb and from one basal limb segment respectively, with different biting actions. So there are three mutually incompatible types of jaw, with any intermediate forms unlikely to have existed because they would be unworkable.

Similarly crustaceans have two-branched (biramous) limbs, the secondary branch usually forming gills, while uniramians and chelicerates now both have uniramous

limbs, but with different origins. Again three separate designs are apparent. The different growth patterns of crustaceans and insects are also incompatible with a common evolutionary history.

Despite this evidence for multiple arthropod origins, two critical problems remain. Firstly, can the extensive similarities between groups really be dismissed as convergence? Different groups have evolved separately but arrived at very similar endpoints because they are the only feasible solutions to common problems, given the constraints of an exoskeleton. So for a worm to evolve a stiff cuticle inevitably entrains all the other changes, including the appearance of appendages (legs) required for locomotion, and the capacity to molt, allowing growth. The result is the evolution of what we call an arthropod. Furthermore, there are classic examples of indisputable arthropodan convergence, since both tracheal and Malpighian tubules have arisen independently in different groups, thus permitting life on land. In other words, remarkably precise convergence should and does happen. Arthropods merely show it particularly clearly because their design severely limits the number of possible solutions to common problems.

The second objection is why should "arthropodization" have happened several times over anyway? To answer this, polyphyleticists must demonstrate that exoskeletons are a major evolutionary advance, likely to be preserved by natural selection whenever they evolved. If this is the case, then several evolutionary prototypes with a cuticle are to be expected, each diversifying into a separate group of "arthropods." The following pages consider arthropod design in this light, although the very numbers of arthropods must attest to the success of this way of building an animal and lend weight to the idea of multiple origins from their worm-like ancestors.

The Exoskeleton

The evolution of an exoskeleton of hardened cuticle entailed a number of consequences and possibilities in the evolution of arthropods. One of the main effects of an exoskeleton is to keep an animal small. An external tube provides the best mechanical support with limited material, while for large animals internal rods (ie endoskeletons, like bones) are a better solution. Also exoskeletons necessitate growth by molting. Large animals would collapse under their own weight before a newly-secreted skeleton hardened. So external hard cuticles *only* work for small creatures. The arthropod design has this apparent grave limitation – particularly on land, and most of all for flying insects.

Yet small size also has some advantages. The number of individuals can be greater, and rates of reproduction (and hence of evolutionary adaptation) can be higher. Small arthropods also have an enormous range of small niches available to them – they experience the world as an incredibly variable place. Hence they can develop

▲ **A jumping spider** (*Plexippus* species, family Salticidae) and its prey, in Kenya. Spiders and other chelicerates have piercing chelicerae for jaws, rather than the biting mandibles of uniramians (eg insects) and crustaceans. However, insects and spiders have single-branched limbs, while the chelicerate limb has two branches. Such distinctions lead to the conclusion that the arthropod body plan has evolved more than once, resulting today in a number of distinct phyla.

◀ **Newly emerged** from the skin of its last larval stage, a grasshopper, *Taeniopoda auricornis* (Acrididae), in Veracruz state, Mexico, prepares for its first day of adult life.

greater diversity, giving rise to the million or more species currently known, precisely because of the "constraint" imposed by an exoskeleton on their dimensions.

Arthropod skeletons are central to their success, so the design of the cuticle itself must be critical. All arthropod cuticles have a similar three-layered structure, all have joints and articulations of similar types and all have glandular and sensory specializations within the cuticle. The various groups also share a common basic cuticular microstructure and chemistry—the bulk is made of the polysaccharide chitin, with the long, tough, chain-like molecular fibrils laid down in characteristic patterns for maximum multi-directional strength in a matrix of proteins. But the groups differ in their methods of hardening the newly-secreted cuticle after molting, and in the surface layers added (eg only terrestrial arthropods use waterproofing, waxy layers).

Besides this variation between groups, arthropod cuticle is also extremely variable in each individual animal. It is this versatility of cuticle which has made it such a successful material. It can be thick for strength, or thin for flexibility, even elastic in wing and leg hinges; heavy for negative buoyancy or light for flight; colored for camouflage or warning, permeable for aquatic breathing, or extraordinarily resistant to water loss on land. These properties can exist in different parts of the same individual, but they can also occur differentially at each stage of the life cycle,

allowing for metamorphosis in the most successful of all groups, the insects.

The cuticle is the arthropod's ultimate barrier against the world, giving physical protection to soft tissues, defense against parasites, pathogens and predators, and a chemical barrier controlling exchanges of respiratory gases, salts, water and other molecules. Thus, heavily-armored marine lobsters are almost invulnerable (except when molting); freshwater mosquito larvae use their cuticle to assist osmotic balance and prevent swelling; and terrestrial insects or spiders rely on cuticle to prevent desiccation and limit damage from blows and falls.

A rigid exoskeleton has profound effects on locomotion; jointed legs are required for swimming, walking and jumping. Each joint is operated by antagonistic flexor and extensor muscles and joints operate in different planes to give maximum maneuverability. All arthropods use gaits based on waves of leg movements along the body, with the opposite legs of a pair alternating; many forms have several gaits for different speeds. Arthropods also have a characteristic posture, very unlike those of most vertebrates with legs arising from the sides of the lower surface (ventrolaterally); the body sags between the suspending legs, for greater stability and resistance to wind and wave. Cuticle is also an ideal light, but strong, material for wing construction, thus opening up the aerial environment to the insect hordes.

Growth and Molting

Perhaps the most important drawback of an exoskeleton is that it restrains growth. Arthropods must therefore grow intermittently by producing a new and larger cuticle at intervals, sheddding the old one. Many arthropods avoid the waste of good biological material by eating their own discarded shell.

Molting involves a complex sequence of changes; most of the old unhardened endocuticle is broken down and resorbed first (**a, b**), then the new epicuticle is laid down, somewhat crinkled (**c**) to allow later expansion (**d**) under a layer of molting fluid. Some of the bulk protein and chitin is added below the new epicuticle (**c, d**) and when the

new cuticle is reasonably thick the older cuticle outside it splits along specific lines (**e**) and the animal pulls itself out of and sheds the old case. Then it may swallow air or water to expand its own volume and stretch the new skeleton before it hardens. Extra endocuticle may then be added, and in some cases (eg insects) surface waxes or cements are added.

Molting must be carefully controlled and coordinated over the whole body, so it is always governed by hormones. Actual cuticle secretion and the molt cycle are due to ecdysone, a steroid hormone found in all arthropods. In insects this hormone is secreted by a gland in the thorax, which is in turn controlled by a hormone from the brain—

whenever the brain receives appropriate stimuli from the insect's environment, the entire hormonal cycle is therefore triggered, and the animal molts. Insects also have an extra chemical called "juvenile hormone" (JH) to regulate metamorphosis. When this is released from a small gland in the head (the corpus allatum), the new cuticle retains larval characteristics (eg soft, extensible cuticle, as in caterpillars); but once the juvenile hormone secretion stops, the insect produces adult cuticle instead (generally thicker and rigid, with complete wings and adult mouthparts) and metamorphosis is complete. Insects do not molt after reaching maturity, unlike crustaceans, which may molt all their lives.

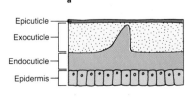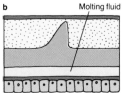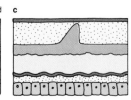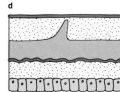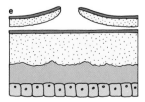

Epicuticle
Exocuticle
Endocuticle
Epidermis

Molting fluid

a b c d e

BODY PLAN OF AN ARTHROPOD

Cuticle

Central to arthropods' success, cuticle comprises chiefly fibrils of polysaccharide chitin, laid down in thin layers, and embedded in a matrix of proteins. The fibrils are parallel within a layer but slightly rotated between successive layers, giving great strength for minimum weight. The exocuticle is hardened by cross-linking ("tanning") of the proteins (with quinones in insects, with sulphur bridges in arachnids), and by impregnation with calcium salts in crustaceans and some myriapods. The endocuticle remains unhardened and is recycled at each molt. On top is the thin epicuticle, made of proteins and lipids. In terrestrial arthropods the epicuticle includes a waterproofing waxy layer and usually a tough protective cement layer.

Segments

Each segment is essentially a box, with the tergum forming the roof, the sternum the floor, and the pleura (sing. pleuron) the sides. Legs emerge from the lower sides of the pleura, and are operated by muscles connected to the main plates of the body to raise or lower the legs (protractor and retractor). Other muscles link adjacent segments, so that the body can flex or curl, or link the roof and floor of the box so the body can flatten. Only the nerve cord, gut and heart run the length of the body, traversing all segments.

Joints

Jointed legs have given arthropods their name (Greek arthron–joint, pous–foot), joints usually moving in only one plane, so that several joints per leg are needed to give full maneuverability. The hard cuticle "tubes," linked at the joint by softer flexible membrane, fit one within the other, so that when fully extended, as shown, one tube "locks" inside the other. When flexed, the outer tube or leg segment rotates about a pivot formed by an extension of the cuticle, usually giving about 90° of movement.

Sensory systems

Most arthropod sense organs are modifications of the cuticle itself. The commonest form is connected with bristles (setae) which may be articulated, so that the nerve ending with its shaft is stimulated when it moves (if touched, or vibrated by water or air movements), or the bristle may carry chemical sensory endings (the latter are particularly common on legs, mouthparts and antennae). Other sense organs involve canals, splits or pits in the exoskeleton, with thin nerve-packed membranes below

which detect strains and tensions, especially at joints. There may also be internal position detectors (proprio-ceptors) attached to the cuticle, tendons or muscles.

The most obvious sense of arthropods, however, is vision. Many arthropods have simple eyes (ocelli) with only one or a few receptors, but in insects and most crustaceans true compound eyes occur also, with many long cylindrical receptors (ommatidia). The cuticle always contributes the outer transparent lens-cornea; hexagonal arrays of these occur in most compound eyes. Behind these are the crystalline cones (helping to focus light), and then the retinular cells, with highly folded inner surfaces bearing the visual pigment, and uniting to form the rhabdome. These cells connect to the optic nerve fibers (axons), and thence to the brain. Such eyes produce mosaic images, more coarsely grained than our own vision, but also more highly sensitive to high frequency flickering (ie to movement). Arthropod eyes are also convex and often very large, giving a huge field of vision; they work at many different light levels, adapting by movements of shielding pigments; and they can be very sensitive to colors, and even to polarization of light.

Nervous system

All arthropods have similar nervous systems—a brain in the top of the head with nerves passing round the gut and uniting underneath as the longitudinal nerve cord, which has ganglia in each segment (though these are fused in many forms). Insect brains have three parts, the first two largely receiving inputs from eyes and antennae respectively; chelicerates (eg spiders) lack antennae, so have no obvious second segment. Each ganglion sends a constant pattern of nerves into the muscles within the segment, and receives sensory information; motor patterns generated centrally can thus be repeated slightly out of phase in adjacent segments to achieve coordinated locomotion.

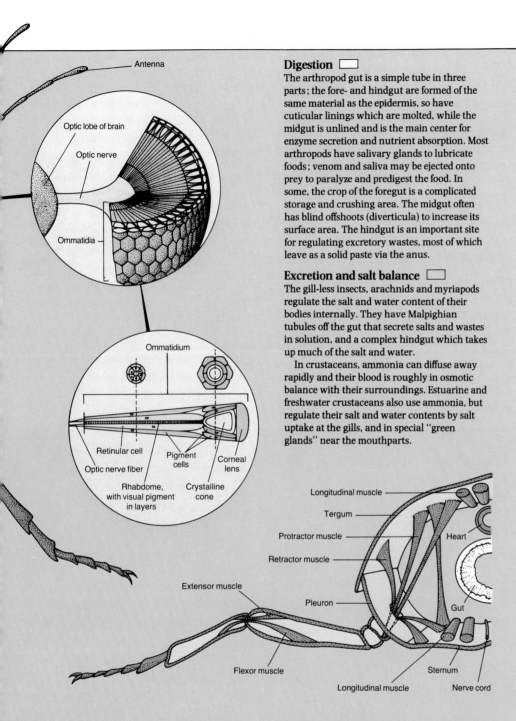

Antenna

Optic lobe of brain

Optic nerve

Ommatidia

Ommatidium

Retinular cell

Optic nerve fiber

Pigment cells

Corneal lens

Rhabdome, with visual pigment in layers

Crystalline cone

Longitudinal muscle

Tergum

Protractor muscle

Retractor muscle

Heart

Extensor muscle

Pleuron

Gut

Flexor muscle

Sternum

Longitudinal muscle

Nerve cord

Digestion

The arthropod gut is a simple tube in three parts; the fore- and hindgut are formed of the same material as the epidermis, so have cuticular linings which are molted, while the midgut is unlined and is the main center for enzyme secretion and nutrient absorption. Most arthropods have salivary glands to lubricate foods; venom and saliva may be ejected onto prey to paralyze and predigest the food. In some, the crop of the foregut is a complicated storage and crushing area. The midgut often has blind offshoots (diverticula) to increase its surface area. The hindgut is an important site for regulating excretory wastes, most of which leave as a solid paste via the anus.

Excretion and salt balance

The gill-less insects, arachnids and myriapods regulate the salt and water content of their bodies internally. They have Malpighian tubules off the gut that secrete salts and wastes in solution, and a complex hindgut which takes up much of the salt and water.

In crustaceans, ammonia can diffuse away rapidly and their blood is roughly in osmotic balance with their surroundings. Estuarine and freshwater crustaceans also use ammonia, but regulate their salt and water contents by salt uptake at the gills, and in special "green glands" near the mouthparts.

Respiration

Most aquatic forms have gills, finely folded extensions of permeable cuticle. These are borne on the legs in crustaceans, usually on the end of the abdomen in aquatic insects. Some arachnids retain a gill-like structure (book gill), while others have a similar breathing apparatus tucked inside a pocket of the body (book lung). But most terrestrial arthropods—insects, myriapods and some spiders—have instead developed a system of fine cuticular tubes (tracheae) that spread inward from breathing vents (spiracles) on the surface of thorax and abdomen, enabling oxygen to travel directly to the tissues. This system is ideal on land (where gills would collapse and dry out) because the closeable spiracles limit water loss: but the tracheae do have to be replaced at each molt.

Circulation

In all arthropods the blood circulates within the body cavity (hemocoel) with few vessels apart from the dorsal heart. This has holes (ostia) which take in the blood before passing it forward to the head and other active areas. The blood then returns to the open cavity of the body, though it may be directed through legs and around the gut by partitioning of the cavity.

The blood (hemolymph) is usually colorless, or yellow-green, and it carries vital nutrients, wastes and hormones to and from all the tissues. (In arthropods other than insects and spiders it also carries the oxygen supply from gills to tissues.) Blood also carries cells to defend against disease and to effect repairs; and in soft-bodied forms it may transmit forces from the muscles, to allow a "hydrostatic" type of locomotion.

The immense versatility of cuticle as a biological building material is perhaps best shown by the range of its uses for feeding. On land, the variety of mouthparts is proverbial, from the hard chelicerae and mandibles of predators, to the piercing and sucking proboscis of biting flies, the delicate flexibly coiled "tongue" of a nectar-feeding butterfly, and the fleshy lapping labellum of a housefly. In aquatic arthropods it can form hard crunching mandibles and pincers, capable of breaking mollusk shells or the carapace of other crustaceans, but it can also be modified as finely structured filtering setae, to net microscopic plankton.

Marine arthropods can disperse numerous eggs and sperm randomly into the sea and expect enough chance fertilizations, but in other habitats specializations are needed. Freshwater crustaceans commonly produce yolky cuticularized (shelled) eggs, or brood the young in special cuticular pouches. On land arthropods must bring egg and sperm together without either drying, so copulation is required. Hence terrestrial arthropods usually have complex genitalia, often using the precise physical match of male and female cuticular appendages (impossible in soft-bodied animals) to ensure that only matings between members of the same species take place. They also use cuticle for egg shells (with elaborate architecture to let the embryo breathe) and, frequently, to make egg-guides or ovipositors, used to lay the eggs into suitable humid habitats—perhaps very long, sharp and sensitive to insert eggs into host animals, or strong and saw-like to penetrate tough plants.

All animals benefit from a stable internal environment (homeostasis) to keep their biochemical systems functioning optimally. Arthropods are aided by their cuticle, since it regulates rates of exchange (eg of heat, gases and other substances) with the outside world, but they are also hindered by their necessarily small size, since temperature and content of smaller bodies inevitably tend to fluctuate more rapidly. So arthropods need very efficient apparatus for gas exchange (usually dependent on cuticular structures) and for salt and water balance, and a good fluid distribution system to keep supplies and wastes in balanced circulation.

Thus, in almost every aspect of their lives, cuticle is what makes the arthropods; it led to their evolution, constrains their design and their size, and yet has above all contributed to their enormous diversity in virtually every habitat on Earth. PGW

MILLIPEDES AND OTHER MYRIAPODS

Superclass Myriapoda
Classes: Chilopoda, Diplopoda, Symphyla,
Pauropoda.
Phylum: Uniramia

The 4 classes are not closely related, but are
known collectively as the myriapods; the trunk
(not divided into thorax and abdomen) bears at
least 9 pairs of simple walking legs. All
myriapods have 1 pair of antennae, 1 pair of
mandibles and 1 or more pairs of maxillae.
Young mostly resemble adults but usually have
fewer segments.

▼ **Mating arthropods may be vulnerable** to
predation and often seek shelter. Chemically
protected species, though, may signal their
distastefulness by warning colors and often
mate in the open, like these giant millipedes,
Epibolus pulchripes, in Kenya.

ONE might expect a creature that bears
anything from nine to over 200 pairs
of legs to run a serious risk of tripping over
itself. To avoid this eventuality, the centipedes and millipedes have evolved a range
of gaits, from scuttling species with some
legs longer than the others, to slower
movers which progress by means of wave-
like movements, either of the legs in
sequence or of the undivided trunk itself.

Millipedes and centipedes are two of the
four classes of arthropods that are grouped
together as the many-legged Myriapoda,
and they include some 95 percent of all
myriapod species. They are easy enough to
find by turning over stones or leaf mold, but
hard to study because they scuttle away to
another dark and moist retreat. Unlike their
relatives, the insects, they lack waxy layers
in the cuticle and breathe through uncloseable spiracles, so are at risk from desiccation
unless they stick to humid sites and night-
time activity. They also differ from inspects
in lacking true compound eyes, or direct

copulatory mechanisms (as do the arachnids) and, most obviously, in having many
more legs and no wings. Nevertheless, they
are extremely common and successful
animals, found from the poles to the
tropics—and there are even some desert
millipedes.

Most **millipedes** are secretive herbivores,
burrowing through soil and leaf litter.
Unlike the more active centipedes, they
rarely expose themselves to danger. Apart
from their very different habits, the two
groups are readily distinguished by the
"diplosegments" of millipedes, two pairs of
legs corresponding to each segment; and the
millipedes have no massive poison claws,
but simple chewing mouthparts. However,
they are much more variable than centipedes, ranging from tiny, soft, tufted
pselaphognaths like *Polyxenus* to bulky
hardened tropical julids, up to 11 in (28cm)
long with more than 100 segments. The size
of a millipede also determines its general
proportions and habits, since the smaller

Life in the Soil

In order to thrive, the soil-dwelling myriapods have had to overcome several problems posed by the medium in which they live. They move either in crevices (flattened, sinuous centipedes), or between soil particles (tiny millipedes), or by pushing soil aside (larger millipedes, especially julids).

The direction and speed of movement are partly controlled by the sensitivity required to locate foods (whether prey or vegetation) and mates. Sight is rarely appropriate, as light is shunned, so only the fast surface-dwelling scutigerimorph centipedes have moderately complex eyes. Others rely on a few simple eyes (ocelli) which merely detect light and shade, or sensitivity to light is spread over the cuticle. It is the chemical and mechanical senses that are preeminent: the antennae have abundant receptors for scents and touch, and the feet or mouthparts may also respond to such stimuli. Sometimes the rearmost legs are particularly sensitive, almost like antennae. Commonly a region near the antennae is also specialized, as the "organ of Tömösvary" thought to respond to vibration. Myriapods may also have receptors that monitor the humidity and temperature of their immediate surroundings.

The soil may seem to us a pleasantly stable, moist habitat relative to more open terrestrial areas, but it is still liable to drought or flooding, and its surface layers can be bakingly hot or frozen solid. Myriapods attempt to keep in favorable regions by migrating vertically—burrowing deeper to cool damp layers in summer droughts or winter frosts, and rising to the surface, or even climbing vegetation and walls, when the soil is waterlogged. They *must* use such behavioral mechanisms to locate suitable microhabitats, because their cuticle (unlike insects') is not waterproof, so they could otherwise easily dehydrate or drown; they might even asphyxiate, if the uncloseable spiracles leading to the breathing tubes (tracheae) became water-filled. Breathing could also be difficult in soils relatively lacking in oxygen, even for slow herbivorous millipedes with their rather slow metabolism.

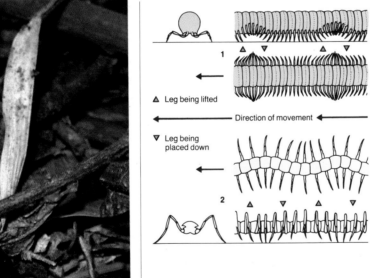

▲ **Varied gaits of myriapods** all involve coordination by wave-like movements along the legs. The herbivorous millipedes are rarely agile, although the number of legs, borne two pairs to each diplosegment, ranges from 40 to over 400. In a typical slow-moving, burrowing cylinder millipede of the order Julida (1), most legs are in contact with the substrate. Leg strokes are long, in phase on each side of the rigid body. One wave of leg movements may involve 22 or more pairs of legs. The short legs arise from close to the midline of the body.

Among the carnivorous centipedes, active runners are more common (2). The body is quite flexible, usually flattened, and fewer legs (often less than half) touch the ground at any one time. Leg strokes are short, out of phase on each side, causing side-to-side undulations, limited by the lateral placing of the legs. A wave may involve just seven pairs of legs (or segments). Scutigeromorphs have longer rear legs which step over the shorter limbs in front.

flattened ones can burrow between soil particles while larger ones must bulldoze the substrate apart into a true burrow and need more streamlined, rigid, but muscular bodies with legs closer to the midline. Few millipedes are really agile, having a slow gait designed for burrowing (with most of the legs pushing at any one time, so that 20–50 legs comprise a single locomotory wave) and a slightly faster but still "low-gear" walking gait, with 10–15 legs per wave. Some millipedes live in caves and rocky places. These types can climb using their strongly gripping legs and are much faster movers; a few even have predatory feeding habits.

The vast majority of millipedes feed on plant material. Most prefer using their stout jaws to scrape and chew at partly decomposed leaves, where the unpalatable tannins and other chemicals have begun to break down; so they are important nutrient recyclers in woodlands. Some have developed a form of sucking mouthparts, and can pierce plants to suck the sap; and quite a number chew the fine roots of living plants, or the whole of a plant at the seedling stage, so making them significant pests to horticulturalists. Such diets keep them protected from many standard control measures (usually involving spraying the large aerial surfaces of plants), and also keep them away from predators for much of their lives. Millipede defense lies in the usually thick, calcium-impregnated cuticle, and in the ability to roll up or coil (see overleaf). Relatively few have defensive secretions, though large polydesmids and julids may produce iodine- or cyanide-based droplets or sprays when severely provoked.

Millipedes use indirect sperm transfer unlike the centipedes, but males have specially modified legs to collect their own sperm and insert it into the female, so the sexes come close together for copulation. This is stimulated by touch (antennal tapping and leg stroking), by pheromones and sometimes by sound signals (leg stridulations). Many millipedes then lay eggs in a prepared nest made of their own excrement, and some use similar nests as molting chambers and as retreats to survive dry spells. Most desert millipedes actually become dormant underground, often massing in some numbers, for several months of the year; a few of them do have waxes in their epicuticle, and can regulate their blood concentrations to survive severe water shortages quite efficiently.

Centipedes are probably best known to the layman in temperate regions (though less common than millipedes), because they are active voracious carnivores, often lightly or brightly colored and so likely to catch the eye. The four orders of centipede range in proportions and habit, from long sinuous burrowers to stouter long-legged runners, but all are rather similar in basic structure. They are all predators, feeding on small soil invertebrates (worms, snails and other arthropods) or even on vertebrates such as lizards, toads and mice in the case of the largest tropical forms up to 13in (33cm) long. The prey is sensed by the antennae (and legs, sometimes) and is captured and paralyzed by the characteristic poison-claws, very large, fanged appendages on the underside of the head. (Some tropical forms have a venom which can be severely painful to humans.) The stunned prey is held while the jaws begin their task, and the centipede will then rest briefly in a humid crevice while its simple gut completes the digestive processes. Because of their abundance and large appetites, centipedes can thus be valuable to gardeners and farmers in keeping down populations of potential pest herbivores, such as root-eating fly larvae and eel worms.

However, life as a small active carnivore reliant on moisture poses certain problems; the soil is not an easy habitat to live in (see box), nor is it very easy to organize rapid movement in a creature with so many legs. Compared with slow burrowing species, the "high-geared" fast runners have shorter bodies and fewer, longer legs. At the extreme, a running scutigeromorph keeps its body fairly straight and provides all the force with its stepping, levering legs, spread laterally to increase stability and prevent rolling. But this is still not enough, as the few long legs must overlap in their strides and could get tangled; so these centipedes have posterior legs that are longer than those at the front and able to step over and outside them—in *Scutigera*, the back pair of legs are twice as long as the first pair. Body rigidity is improved by larger overlapping back plates (tergites), and any slippage against the ground is limited by flattening and ridging of the last few leg segments, which grip the substrate. This design is in sharp contrast to the flexible and extensible geophilomorph type, which burrows, largely by extending and contracting the trunk (like an earthworm), with the legs principally being used just for anchorage.

Small active carnivores expose themselves to danger while capturing prey; so centipedes need defenses against other hunters, especially nocturnal rodents and birds. Apart from the poison-claws (effective against frontal attack), they may have spiny rear legs; and in many of the slower centipedes each segment bears "repugnatorial glands" that secrete adhesives or toxins in the event of disturbance. These chemically defended species are often brightly colored as a warning.

Perhaps again because of their carnivorous habit, many centipedes use courtship behavior to ensure correct recognition—a pair will circle for many minutes, tapping each other with their antennae. Then the male spins a small silk pad and deposits a package of sperm on it, since he lacks copulatory organs, and the female picks up the sperm. After laying her eggs the female frequently broods them until the hatchlings can disperse to prey for themselves. PGW

▲ **Giant South African millipede** coiled up for protection. The bright colors signal that defense in this species is no passive matter. Segmentally arranged glands secrete a bitter, foul-smelling poison which deters most predators. Birds such as quail and rails, however, seem to cope with the noxious substances and often eat millipedes.

► **Massive jaws, and legs adapted for running**, of *Ethmostigmus rubripes*, a large centipede from Australia. Their rapid gait and powerful venom combine to make large centipedes voracious predators. They are found under stones, loose bark and leaf litter. Larger species still, up to 8in (20cm) long, will attack small lizards and frogs.

The 4 Classes of Myriapods

Millipedes
Class Diplopoda

8,000 species in 2 subclasses and 10 orders; slow-moving herbivores, mostly 0.08–4in (2mm–10cm) long with at least 11 leg-bearing segments all but the first 3 of which are "diplosegments" with two pairs of legs; 2 pairs of true mouthparts.

Subclass Pselaphognatha (1 order): tiny, with soft cuticle, tufted hairs and 13–17 pairs of legs. Cryptic, in humus, soils and crevices.

Subclass Chilognatha (9 orders): larger forms with hard cuticle containing calcium salts. Includes **pill-millipedes** (order Glomerida) with 11–12 arched segments allowing rolling-up; **flat-backed millipedes** (order Polydesmida) with usually 20 trunk segments bearing lateral keels; **cylinder-millipedes** (order Julida) with 40 or more segments bearing short legs on mid-underside, in humus, litter and beneath stones or logs.

Centipedes
Class Chilopoda

3,000 species in 4 orders; active carnivores, mostly 0.04–2.4in (1–6cm) long, with at least 15 leg-bearing segments (always an odd number), 3 pairs of true mouthparts, and large poison claws (first pair of "legs").

Order Geophilomorpha: long, thread-like soil-dwelling burrowers with 31–177 pairs of short legs.

Order Scolopendromorpha: heavy-bodied, flattened burrowers or crevice dwellers with 21–23 pairs of legs.

Order Lithobiomorpha: heavy-bodied, flattened crevice dwellers with 15 pairs of legs.

Order Scutigeromorpha: active, fast runners in varied habitats with 15 pairs of long legs.

Symphyla

120 species of small, scuttling herbivores, 0.08–0.4in (2–10mm) long, with 12 leg-bearing segments (but extra tergites or back plates), 3 pairs of mouthparts resembling those of insects; eyeless. In soil and leaf mold.

Pauropoda

380 species of tiny, soft-bodied scavengers, 0.02–0.08in (0.5–2mm) long, with 9 leg-bearing segments (but fewer tergites), 2 pairs of mouthparts, branched antennae; eyeless. In soil and leaf mold.

Rolling Up

Curling into a tight ball (conglobation) is an excellent defense for a small arthropod with thick back plates of cuticle. All the softer parts and the vulnerable sense organs can be tucked in and protected against predators, and water loss can be reduced. So it is not surprising that many forms have developed this trick; the pill millipedes (glomerids) and the woodlice (or "pill bugs"—actually crustaceans) are the best-known examples, but other living arthropods also curl up, and millions of years ago many trilobites were equally expert at the defensive roll.

All these animals are hemispherical in section and they curl up about their flat under-surface, stretching apart the overlapping back plates (tergites) and enclosing the legs in a small central space.

In pill millipedes, the head is tucked in (1) and the tergites are shaped especially to create a smooth exposed surface during the roll. The tergites are also staggered relative to the plates on the underside (sternites), so improving flexibility. By contrast woodlice (2) cannot tuck the head in. They achieve the necessary trunk flexing with normally shaped segments which overlap backward dorsally but in the opposite direction underneath, so the belly concertinas together as the back extends.

The extinct trilobites (3) achieved their roll using special peg-and-socket joints between segments; but the head was not tucked in, being itself heavily armored.

So three separate, independently evolved mechanisms all achieve the same end—another example of precise convergent evolution in the arthropods.

Many longer-bodied arthropods, unable to achieve a globular shape by rolling, use spiral coiling for defense instead. Longer millipedes are particularly good examples—they can use a similar technique to the rolling pill millipedes to arrange themselves as a flat spiral (4), like a catherine wheel, with the head in the center and all legs tucked away, leaving only tough, unpalatable surfaces exposed to would-be predators.

1

2

3

4

SUPERCLASS: HEXAPODA
Phylum: Uniramia

Proturans
Class: Protura
About 70 species

Diplurans
Class: Diplura
About 400 species

Springtails
Class: Collembola
Over 2,000 species

Insects
Class: Insecta
Nearly 1,000,000 species described, in 2 subclasses and 28 orders.

Subclass Apterygota (wingless)
Bristletails—Archaeognatha
Bristletails, silverfish—Thysanura

Subclass Pterygota (adults winged, though wings lost in some groups)

Palaeoptera (wings held at right angles to body)
Mayflies—Ephemeroptera
Dragonflies—Odonata

Neoptera (wings fold back)

Wings develop externally (exopterygote); metamorphosis incomplete (hemimetabolous):

Cockroaches—Blattodea
Termites—Isoptera
Mantids—Mantodea
Earwigs—Dermaptera
Stone flies—Plecoptera
Crickets, grasshoppers—Orthoptera
Stick and leaf insects—Phasmatoidea
Book lice—Psocoptera
Web spinners—Embioptera
Zorapterans—Zoraptera
Thrips—Thysanoptera
Parasitic lice—Phthiraptera

IF arthropods are the success story of the planet, then pride of place among them must go to the insects. While nearly a million species have been described, several million more await discovery. About 7,000 new insect species are described every year, but this figure is probably exceeded by the annual losses of unknown species, which results from the destruction of habitats, mainly tropical forests.

Most authorities now agree that the wingless Collembola (the springtails), Protura and Diplura are not insects (see box). They are best viewed as separate classes within a superclass (Hexapoda) of the phylum Uniramia. Hexapods are distinguished from the much less numerous myriapods (centipedes and millipedes) by having the body divided into three distinct regions—head, thorax and abdomen, the presence of six legs (hence "hexapod") on the three-segmented thorax, and possession of a tracheal system.

The insects themselves are divided into the small wingless subclass Apterygota (archaeognathans and bristletails), and the winged Pterygota, which comprise the other 99.9 percent of known insect species. The wings are borne on the second and third thoracic segments which are often fused together to form a rigid box that withstands the forces exerted in flight.

There are several theories about the origins of insects, but it is likely that they evolved from myriapods, and that their immediate ancestors resembled symphylans. Beside the arthropod exoskeleton, the main features of early insects included mouthparts not enclosed in a cavity (ectognathous), a hypognathous head (with the mouthparts facing downward), one pair of antennae with muscles only at the base, six legs with more than five segments, a thorax with three and an abdomen with 11 segments (one or more usually fused), and a genital

Hexapods Other Than Insects —The Classes Protura, Diplura and Collembola

There are three groups of hexapods distinguished from insects in having their mouthparts enclosed (entognathous) within a cavity formed by the sides of the head fused to the labium. Most, unlike insects, have muscles within the antennae, and none can fly. Representatives of all three classes bear appendages on at least some segments of the abdomen.

The **proturans** (class Protura) (1) are minute white animals living in soil, usually less than 0.08in (2mm) long. They have a cosmopolitan distribution. They have no antennae, but the forelegs function for sensory purposes, while the mid- and hindlegs are used for locomotion. The legs have five joints and there is a single process (telson) at the tip of the abdomen. Their tracheal respiratory system is simplified and some species possess only a single pair of spiracles. Segments are added to their body as they mature. Proturans are retiring animals and not much is known of their biology, although they occur so widely. They have sucking mouthparts and feed mainly on fungi. There are some 70 species in 7 or 8 genera, including *Acerentomon*, *Acerentulus*, *Eosentomon*, *Protapteron*.

The **diplurans** or **two-pronged bristletails** (class Diplura) (2) number about 400 species, some of which are widespread and common. *Campodea* reaches a length of 0.28in (7mm), but *Heterojapax* can be up to 2in (50mm) long and has its pair of cerci modified as prey-catching pincers; the biting mouthparts are reduced. Diplurans live in damp places under logs or stones and appear to be blind. They have a tracheal system usually with two or four spiracles but up to 11 pairs in *Heterojapax*. The antennae and (usually) cerci are long and there may be rudimentary abdominal legs in addition to the three pairs of five-jointed thoracic legs. The male places his sperm in a stalked packet on the ground and the female then picks this up.

Worldwide, more than 2,000 species of (3) **collembolans** or **springtails** (class Collembola)

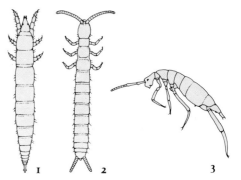

occur in concealed, damp places and on the surface of pools of fresh and salt water. They are usually less than 0.12in and never more than 0.2in (3–5mm) long. In addition to the six four-segmented legs of the thorax, most species bear on the fourth abdominal segment a forked tail (furca) which when released by an appendage (retinaculum) on segment three, springs downward, causing the insect to leap up—hence the name springtail. Springtails also possess, on the first abdominal segment, a ventral tube through which they can take up water and which also in aquatic forms allows them to grip the water meniscus.

Springtails eat decomposing organic matter and many also feed on living plants, using their biting mouthparts. Some collembolans are serious pests of sugarcane, tobacco or mushrooms, and one common species feeds on duckweed. Others feed on pollen, fungi, bacteria or algae. They are often very abundant—for example a million individuals may occur in an acre of meadow, and some soils contain 1,000 per pint. They may suddenly appear in vast numbers on snowfields, where they may look like soot. Some construct elaborate chambers from their own fecal material which they occupy in times of drought. Most collembolans have a tracheal system with a single pair of spiracles, and there are two groups of up to eight simple eyes (ocelli) on the head. Genera include *Achorutes*, *Anurida*, *Podura*, *Sminthurus*.

IER HEXAPODS

▲ Diversity and success of insects stems from, among other factors, the ability to fly, withstand desiccation, and reproduce in large numbers, all of which are characteristic of the Desert locust, *Schistocerca gregaria* (Acrididae), vast swarms of which may number hundreds of millions of individuals.

Bugs—Hemiptera

Wings develop internally (endopterygote); metamorphosis complete (holometabolous):
Snake flies—Raphidioptera
Alderflies—Megaloptera
Lacewings, ant lions—Neuroptera
Beetles—Coleoptera
Strepsipterans, stylopids—Strepsiptera
Scorpion flies—Mecoptera
Fleas—Siphonaptera
Two-winged flies—Diptera
Caddis flies—Trichoptera
Moths and butterflies—Lepidoptera
Sawflies, wasps, ants and bees—Hymenoptera

usually short life cycle which includes metamorphosis, a high reproductive rate, and the capacity to survive unfavorable seasons; and cooperation between individuals of the social termites, ants, wasps and bees.

Modern insects have been able to radiate into a very large number of terrestrial habitats largely as a result of their characteristic combination of a waterproof cuticle and a respiratory system of valved tracheae. So important and versatile a tissue is cuticle in insects that the adaptive radiation of insects can be viewed as the radiation of the cuticle and the structures it forms, not least the exoskeleton typical of all arthropods. It varies from very hard in claws and mandibles, to being soft and pliant in leg joints, intersegmental membranes and, within the insect, linings of the tracheal system, the fore- and hindguts, parts of the genital system, and the ducts of skin glands. Although increase in an insect's size is normally limited to a short period just after a molt, caterpillars and other soft larvae can increase in length between molts. Even some adult insects can enlarge: the abdomen of a queen termite may elongate by about 10 times after she has founded a nest and raised an initial brood of workers.

Cuticle forms the many types of hair, bristle and scale which adorn the external surfaces of insects, and which are responsible for such features as the exquisite colors of butterflies' wings, the furry coats of bees and the protective spines of beetles. It also forms many types of sensory structure including the lenses of eyes, the tympanic membranes of ears and the perforated hairs which serve for olfaction and taste.

Cuticle can be elastic and rubbery so as to store and release energy for jumping or to assist in flapping the wings. The rubbery cuticle is made from a special protein, resilin. In addition to providing the

opening (gonopore) on the eight abdominal segment of the female and the ninth segment of the male. All of these distinguish insects from other hexapods.

The success and great diversity of insects depend on a number of key features, including: adaptations to prevent or withstand desiccation; fast, maneuverable flight, which may be sustained for long periods; a

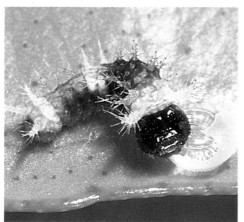

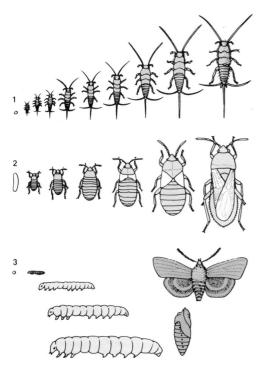

▲ **Number of larval stages** (instars) ranges from 33 in some stone flies to the five molts common in advanced orders. In primitive insects such as silverfish (**1**) there is little change in form between first stage and adult (*ametabolous* development). The larva (nymph) of exopterygote insects such as bugs (**2**) resembles a miniature wingless adult; as it grows, the wings develop externally. In contrast with this *hemimetabolous* development, more advanced insects (**3**) go through a complete metamorphosis—the larva undergoes a pupal stage, before an adult (imago) emerges that may be quite different in form, habitat and feeding habits (*holometabolous* development). Internally developing (endopterygote) wing buds occur in the later larval stages.

◄ ▼ **Developmental stages** of the Orchard swallowtail, *Papilio aegus* (Papilionidae), in eastern Australia: an adult laying a single egg; larvae (newly hatched, eating egg case; second stage with molted first stage skin; late stage displaying pungent-smelling red osmeterium to deter predators); and pupa (chrysalis) attached by silken pad at tip of abdomen and thread round thorax and wings to leaf stem of cultivated citrus.

exoskeleton, cuticle may also form an extensive endoskeleton, particularly in larger insects, providing sites for the attachment of jaw or body muscles, bracing thoracic walls internally, and forming long tendon-like apodemes for the remote control of tarsi or claws.

Like other arthropods, insects breathe by means of air-filled, cuticle-lined tubes which ramify throughout the body and open to the outside, usually in insects through 10 pairs of spiracles positioned along the sides, each controlled by a small valve. The main tubes (tracheae) which open to the exterior give rise to myriad smaller blind-ending tracheoles tapering to less than $0.1\mu m$ in diameter. The terminal portions of tracheoles may contain a liquid, sucked into the tubes from surrounding tissues by capillarity: the liquid retreats towards the tip when the tissues become active as a result of changing osmotic pressure or pH.

The tracheal system can both meet very high oxygen demands for flight and minimize water loss during periods of inactivity. In flight some insects burn more than 0.1 liter of oxygen per gram of body weight per hour ($100l/kg/h$), a higher metabolic rate than occurs in any other multicellular organism. Air sacs and tracheae are very abundant in the thorax, which automatically ventilates itself as a result of the wing movements, in the locust for example, exchanging about $20\mu l$ (0.002cc) of air with each stroke. Some large beetles in addition have two pairs of giant tracheae in the thorax through which air is ducted in flight: this not only helps to supply oxygen but it also cools the thorax, as in an air-cooled engine.

Tracheal systems function well in aquatic environments, allowing insects either to depend on dissolved oxygen through the use of gills, or to acquire oxygen at the water surface and thus be able to exploit anaerobic habitats. Modified tracheae also serve as reflecting tapeta behind the eyes, as sound resonators, as heat insulators and even as variable buoyancy tanks in some freshwater species.

The metamorphosis, complete or incomplete, that is characteristic of most insects allows the adult to act primarily as a reproductive and dispersal stage whereas the larva is a developmental and feeding stage. It also allows larva and adult to exploit very different habitats and sources of food.

Although parthenogenesis (asexual reproduction) occurs in a few insects, most reproduce sexually. Early terrestrial arthropod males protected their sperm in a special

covering, the spermatophore, which was deposited on the ground and taken up by the female. Some primitive hexapods (eg Collembola or Diplura) still use this method. In those modern insects which continue to use a spermatophore, however, the male places it within the female. Females produce eggs in one large batch or in a succession of clutches, and they may mate again between clutches. In some cockroaches the eggs hatch within the female and emerge as first-stage larvae; in the tsetse fly a single larva develops within the female, emerges when fully grown and pupates immediately; in the live-born female Black bean aphid, embryos are already developing—parthenogenesis and telescoping of generations combining to produce a very high rate of population growth.

In some species the sexes encounter each other at feeding or egg-laying sites. Dung flies may meet on dung, tsetse flies on mammals, dragonflies by the waterside. Other species use landmarks such as hilltops, bushes or trees to rendezvous with the opposite sex. Large, smoke-like swarms of midges over church towers have even resulted in calls for the fire brigade! In parts of East Africa, where lake flies swarm in thousands of millions, they are gathered, compressed into cakes and eaten by the local people. The sexes of many species "call" to each other to mate. Fireflies flash their lanterns, cicadas, crickets and grasshoppers stridulate noisily, and many moths release pheromones.

Courtship, widespread in insects, may be a prolonged and complex sequence of activities. It may be more important for allowing the female to assess the "fitness" of a male than for ensuring correct species and sexual identification between the pair. Courting males may display prominent colored wings or other structures, they may sing, perform courtship dance flights, or release chemicals. Males also compete for females by fighting, the male of some species of horned beetles, for example, trying to overturn his rival, and such battles can lead to the death of the loser. In most species conflicts are more often ritualized, and males may be able to assess the size or strength of a rival, while displaying, without physical contact.

A male sometimes guards a female before copulation, waiting until she becomes ready to mate. He may continue to guard her afterward while she lays eggs, thus ensuring his paternity of the eggs, for a male's sperm may be displaced by that of a male which mates subsequently. Alternatively, a male may insert a plug into the female or inject a chemical which renders her unattractive or unreceptive to other males.

The insect head contains a brain and a sub-oesophagal ganglion, each formed from fusion of three or more primitive ganglia. Fusion also occurs among thoracic and abdominal ganglia. Fusion probably allows incoming information to be integrated more rapidly and may economize in the number of neurones (nerve cells) required.

The brain of some species contains over a million neurones, most of which (97 percent in some flies) analyze information from the eyes and antennae. A pair of mushroom-shaped bodies in the front part (protocerebrum) contains an abundance of tiny neurones and this region may not only integrate input from sense organs but also initiate some behavior patterns. In bees and other social insects whose mushroom bodies are much larger than in solitary species it may also act as a storehouse for memories.

The most striking features of insect nervous systems are the relatively small numbers of neurones available for the complex behavior insects show, the high degree of specificity and individuality of neurones, and their structural complexity, with branching processes (dendrites) sometimes spreading across half a ganglion, allowing interaction with hundreds of other neurones.

Most sensory neurones are closely associated with minute cuticular structures upon which they depend for their functioning. Among these are mechanoreceptors including hairs, bristles, deformable caps (or campaniform sensilla), and tympanic membranes sensitive to sound waves. Some mechanoreceptors respond to strains within the cuticle or to stretch across joints arising from movement of the insect itself.

Insects are exceptionally well endowed with visual organs, whose responsiveness extends well into the ultraviolet to which we are blind. Many insects locate food, mates, rivals, nests, egg-laying sites and predators all visually, and they may be able to learn the geography of their neighborhood. The eyes, which may occupy much of the surface of the head, can provide all-round vision, color discrimination, high acuity (ie resolution of fine details), good sensitivity (ability to see at night), and can function well at different light intensities. Many species can also detect the plane of polarized light, information which they use for orientation, while in others overlap in fields of vision of widely separated eyes gives good stereoscopic vision and the ability to judge distances. In addition, most flying insects

have three small simple eyes (ocelli) near the top of the head, each with a single lens. They provide a highly sensitive and fast-reacting system which helps the insect to preserve stability in flight.

More difficult for us to appreciate is the insect world of scents and tastes. Insects also respond to gravity, to the earth's magnetic field, to temperature and humidity. Furthermore, while vision is the prime sensory system of some species, chemoreception is dominant in others. Chemoreceptors are located mainly on the antennae, mouthparts, feet, and in some cases on the egg-laying tube (ovipositor). Insects may taste food with tarsal receptors, or smell it at a distance with receptors on the antennae. Chemicals (pheromones) released by members of some species are also detected by the antennae, sometimes at very low concentrations.

Adult insects range in length from less than 0.08in (0.2mm) in tiny parasitic wasps—smaller than some protozoans—to over 12in (30cm) in some stick insects; the largest insects reach weights of 2.5oz (70g). It is often asked why no modern species is larger than this, since much larger species did occur 30 million years ago. The explanation may be that niches for larger species are

▶ **Compound eyes** enable many insects, such as this horsefly (Tabanidae) to locate food, mates, rivals, egg-laying sites, and predators. Taking up much of the head surface, the eyes may provide all-round vision, color discrimination, good resolution, sensitivity to low light intensity (night vision), to ultraviolet light and to polarized light (for direction-finding on cloudy days).

◀ **Mating day-flying moths,** *Aletis erici* (Geometridae), in Kenyan rain forest. The black and orange pattern, which deters predators with its warning of poisons, mimics that of the butterfly *Danaus chrysippus* (Nymphalidae). Such mimicry by one toxic species of another is called Müllerian, after the Müller brothers who described it first in 1877. The mimic benefits because, since predators need learn only one "poisonous" pattern, the numbers of poisonous individuals killed is reduced.

▼ **Working in cooperation,** Green tree ants, *Oecophylla smaragdina* (Formicidae), draw two leaves together to form their nest. The size and complexity of societies of social termites, ants, wasps and bees are rivalled only in humans. The "selfless service" of hymenopteran workers may be explained by an unusual mechanism determining sex (haplodiploidy), whereby sterile sisters (the workers) are more closely related than sisters or brothers are in other insect orders.

now occupied by more successful vertebrates such as birds. But if insects are limited in size, they are not limited in the diversity of habitats which they successfully colonize, or in the multitude of ways of life they exemplify.

By perfecting a waterproof cuticle and by the development of valved spiracles, insects have been able to colonize dry terrestrial habitats including both very hot and very cold regions. Relatives of crickets can be found living very actively in snow, while various beetles and cockroaches colonize the hot sands of deserts. Many other insects survive adverse periods by hibernation or aestivation, sometimes in the egg or pupal stage and sometimes as inactive larvae or adults. Frost resistance may be improved by the addition of anti-freezes such as glycerol, while dry seasons can be overcome by burrowing and remaining inactive, or, as in the case of larvae of the African chironomid midge *Polypedilum vanderplancki*, by allowing the tissues to dry out completely. These remarkable larvae can revive quickly when placed in water after years in a dry cryptobiotic state. Flies, including midges, and several other orders, have become secondarily aquatic as larvae and even in the adult stages of some species, inhabiting a variety of freshwater habitats.

Evolution of the ability to fly has enabled insects to reach small and scattered habitats, such as piles of dung, dead carcasses, or rare plants where they can feed and lay eggs. Every part of higher plants may be consumed by some insect, including root (eg cicadas), stem (stem borers), trunk (timber beetles), branch, leaf (moth larvae), flowers (butterfly larvae), fruit (tephritid flies) and seed (bruchid beetles). Other insects specialize in feeding on conifers (spruce budworm), ferns (sawflies), cycads, mosses (some lycaenid beetle larvae), algae and lichens, fungi (termites) and bacteria. The breakdown of intractable animal or plant material may be carried out by internal gut symbionts, or by the cultivation of external fungal gardens (ants, termites). Although many plants produce an assembly of toxic chemicals with which to deter herbivores, or are armed with thick cuticles, spines, prickles and viscous fluids, there always seems to be at least one insect species which has overcome the defenses and which may thereby have exclusive grazing rights on a plant. Sometimes the plant toxins are taken over by insects for their own defenses, as in the case of burnet moths. Even the parasites of such insects may in turn utilize the same toxins.

While some insects feed on plants, others devour animal products such as hoof, horn, skin, hair, feathers, scales, wax or dung. Parasites, many of which have lost the wings of their ancestors, may specialize on certain tissues such as blood, while predators normally consume the greater part of their prey.

Rapid dispersal and a short generation time are key features which allow many insects to exploit newly formed habitats, such as those created by retreating glaciers, volcanic eruptions, earthquakes or fires.

PLM

The Power of Flight

A major factor in the success of insects

Flying dominates the adult life of most insects, allowing them to exploit otherwise inaccessible habitats and to be highly active in a three-dimensional world. The ability to fly evolved early in the Carboniferous period 350–280 million years ago. One theory is that early large insects glided on fixed side extensions of the body which then came to be twisted for greater control, and finally to be flapped. Another suggestion is that wings evolved in smaller species from the use of structures already flapped for other functions, such as gills for ventilation or extensions of the thorax for sexual signaling. Flight probably arose only once and it made use of muscles whose equivalents can in the main be identified in the flightless bristletails (order Thysanura).

Several trends mark the evolution in flying insects toward greater speed and maneuverability. The originally net-like wing venation became simplified, with fewer of the longitudinal corrugations or flutes in the wings which gave longitudinal stiffness. A single pair of beating structures evolved, either by the coupling of the two wings of one side, or by reduction in size of one pair of wings to form wing shields (eg in earwigs, beetles) or the balancing organs known as halteres (in dipteran flies). Power-producing muscles came to be distinct from controlling muscles, whereas both functions had primitively been carried out by the same muscles (eg in dragonflies). There has also been a tendency toward a shorter and thicker body, with a consequent reduction of inherent stability but a great increase in potential maneuverability. Finally, success in flight owes much to the development of a specialized type of wing muscle which is able to contract at much higher rates than is normal for other muscle—for example at up to 1,000 times a second in some small flies.

The form of a wing stroke is complex. The leading edge of the wing is tilted down during the downstroke and up during the upstroke. In flies, wing twisting at each end of the stroke is automatic, but the degree of twisting can be adjusted by small muscles. Much of the power is developed indirectly by muscles which act on the plates (sclerites) of the cuticle exoskeleton of the thorax in all but the most primitive insects.

The wingbeats are assisted, first, by rubbery hinges (of resilin) which cause the wings to bounce at the top and bottom of the strokes; second, by elasticity resulting from a click mechanism which makes the wings unstable about the mid-position (like a light switch); and, third, by elasticity within the muscles themselves. Power can be raised by increasing the amount of wing twist and by increasing the beat frequency. Turns in flight are achieved usually by altering the amplitude or twist on one side, and they may be aided, as in locusts, by using the long abdomen or legs as rudders.

Some insects can hover using a helicopter-like stroke with the body nearly vertical and the wings turning over on the upstroke. Other species clap the wings together at the top of the stroke and then separate the leading edges, so causing the circulation of the air vortices upon which lift depends. Dragonflies, hoverflies and some wasps hover with the body horizontal, using a shallow stroke whose aerodynamics are not yet fully understood.

In terms of energy costs for distance traveled, flight may be relatively cheap, perhaps cheaper than walking or running. However, in cost per unit of time it is expensive, particularly during hovering when heavy loads are carried (eg wasps carrying prey), or at very high speeds—some insects may fly at up to 45mph (72km/h or 20m/sec). Bees may have a power output of 68 watts per pound (150w/kg) and hence flight muscles are furnished with a very efficient system for supplying oxygen. Adequate fuel supplies are ensured by having high concentrations of carbohydrates in the hemolymph and by using hormones to boost fuel mobilization.

The high rate of energy use in flying produces much heat, which may be quickly dissipated in small species but which accumulates in large ones. Flight muscles are adapted to working at temperatures of up to 104°F (40°C) in, for example, bumblebees, and they need to be warmed up, by basking in the sun or by shivering, before takeoff is possible. Once in flight, some species can avoid overheating by shunting hot blood from the thorax into the abdomen. In species which lack this mechanism, flight may be confined to cool periods such as the night. Daytime fliers, such as butterflies, dragonflies and locusts may both save energy and prevent overheating by making glides between intermittent wing flaps, and they often have an expanded posterior lobe of the hindwing which assists gliding.

Flying insects must have mechanisms which counter tendencies to roll, pitch or yaw, yet allow them to be maneuverable. Sense organs which help to preserve stability include the compound eyes and ocelli, and various mechanoreceptors on the antennae, head, wings, and cerci at the tip of the abdomen. Many cup-shaped

▲ **In full flight,** a male European cockchafer, *Melolontha melolontha* (Scarabaeidae). The hardened forewings or elytra are held aloft, while the beating of the transparent, membranous hindwings provides the thrust for flight.

▶ **Mechanism of the basic wing stroke** in a stylized neopteran insect. On the upstroke (**a**) the vertical dorso-ventral muscles pull down the tergum, raising the wings; the thoracic box is lengthened, stretching the horizontal muscles. When these contract, the tergum is moved up, pushing the wings into the down stroke (**b**). These indirect flight muscles are supplemented in some insects by muscles that vary the slope or pitch of the wings.

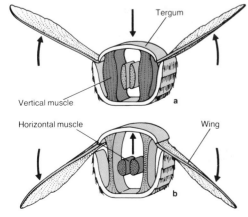

Tergum

Vertical muscle

Horizontal muscle

Wing

a

b

campaniform sensilla occur on the club-shaped haunches haltes of flies, organs which act like gyroscopes registering deviations in all three planes. Scales and strepsipterans may use a similar mechanism in their reduced forewings. Flightless species are to be found in many insect orders, and a few entire orders have become flightless, such as the fleas. Flight has a high cost both to develop, for the pre-adult stages, and energetically in the adult, and is quickly selected out when no longer valuable. Insects which have lost the power of flight include those which have become aquatic, those which burrow and have deformable bodies, parasites on vertebrate hosts, and inhabitants of small islands where winds endanger flying forms. Even in flightless individuals, dispersal can sometimes still be achieved by clinging to other flying animals (phoresy), or by being transported by a winged partner of the same species (usually the male). In other insects, flight may be limited to a certain phase of adult life, after which the flight muscles may atrophy and the wings be discarded (eg termites), or some generations may fly and others be flightless according to season (eg some water bugs or aphids).   PLM

Pheromones

Chemical messengers between individuals of a species

A pheromone is a specific chemical messenger produced by one animal that affects the behavior of other individuals of the same species. Pheromones probably arose early in the evolution of animal communication and the greatest number is found in insects. Pheromones are secreted as liquids or gases. Some are detected at a distance by smell (olfaction), others through direct contact with the body surface of the receiving insect, by smell or taste. Some are encountered in a liquid phase as olfactory "signals" to be smelled over relatively long periods.

Pheromones of various kinds dominate behavior and physiology in all aspects of insect life. Sex pheromones trigger behavior that leads to mating. When such a chemical is the means by which a mate is found at long ranges it is called a sex attractant. Usually, sex attractants are released by females, the pheromone stimulating males to fly upwind toward them. On arrival, there is a switch to courtship behavior, often with visual displays, which functions to establish mate identity and quality. Aggregation pheromones release behavior leading to an increase in numbers of a species near the pheromone source. Such pheromones are found in cockroaches, beetles, especially bark beetles (Scolytidae), and both solitary and social bees and wasps. Dispersal pheromones stimulate behavior that leads to a wider spacing between individuals. For example, a female of the Apple maggot fly, *Rhagioletis pomonella*, applies a pheromone to the fruit in which she has just laid an egg, so deterring other egg-laying females and reducing competition for food between larvae. Alarm pheromones stimulate escape or defensive behavior, especially in social insects. An injured or attacked honeybee releases a pheromone which triggers stinging behavior by nest mates. Typically, alarm pheromones are of low molecular weight and high volatility, so that the "message" spreads quickly but does not persist once danger has passed. Trail pheromones are common in termites, ants and stingless bees. When a worker finds a food source, it lays down a pheromone trail as it returns to the colony. Other workers are recruited to the food source by following this chemical trail. Trail pheromones are also used to facilitate migration of the colony to a new nest site.

The physiological state of individuals can be recognized by other insects via pheromones. A sexually mature male bark beetle, for instance, bores into a host log, releases pheromone and attracts females; immature males may bore and feed, but do not attract females.

The behavior of insects is typically very stereotyped or programmed. A female moth may release a pheromone only during one or two hours each night, and the males may respond only during a similarly narrow time period. The behavior of the two sexes may therefore be synchronous, but each is often controlled independently by outside stimuli, such as temperature or light. If a male moth encounters female sex pheromone at the optimum concentration, but outside the appropriate response period, no response will be triggered.

The chemistry of insect pheromones is usually simpler than that of mammals and comprises a few chemicals whose composition is well defined. Insect pheromone systems have become so finely tuned through evolution that their components are synthesized to a high degree of chemical

▼▶ **Antennae of some male giant silkworm moths** (Saturniidae) are large and finely branched (here the African *Argema muinosae*). This greatly increases the surface area and enhances efficiency. The antennae remove a third of all the pheromone molecules that pass over them and males can detect a "calling" female several miles away. Pheromones are perceived via the olfactory sensillae (shown here, greatly magnified, in the Southwestern corn borer moth, *Diatraea grandisosella*, family Pyralidae), cuticular pegs or hairs on the antennae, which support the sensory nerve fibers that ultimately transmit impulses to the central nervous system. The thin walls of these sensillae are perforated by pores. Pheromones are released in very small quantities, so antennae show a high degree of selectivity. Out of the many odors in the environment, the insect responds only to a narrow range of compounds relevant to behavior in its own species.

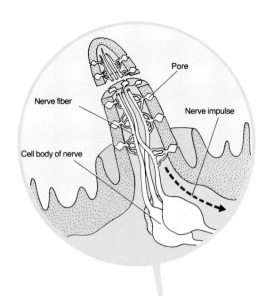

purity. Moreover, different geometric configurations of the same molecule (isomers) can also evoke very different behavior patterns, so that discrimination between these molecules must occur at the molecular level, in the antennae or the central nervous system.

The composition of pheromones is also critical. Some moths and bees use a blend of two or more chemicals as a sex attractant. The ratio between these components must be within a few percent of the natural ratio if there is to be a response. In social insects, where the pheromone blends can be complex, the discrimination and reactions are equally complicated: different concentrations may trigger distinct behavior.

Insects have a wide range of sometimes complex glands for the manufacture and storage of chemical messengers. Often, the exocrine gland openings are associated with special structures, eg modified hairs, which act as wicks to disperse the pheromone.

Pheromones have an important role to play in pest control. Pheromone-baited traps are used to detect and monitor the populations of pest insects. This enables pest control measures to be deployed more effectively. More directly, the mass application of synthetic pheromones can be used to disrupt mate finding by the males of pest insects and reduce mating success. This has been effective in controlling populations of the Pink bollworm moth, *Pectinophora gossypiella*, on cotton and, on a small-scale trial basis, of the Artichoke plume moth, *Platyptilia carduidactyla*, in California. Thus, pheromones offer the exciting prospect of highly specific and environmentally "clean" methods of pest control.   MCB

BRISTLETAILS

Orders: Archaeognatha; Thysanura

Class: Insecta, subclass Apterygota.
About 580 species.
Phylum: Uniramia.
Distribution: worldwide, even at high altitudes, in coastal areas and in polar regions.

Features: wingless; adults 0.1–0.6in (3–16mm) long; flattened and oval or elongated; brownish-gray or white, often with metallic sheen (silverfish); antennae long and thread-like, mouthparts projecting, well developed; can run fast on the 3 pairs of legs; abdomen has 11 segments and bears a pair of thread-like cerci and, at the tip, a long segmented filament (the "bristle"). Terrestrial, generally night-active, free living. Larvae do not metamorphose.

Bristletails

Order Archaeognatha
250 species in 2 families, Meinertellidae and Machilidae.

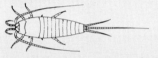

Jaws are long, simple, with a single point of articulation and rolling action.

Bristletails, silverfish, firebrat

Order Thysanura
330 species in 5 families, among them the Leptothricidae, Nicoletiidae and Lepismatidae, including the **House silverfish** (*Lepisma saccharina*) and **firebrat** (*Lepismodes inquilinus*).

The jaws are primitive, with two points of articulation and transverse action.

THE insects may be divided into two main subclasses of very unequal size, the winged Pterygota and the much smaller Apterygota (*a–pterous*, not winged). The latter grouping includes all primitively wingless insects whose ancestors have never borne wings since their first known appearance in the Devonian period, 405–345 million years ago. (Secondarily wingless insects, such as fleas and some flies, have become wingless due to a parasitic life-style. Such loss of wings has occurred independently many times and in many insect orders and for a variety of reasons.)

The Apterygota comprises two orders of three-pronged bristletails, the Archaeognatha and the Thysanura. At one time three other orders were included, the proturans, the two-pronged bristletails or Diplura and the springtails or Collembola. However, these groups lack the projecting mouthparts that today are taken to characterize insects.

Three-pronged bristletails have long-thread-like antennae, and three segments on the thorax bearing small hardened plates (sclerites) on the sides. The abdomen has 11 segments, at least some of which bear rudimentary limbs (styles) which in some species supplement the legs when running quickly over uneven or steep surfaces. Toward the tip of the abdomen projects a pair of long appendages (cerci) and from the tip itself a long, many-segmented filament, the "bristle" proper, or appendix dorsalis.

Insects of the subclass Apterygota mate by transferring a sperm packet (or spermatophore) indirectly from the male to the female. Larval development is direct (ametabolous), molting occurs throughout life, and there is little difference between larvae and adults except sexual maturity. The distribution of respiratory tubules on the side projections from the upper surface of the thorax segments is similar to that found in the wing parts of primitive insects; it has been suggested that these "paranotal lobes" gave rise to wings.

The order **Archaeognatha** is small and homogeneous. It comprises two present-day families, the Meinertellidae and the Machilidae. The body of most of these insects is a flattened cylinder with the abdomen tapering. The body is covered with pigmented scales and the thorax is strongly arched. The compound eyes are large and often touching, and there are simple eyes (ocelli) consisting of a few sensory cells and a lens. The jaws are long and simple, have a single point of articulation and work with a rolling or auger-like action, as opposed to a transverse biting, as in thysanurans. The second to ninth abdominal segments bear rudimentary limbs (styles) and the thread-like appendix dorsalis is longer than the cerci.

Archaeognathans are mostly nocturnal, living under bark, litter and in rock crevices, often on coastal cliffs. Their diet consists of algae, lichens and decaying vegetable matter. Most can run fast and many jump 4in (10cm) or so by means of a rapid downward movement of the abdomen. They reproduce

▲ **A flash of silver reveals** the House silverfish, a cosmopolitan pest of the order Thysanura, living in damp places, where it feeds on wallpaper paste and bookbindings etc. Being nocturnal, silverfish are rarely seen, except when disturbed by light. The shiny, silvery sheen is due to reflectant scales. Another pest species of the silverfish family Lepismatidae, the firebrat, prefers warm places such as kitchens and bakeries.

◄ **A well-camouflaged marine bristletail,** *Petrobius maritimus* (order Archaeognatha, Machilidae), common along rocky coasts in the Northern Hemisphere. It grazes on lichens and algae encrusting rocks just above the waterline.

sexually. Male archaeognathans deposit spermatophores on the substrate which are picked up by the females. Batches of 15 or so soft, globular, orange eggs are laid in crevices. They become hard and black and assume the shape of the surrounding crevice. Larvae pass through a number of molts (8–9 in *Petrobius maritimus*, a rocky-shore dweller), before becoming sexually mature. Archaeognathans are preyed upon by spiders, centipedes and some beetles.

The order **Thysanura** is more diverse than the Archaeognatha, but the two have many points of similarity. Silverfish are members of the family Lepismatidae but the name sometimes extends to cover all thysanurans. The general shape of the body is as in archaeognathans, but it may be with or without scales or pigmentation and the thorax is not strongly arched. The eyes are small and compound, or entirely absent—there are no ocelli. The primitive jaws have two points of articulation and bite transversely. The rudimentary limbs are similar to those in

Archaeognatha but the appendix dorsalis is the same length as the cerci.

Thysanurans are free-living and agile; they can run fast but not jump. Members of the family Leptothricidae and most of the Lepismatidae are cryptically colored and live under bark or litter, while species in the family Nicoletiidae are cave-dwelling or subterranean. Some species even live in ant and termite nests. Thysanurans are omnivorous, feeding mainly on vegetable material and starchy compounds. Some are household pests, attacking glues, bookbindings, linens, silks and wallpapers, and can produce a cellulose-digesting enzyme called cellulase.

Reproduction is generally sexual but can be parthenogenetic (ie not requiring males, even indirectly, to fertilize eggs) and the reproductive potential is large, as some species can live up to four years. The common and cosmopolitan households pests occur in the family Lepismatidae. Thysanurans are preyed upon mainly by spiders.   GCM

MAYFLIES AND DRAGONFLIES

Orders: Ephemeroptera, Odonata
Class: Insecta, subclass Pterygota.
Phylum: Uniramia.

Mayflies

Order Ephemeroptera
About 2,000 species in 19 families.
Distribution: worldwide except Antarctica, some oceanic islands.

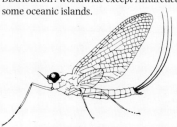

Features: medium-sized, delicate insects with biting mouthparts, vestigial in adult which does not eat; antennae bristle-like (setaceous); two pairs of richly veined clear wings (hindwings smaller, may be absent) held vertically at rest, span from under 0.4–2in (1–5cm); adults and larvae typically with three "tails" (cerci) at the tip of abdomen; larvae (nymphs) aquatic; unique pre-adult winged stage (subimago, dun); incomplete metamorphosis (hemimetabolous); wings develop externally (exopterygote).

Includes families Ephemeridae (eg **Spent gnat** or **greendrake**, *Ephemera danica*); Baetidae (eg **Medium olive**, *Baetis vernus*); Caenidae; Siphlonuridae; Heptageniidae (eg **Pond olive**, *Cloeon dipterum*, and **Lake olive**, *C. simile*); Ecdyonuridae (eg **Late March brown**, *Ecdyonurus vernasus*).

Dragonflies and damselflies

Order Odonata
About 5,000 species; 3 suborders, 29 families.
Distribution: worldwide, abundant in tropics and Far East.

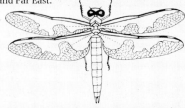

Features: generally large, length up to 6in (15cm), wingspan up to 7.5in (19cm); biting mouthparts retained in predatory adult; antennae very short, eyes very large; two pairs of richly veined wings, sometimes brightly colored, of similar shape, narrow at base and at rest held vertically (damselflies) or of different shapes, broadly attached at base and held out horizontally (dragonflies); legs directed forward; abdomen long, in male bearing secondary genitalia on 2nd and 3rd segments; metamorphosis incomplete; larvae aquatic, capturing prey by shooting out labial mask.

Includes the **damselflies** (suborder Zygoptera), (eg Calopterygidae, including **blackwings**, *Calopteryx* species); **dragonflies** (Anisoptera), including the **hawkers** (family Aeshnidae), **darters** and **skimmers** (Libellulidae), **clubtails** (Gomphidae), **emeralds** (Corduliidae) and Petaluridae; and **primitive dragonflies** (Anisozygoptera).

MAYFLIES and dragonflies represent the most ancient flying insects. Their ancestors first appeared in the Carboniferous period 350–280 million years ago, and forms similar to modern genera can be found in deposits of the subsequent Permian period (to 225 million years ago). The adult life of a mayfly or dragonfly is dominated by aerial activities and since its wings cannot be folded the insect is generally inactive on the ground. The typically large fore- and hindwings are articulated by plates which are fused to the main veins, and they have a rich venation including many triple-branched veinlets. The larvae are aquatic; they have a closed tracheal system and breathe by means of gills.

The delicate adult **mayflies** (order Ephemeroptera) do not feed, and they live only for a few days, spent in an airborne quest for mates. Underwater, however, the larva may take a year or more to pass through a series of molts before it emerges to form a winged terrestrial pre-adult stage that is unique to mayflies, then molts to become the sexually mature adult.

Mayfly larvae are to be found in a wide variety of freshwater habitats, and a few occur in brackish water; one is even terrestrial. They typically possess three long "tails" (cerci) at the tip of the abdomen and lack eyes. In their general morphology they are rather like bristletails of the order Thysanura. They pass through 15–25 molts and normally take 1–3 years to develop, although some small species may have up to three generations per year in warm regions.

Some mayfly larvae live in still water and swim about by active vertical undulations of the body aided by the tail; a few can assist swimming by squirting water from the anus, a trick perfected by dragonflies. Others crawl about on the muddy bottom of their habitat or live in U-shaped burrows which they dig with special tusks attached to the

Sperm Competition

Male dragon- and damselflies compete intensely for females by defending territories, fighting rivals, even by attempting to take over females already in copulation. But competition does not end with success or failure in finding a mate. Females can store live sperm for many days and one mating may provide enough sperm to fertilize all the eggs she lays. However, females may mate many times in order to gain access to egg-laying sites controlled by males. If a second male mates with a female before she lays eggs shortly afterward he may fertilize all the eggs because his sperm are the first to be used.

In some species of damselflies the copulating male may first scoop out the sperm of rivals from the female before he transfers his own. There are indications that some dragonflies too do the same during copulation. In this way a male can guarantee that he fathers all the eggs laid by a female until she mates with another male.

Male dragonflies are unique in their

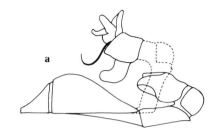

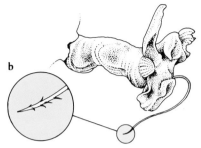

possession of secondary genitalia on the second and third abdominal segments. The store on the third segment is provisioned with sperm from the primary genitalia on the ninth segment by bending the abdomen up. In damselflies the penis on the second segment is a hard structure bearing a variety of hooks and backwardly directed bristles: much of copulation (1–2 minutes to several hours, according to species) may be spent in scooping out sperm from the female, with fresh sperm being deposited only toward the end.

In dragonflies the penis is a four-segmented inflatable structure (**a**) in which the first

segment stores sperm. When inflated the terminal segment expands and in a few species it extends a barbed flagellum (**b**) which may be able to enter the female's sperm storage organs and withdraw sperm.

The males of many species guard their mates closely during oviposition, preventing other males from gaining access to them and displacing their sperm. In non-territorial species the male may guard by remaining in tandem with the female, whereas in territorial species the male commonly guards by hovering over her or sitting close by, driving away rivals.

◄ **A subimago of a common Eurasian mayfly,** *Ephemera danica* (Ephemeridae). The short-lived subimago stage is unique to mayflies and bridges the period between larval life and the final molt to adulthood.

▼ **Dragonfly nymphs** are among the most important of invertebrate predators in ponds and rivers. This one stalks a tadpole. They also take other insects and small fish.

mandibles. Others again live in fast streams and they may be flattened, offering little resistance to the water flow as they stick with adhesive disks to the undersides of stones. Mayfly larvae possess up to nine pairs of gills which are either free or concealed under an operculum in a branchial chamber through which water is passed. Mayfly larvae are primary consumers: some are filter feeders collecting suspended matter with setae on the forelegs and mouthparts, while others are fine-particle detrivores or scrapers, rasping algae of rocks; a few are predatory.

The species composition of a habitat can give a valuable measure of pollution, since many species are very sensitive to lack of oxygen and to acidity. Acid rain has probably eliminated mayfly larvae from many habitats in North America and Europe, and thus contributed to the diminution of fish stocks, since larvae are important items in the diet of fish. When in 1675 the Dutch biologist Jan Swammerdam gave the first accurate description of a mayfly, he used *Palingenia*, a genus then abundant in Holland but now extinct in western Europe.

In temperate regions different species emerge throughout the summer, while in the tropics emergence may be seasonal or it may occur throughout the year in time with phases of the moon. The last larval stage either climbs out of the water, or in small species it emerges directly from the water surface. It molts into a subimago, a stage unique in insects, the smoky-winged dun of fishermen. This flies a short distance

and then molts again, in some species after only a few minutes, but in others after several hours, to form the clear-winged sexually mature adult (the spinner of anglers). The hindwings are much reduced in some species but the forewings are large and highly fluted, with alternating convex and concave veins. Adults do not feed and the guts remain air-filled after the molt, thereby reducing the density of the insect.

Swarms of males gather when the temperature is suitable and they perform striking aerial dances, flying upwards and slowly parachuting down, aided by their three long cerci. The males have eyes with a specially adapted dorsal region, sometimes forming a separate eye, in which the large ommatidia look upward and have high acuity—an adaptation for seeing females flying above them. When a female enters a swarm she is quickly seized by a male from below and he passes his elongated forelegs round her thorax, locking the tarsal claws into special recesses in the female's pleura. The genitalia then link together and they mate as they sink slowly towards the ground. The male has paired penes which are inserted into the two female genital openings, side by side. No sperm packet (spermatophore) is produced and copulation takes only a few seconds. The female then releases her fertilized eggs into the water either in a large mass, or more usually in small packets as she repeatedly dips her abdomen. In a few species which inhabit streams, the female descends below the water surface to lay eggs. About 50 species are known which

can reproduce without fertilization by the male (parthenogenetically), and in five this is the only method of reproduction, males being unknown.

Dragonflies have been appreciated aesthetically for many centuries. They have been depicted in medieval manuscripts, Dutch tiles, Flemish flower paintings and Japanese stamps, and have been the subjects of many songs and poems. They are also used as nose ornaments in the Far East, and their larvae are relished as delicacies in China.

Dragonflies are indeed the dragons of the air, with their magnificent powers of flight, often brightly colored wings, acute vision and large size. Some dragonflies of the Carboniferous reached a wingspan of 2ft 6in (75cm)! The largest Odonata today, rather untypically a damselfly (*Megalopropus* species), measures a quarter of this.

The order is divided into the more delicate, weakly flying damselflies (Zygoptera) in which fore- and hindwings are of similar

shape, the usually bigger and more robust dragonflies (Anisoptera) in which the wings are of different shapes, and a relict group of primitive dragonflies (Anisozygoptera) found in the Far East which has some characteristics of each of the other two suborders.

The aquatic larvae of dragonflies and damselflies have exploited a great variety of habitats; one or two are partially terrestrial. The larvae pass through 9–15 stages (instars) and may grow to a length of 2–2.4in (5–6cm) in the largest species. Life as a larva may last 5–6 years in the primitive Petaluridae, or can be as brief as 30–40 days in some darters, inhabitants of temporary pools. Temperate hawkers spend 1–2 years as larvae, whereas some of their tropical counterparts can complete development in under 100 days. Development times are strongly dependent on food abundance and temperature. Temperate damselflies may take two years to complete development in the northern parts of their range but can

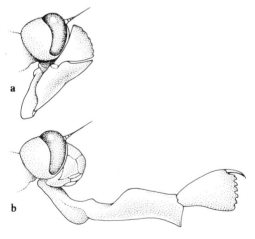

▲ **The "mask" of dragonfly larvae** is so-called because when folded at rest (**a**), it covers the other mouthparts. The mask can be extended with extreme rapidity (**b**) to grasp prey and bring it within reach of the powerful jaws. Armed at its apex with a pair of movable hooks, it is a hinged unit comprising the postmentum and prementum.

◀ **A denizen of slow-moving rivers and canals,** this damselfly, *Calopteryx splendens* (Calopterygidae), with its metallic splendor and fluttering flight, is a common sight in high summer. This male perches on waterside vegetation, a vantage point from which he will make sorties in search of females and insect prey.

▶ **Large red damselfly** male, *Pyrrhosoma nymphula* (Coenagrionidae), with its caddis fly prey, in England. Damselflies unlike dragonflies hold their wings together at rest. All Odonata are hunters, catching other insects in flight in a prey basket formed by the spiny legs held out in front of the insect. Damselflies in addition take non-flying insect prey.

▶ **Resting on a waterside plant** OVERLEAF, a female Broad-bodied darter dragonfly, *Libellula depressa* (Libellulidae). Females of this species are not attended by their mates when laying eggs on floating plants. However, they are frequently molested by roving males while egg-laying. They often avoid this interference by leaving the area immediately after mating, returning later to lay when the males have dispersed. Males of *L. depressa* are rapacious—one was once seen attempting to mate with a hornet! This behavior was probably released by the orange and yellow markings of the hornet, which resemble those of the female dragonfly.

have up to three generations a year at the southern end. Some species normally overwinter in the last larval instar and then emerge in a burst in late spring, while others overwinter at an earlier stage and emerge later in the summer, sometimes over an extended period.

Dragonfly larvae use many types of habitat, including lakes, ponds, bogs, marshes, tree holes and bromeliad leaf-bases, as well as rivers, streams, and even waterfalls. For example, larvae of one hawker species of the genus *Zygonyx* flourish in the spray and splash zones of the Victoria Falls in Zimbabwe, while the adults patrol along the brink of the falls.

Dragonfly larvae are typically opportunistic hunters, and their diet may include oligochaete worms, gastropods, crustaceans, tadpoles and fish as well as all sorts of insects, although they are seldom cannibals. Some species hunt mainly by sight, and their compound eyes develop early. An *Aeshna* larva typically remains motionless,

Defending a Patch

A territorial dragonfly male commonly adopts a stretch of the bank of a river, stream or pond which includes suitable egg-laying sites. He normally allows only a female with which he has recently mated to oviposit on his patch. The territory may extend for tens of yards along a bank or be limited to a much smaller holding in the vicinity of a water plant, tree hole or bromeliad leaf base. In some species a male may hold the same territory for many days or even weeks and clearly must have a good memory for landmarks, but in others there can be a rapid turnover of males. Some tropical darters are reproductively and territorially active only in the morning, others only in the afternoon or evening.

A territory holder commonly perches prominently and makes periodic patrols with much hovering along his beat. Intruding rivals may be challenged and pursued until they leave the area. Contests sometimes escalate and clashes may develop with one male being knocked into the water where it is at risk from fish or other predators. Sometimes conflicts are highly ritualized, and a variety of special flight pattterns have been identified: two males may fly toward each other displaying brightly colored abdomens or flashy legs, or one may fly in circles around another which hovers, or again they may perform elaborate zig-zagging dances, spiraling upward.

Copulation often occurs in the middle of the territory, the male either hovering or settled, but remaining visible to intruding males. At high population densities territories tend to be smaller and the intensity of male interactions declines, preventing incessant conflicts.

In some species only a small proportion of the males, usually the largest ones, are able to hold territories and most other males act either as satellites, sitting apparently unobserved in the territories of other males, or wander with no fixed address, seizing females whenever opportunity offers, sometimes away from the water-side. Territorial males normally obtain many more matings than other males.

but when prey draws near it stalks slowly until within range and then shoots out its "mask," a modified labium, whose long basal segments are folded under the head and thorax when at rest. The distance is gauged by stereoscopic vision and the mask extends in 25 milliseconds. It is controlled by labial muscles and the action of abdominal contractions which force blood forward. The mask has terminal hooks which grasp prey. Other species detect vibrations of moving prey with the antennae or tarsi; they can live in turbid waters, finding prey in mud, and their eyes develop later. All larvae use the labial mask for prey capture, but its shape and size vary considerably according to the habitat and the type of prey commonly sought.

Damselfly larvae swim by side-to-side body undulations assisted by the three leaf-like appendages at the tip of the abdomen. These are the tracheal gills. Dragonfly larvae can jet themselves along by forcing water from the rectal chamber out of the anus. This provides them with a high-speed escape mechanism, which may also be used to swim to the shore before emergence. The rectal chamber also contains the gills. Some dragonfly larvae seek protection by burrowing in mud or sand, and a few clubtails have the last abdominal segment extended into a respiratory siphon which remains above the mud surface. Shortly before emergence, larvae cease to feed, tissue is withdrawn from the labium and the compound eyes develop rapidly. They seek emergence sites provided by waterside plants, rocks, or the shore itself, but larvae will also sometimes climb out on boats, stakes, jetties, anchor chains or on waterlily leaves. Tropical species normally emerge at night and fly off at dawn, while temperate species may do so at night or during the day. Most species require a vertical support for emergence, but clubtails and some damselfly larvae can molt and expand their wings on a horizontal surface, and their casts are sometimes found in large numbers just above water level in lakes and rivers.

Dragonfly numbers are controlled by predators such as water bugs, beetles and fish. In some damselfly species the larvae establish feeding territories and defend them against conspecifics. This remarkable behavior probably allows them to develop more rapidly and to grow into larger adults.

Like mayflies, larval dragonflies do not tolerate pollution of their habitats. If quantities of nutrients in water rise, a consequent increase in algal growth may result in the disappearance of higher plants upon which

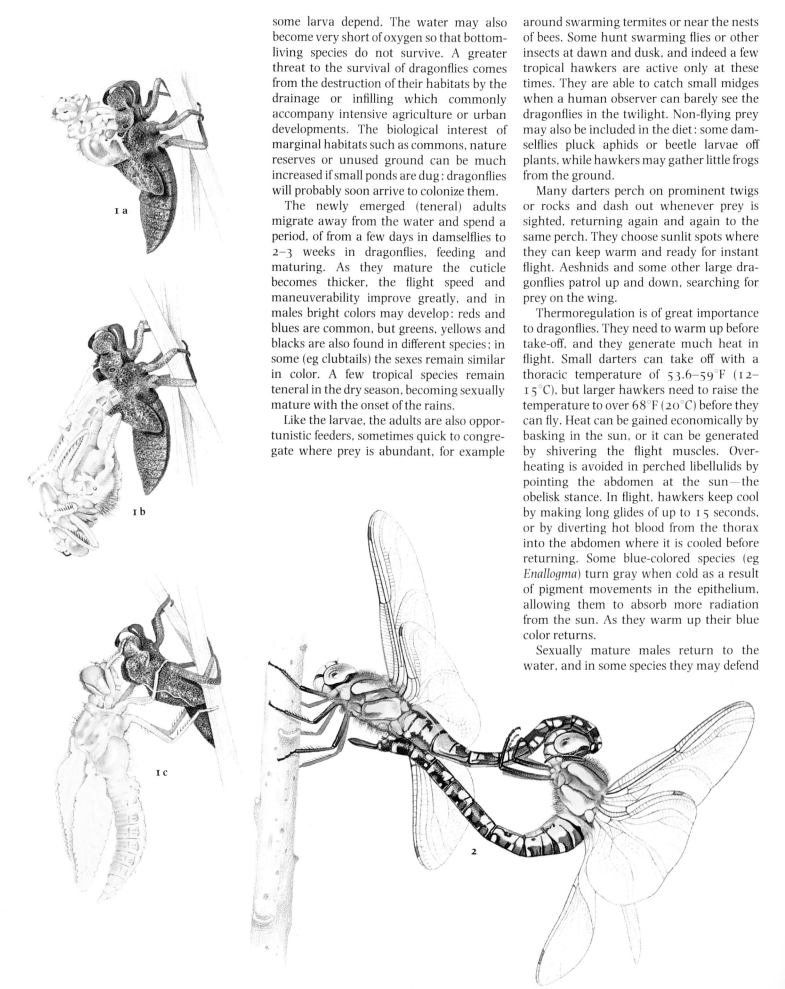

some larva depend. The water may also become very short of oxygen so that bottom-living species do not survive. A greater threat to the survival of dragonflies comes from the destruction of their habitats by the drainage or infilling which commonly accompany intensive agriculture or urban developments. The biological interest of marginal habitats such as commons, nature reserves or unused ground can be much increased if small ponds are dug: dragonflies will probably soon arrive to colonize them.

The newly emerged (teneral) adults migrate away from the water and spend a period, of from a few days in damselflies to 2–3 weeks in dragonflies, feeding and maturing. As they mature the cuticle becomes thicker, the flight speed and maneuverability improve greatly, and in males bright colors may develop: reds and blues are common, but greens, yellows and blacks are also found in different species; in some (eg clubtails) the sexes remain similar in color. A few tropical species remain teneral in the dry season, becoming sexually mature with the onset of the rains.

Like the larvae, the adults are also opportunistic feeders, sometimes quick to congregate where prey is abundant, for example around swarming termites or near the nests of bees. Some hunt swarming flies or other insects at dawn and dusk, and indeed a few tropical hawkers are active only at these times. They are able to catch small midges when a human observer can barely see the dragonflies in the twilight. Non-flying prey may also be included in the diet: some damselflies pluck aphids or beetle larvae off plants, while hawkers may gather little frogs from the ground.

Many darters perch on prominent twigs or rocks and dash out whenever prey is sighted, returning again and again to the same perch. They choose sunlit spots where they can keep warm and ready for instant flight. Aeshnids and some other large dragonflies patrol up and down, searching for prey on the wing.

Thermoregulation is of great importance to dragonflies. They need to warm up before take-off, and they generate much heat in flight. Small darters can take off with a thoracic temperature of 53.6–59°F (12–15°C), but larger hawkers need to raise the temperature to over 68°F (20°C) before they can fly. Heat can be gained economically by basking in the sun, or it can be generated by shivering the flight muscles. Overheating is avoided in perched libellulids by pointing the abdomen at the sun—the obelisk stance. In flight, hawkers keep cool by making long glides of up to 15 seconds, or by diverting hot blood from the thorax into the abdomen where it is cooled before returning. Some blue-colored species (eg *Enallogma*) turn gray when cold as a result of pigment movements in the epithelium, allowing them to absorb more radiation from the sun. As they warm up their blue color returns.

Sexually mature males return to the water, and in some species they may defend

territories along the margins against rivals. Females arrive later and they tend to stay only long enough to mate and oviposit. The arrival of a female signals intense competition among males for her possession, and, even if she has mated previously, she will mate again. She then lays her eggs in the territory of the successful male while he guards her from other males. There are many variations to this general picture in different species: for example in some damselflies and a few dragonflies an elaborate courtship precedes copulation. The male first induces the female to enter his territory and then may indicate a suitable oviposition site, using a distinctive flight with either an abnormal wing beat frequency or flying with only one pair of wings. The female may then permit the male to form a tandem and copulate with her. Such courtship contrasts with the more usual rush-and-grab tactics of the males of many other species which occasionally form tandems with females of the wrong species. A male forms the tandem in flight by grasping a female with his legs and then locking his abdominal claspers onto her prothorax (in damselflies) or head (dragonflies). They may fly in tandem for some time or immediately go into the "wheel" copulatory position in which the female's abdomen is swung up and their genitalia interlock. Copulation may take place entirely on the wing but is often completed after settling.

A female produces successive batches of eggs throughout her life and she is normally ready to oviposit soon after copulation. Damselfly and hawker females possess egg-laying tubes (ovipositors) which can pierce and then insert eggs into plant tissues—a relatively slow process but one which provides considerable protection for each egg. Some damselflies crawl underwater and oviposit well below the surface, remaining submerged for over an hour to do so. Darters, by contrast, have no ovipositor and tend to scatter eggs widely onto the water or nearby. They may repeatedly dip the abdomen into the water, or extrude eggs above the water surface—the latter being a safer procedure since predators lurk close to the surface. A few settle and glue eggs onto plants or rocks at or above water level, while others again scoop up water drops and flick them together with eggs onto the bank. In general these strategies may help to prevent eggs from being washed downstream, or from sinking into soft bottom deposits short of oxygen, as well as giving them some protection against egg parasites and predators.

◀▲ **Emergence, mating and egg-laying** in dragonflies and damselflies. The final instar larvae of dragonflies and damselflies climb out of the water on emergent vegetation just before the adults hatch: (**1a–c**) *Orthetrum coerulescens* (Libellulidae) and (**6**) *Coenagrion puella* (Coenagrionidae). (**2**) Mating *Aeshna mixta* (Aeshnidae), the female (RIGHT) receiving sperm from the male's secondary genitalia, while the male clasps the back of his mate's head. (**3**) A female Golden-ringed dragonfly, *Cordulegaster boltoni* (Cordulegasteridae) uses her ovipositor specially modified for laying eggs in the gravel beds of shallow streams. (**4**) Male-assisted egg-laying in *Coenagrion puella*. (**5**) A female *Aeshna cyanea* lays eggs in a soft, water-logged tree stump.

PLM

COCKROACHES

Order: Blattodea
Class: Insecta, subclass Pterygota.
Phylum: Uniramia.
About 3,500 species described in 5 families,
probably at least as many species undescribed.
Distribution: cosmopolitan, except polar regions.

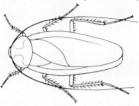

Features: adults medium to large, about 0.4–
2.4in (1–6cm) long, with flattened body, and
usually forewings dark in color and hard; head
directed downward, protected by back plate
extending forward from prothorax; long
antennae. Eggs laid in hardened capsule
(ootheca) sometimes carried by female. Chiefly
nocturnal omnivores, often scavengers. Inhabit
great variety of places; some species are
domestic pests.

Family Blattidae
Medium-sized cockroaches, including the
American cockroach (*Periplaneta americana*).

Family Blattellidae
Small to medium-sized, slender. The **German
cockroach** (*Blatella germanica*) and **Oriental
cockroach** (*B. orientalis*) are common domestic
pests.

Family Blaberidae
Includes the largest cockroaches; many are
stout, wingless, and burrow in the soil and in
rotting logs. Some, such as the **Madeira
cockroach** (*Leucophaea maderae*), live in
association with man.

Family Polyphagidae
Small, delicate cockroaches, some living in
ants' nests.

Family Cryptocercidae
1 genus (*Cryptocercus*) of wood-eating
cockroaches from N America.

Not only are cockroaches found just about everywhere, they also eat just about anything. They have adapted successfully to an enormous range of environments. Found from sea level up to almost 6,500ft (2,000m) in the mountains, they inhabit deserts, tundras, grasslands, swamps and forests. They live in, on, and under trees. They burrow in the ground and live in caves. Some Asian species are even amphibious.

The versatile cockroaches are among the most ancient of all insect groups, and fossils from the Carboniferous period 345–280 million years ago are known. Each species is built for its particular habitat: burrowing cockroaches tend to be stocky and wingless, with strong spade-like limbs. Tree-dwelling insects are slim, with well-developed wings and long, slender legs for fast running. Species living under bark are highly flattened. Many cockroaches are true omnivores, feeding with their relatively unspecialized chewing mouthparts, on living or dead plant and animal material.

More specialized feeders include the wood-eating *Cryptocercus* species from Asia and North America. Although many insects feed on wood, most are unable to digest its major component, cellulose. *Cryptocercus* has solved this problem by keeping a population of protozoans in a special sac off its gut. These microorganisms digest cellulose for the cockroach and release the nutrients back into the gut in a form which the insect can absorb. In return for their services, the cockroach provides the protozoans with food and a stable, secure environment.

The only other group of insects (apart from some beetles) which has this relationship with protozoans is the termites, which have exactly the same types of gut organisms as *Cryptocercus*. Structural similarities, and the greater age of known cockroach fossils, suggest that termites evolved from cockroaches.

Larvae of the genus *Cryptocercus* are not born with the protozoans in their gut. They become infected by feeding on droplets of fecal material exuded from the anus of adults. This requires young and adults to live together, and it is suggested that this behavior may have led to the development of true sociality in termites. However, although *Cryptocercus* and some other cockroaches live in aggregations, none exhibits the termites' communal care of eggs and young and other division of labor.

The reproductive life of cockroaches shows as much diversity as other aspects of their biology. The five families are divided on the basis of differences in the genitalia, egg-laying behavior, and foregut structure.

Many cockroaches are oviparous—they deposit their eggs along with glandular secretions which harden to form a tough protective capsule; this ootheca may be stuck to the substrate and concealed with bits of debris, or else carried around on the end of the female's abdomen. Other species are ovoviviparous—the females incubate their eggs within a special brood sac until they hatch. One species (*Diploptera punctata*) even produces live young, the mother providing nutrients for the developing hatchlings which she keeps within her brood sac.

The eggs of cockroaches are parasitized by a number of other insect species, most commonly wasps. Oothecae which are left in exposed positions are particularly at risk. Cockroaches are considered tasty morsels, as young and adults, by insects and other arthropod predators, as well as by frogs, toads, lizards, snakes, birds and insectivorous mammals.   ssi

---

Insect "Rats and Mice"

Cockroaches, such as the large American cockroach and the smaller German and Oriental cockroaches, are the insect equivalent of rats and mice. They have become extraordinarily successful at living in association with man, thriving in the same warm, humid, sheltered environments which we ourselves enjoy.

Because of their flattened bodies, cockroaches are able to crawl into narrow crevices, behind cupboards, under floorboards and into drains and sewers, where they hide during the day. At night they become active and roam around in search of food. Being catholic in their tastes, they will eat any accessible household foods as well as papers, documents and book bindings.

More seriously, cockroaches foul with their excreta and dirty feet those sites where they walk and feed. A cockroach which has crawled out of a drain or sewer and then wanders over exposed foodstuff may transmit disease. Cockroaches have been reported to carry poliomyelitis virus and *Salmonella*, the food poisoning bacterium.

In addition to damaging stored food, books and papers, and transmitting disease, cockroaches are difficult to eradicate. They are very adaptable and after one nasty but not fatal experience will learn to avoid areas where poisons have been placed.

Cockroaches are also difficult to catch. They are extremely sensitive to vibration of the surface on which they stand, being able to detect a movement of less than one twenty-five millionth of an inch. They also respond to very slight air movements which they sense through hairs on the two appendages (cerci) which project from the tip of the abdomen. A cockroach can detect vibration of air movements long before the would-be attacker is anywhere near and can run swiftly to cover in inaccessible cracks and crevices.

Cockroaches are also long-lived and produce large numbers of offspring. The American cockroach holds the record. It can live for over four years, during which time a female may lay more than 1,000 eggs.

No wonder cockroaches are such successful pests and so unpopular with their human hosts.

▲ **Anti-predator devices** are a recurrent theme in the story of insect survival. One is to mimic other species which are poisonous and have a warning coloration. As its name suggests, this South American cockroach, *Paratropes lycoides* (Blaberidae), mimics the color pattern of noxious beetles of the family Lycidae.

▶ **Safety-in-numbers principle** is exploited here by a dense cluster of cockroach nymphs in Kenya. The larger the aggregation, the lower the risk of predation to the individual. This protection is enhanced by the bright colors, which signal to would-be predators that the nymphs are distasteful.

Cockroach larvae resemble small adults in appearance and habits, and go through a number of molts. In winged species, wing buds appear on the thorax of the larva in later stages. The wings are fully developed by the final molt.

TERMITES

Order: Isoptera
Class: Insecta, subclass Pterygota.
Phylum: Uniramia.
About 2,230 species described in 7 families.
Distribution: worldwide from Equator to
45–50°N and S.

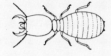

Features: highly social in large, permanent
communities with various "castes," each
distinct in form. Mostly slender, 0.8–8.7in (2–
22mm) long to 5.5in (14cm) in some "queens";
reproductive adults darker with 2 similar-shaped
pairs of wings spanning 0.4–3.5in
(10–90mm) that drop off after the swarm flight;
head with biting mouthparts for diet of dead
plant material, often wood, set at right angles
to rest of body; larvae (nymphs) resemble
adults, no pupal stage.

TERMITES not only feed, groom and protect each other, but the offspring of one generation assist the parents in raising the next, the mark of truly social animals.

Termites live in colonies ranging in size from a few hundred to as many as seven million individuals. Each termite society is divided between several castes—the winged and sighted reproductives (queen and king, and young reproductives the vast majority of which will perish without mating), and the wingless and usually blind workers and soldiers, which feed, maintain and protect the colony. The termites share this characteristic of social life with the ants, but in each termite caste either sex may occur, whereas ant and bee workers are always female.

The similarities between colonies of termites and ants are all the more remarkable because the termites evolved quite independently, and much earlier than ants. Furthermore, ants are also termites' worst enemies (see below). The termites are "social cockroaches," having evolved from a common stem with cockroaches during the early Mesozoic or late Palaeozoic about 220 million years ago. This close relationship is illustrated by the primitive Australian Darwin termite and the colonial, wood feeding Brown-hooded cockroach (*Cryptocercus punctulatus*) of North America, which share an astonishing number of characteristics, including not only the general structure of their wings, genitalia and jaws, but even the habit of laying batches of eggs in a double-row of 20–35. Perhaps most significant of all, both species have similar colonies of single-celled animals (protozoa) living in their guts and giving essential assistance in the digestion of food. Both the cockroach and termite adults pass the protozoa on to young individuals in their feces. This reliance of younger on the older members of the colony has been a key factor favoring the evolution of social behavior in termites.

A termite colony begins when a flying sexually mature male is attracted to a female by an odor secreted from a gland on her underside. If they have not already done so, they then shed their wings, whose brief job of carrying them away from the parent nest is now completed. They run off in a "tandem pair," the male close behind the female, in search of a suitable location to build a nest and raise young.

The first larvae are always destined to be workers in one form or another. In the six

The 7 Families of Termites

Darwin termite
Family Mastotermitidae

I species (*Mastotermes darwiniensis*) in Australia; primitive, nests in tree stumps; food mainly wood but pests of many materials.

Dry-wood termites
Family Kalotermitidae

350 species, distribution as order; nest in dead branches; food dry, mainly dead, wood; also pests in plantations, building timbers.

Termopsidae
17 species in Australia, Asia, S Africa, USA, Chile; nest in rotten stumps and logs; food rotten wood; pests of timber.

Harvester termites
Family Hodotermitidae

17 species in drier areas of Africa, Arabia, Asia; nest underground; food grass; pests of grasslands.

Damp-wood termites
Rhinotermitidae

206 species, same range as order;

nest in and feed on rotten wood; some very destructive in buildings and crops.

Sawtooth termite
Family Serritermitidae

I species (*Serritermes serrifer*) in Brazil; nest in walls of mounds of other termites (usually the snouted termite *Cornitermes*); food not known.

Higher termites
Family Termitidae

1,639 species (over 70 percent of termite species) in tropical and subtropical regions worldwide; nest very variable, in trees, surface mounds or underground chambers; food very variable, dead wood, grass, leaves, soil, humus and other organic matter. Four large subfamilies: **soldierless termites** and relatives (subfamily Apicotermitinae); **termitines** or **subterranean termites** (Termitinae); **snouted termites**, some **harvester termites** (Nasutitermitinae); and **fungus-growing termites** (Macrotermitinae).

▼ **Inside the royal chamber** of an African termite, *Macrotermes subhyalinus* (Termitidae). The male or "king" dwarfs the workers, but is in turn dwarfed by the grotesquely swollen abdomen of his mate, the queen. The king remains with the queen and both are tended by a court of workers which feed and clean them.

families of more primitive "lower termites" even the immature forms can behave like workers and contribute to the well-being of the colony.

Once a few workers have been raised and are able to build, nurse young and finally collect food, soldiers are reared to defend the colony. Soldiers are usually armed with enlarged, biting or snapping jaws and armored heads, and are sometimes capable of squirting defensive secretions at their enemies from special head glands. However, they are wholly dependent upon their workers for food, which is regurgitated or fed in an anal secretion. The original two flying termites, surrounded with their subjects, have now truly earned the titles of "king" and "queen" of the colony.

In most termite species both soldiers and workers are blind, although they are sensitive to light directly through the cuticle of the head capsule. In a mature colony fully developed adults capable of reproduction (reproductives) are raised, equipped with wings and proper eyes, unlike their brothers and sisters. At this stage the queen may be laying over 30,000 eggs a day, her body hugely enlarged into an egg-producing machine up to 5.5in (14cm) long and 1.4in (3.5cm) across. Her king, still constantly in attendance at her side, remains his normal size, by now dwarfed by his massive, white, pulsating spouse.

When conditions are right, often after a heavy storm, the workers open holes in the nest and release the young reproductives, which fly off in all directions to complete the cycle of renewal. The exposed and weak-flying termites are at their most vulnerable, and this is a time of plenty for predators like ants, spiders, geckos and other lizards, shrews and other insectivorous mammals, and a host of birds from francolins to falcons; in many parts of the tropics flying termites are also eaten by people. Perhaps fewer than one flying termite in a thousand survives to raise a mature colony.

Except during their annual swarms, termites are secretive insects, yet they are all too familiar to people in tropical and subtropical regions because of the extensive damage they can cause. Termites depend on dead plant material for food, and often for a nesting place too. Man usually replaces natural vegetation by crops, forestry plantations, factories and homes, all of which can provide the termites with substitute foods in one form or another. Not easily dislodged, termites damage wood and wood-derived materials in exotic trees, building timbers, furniture, books, packing cases and even rifles and cricket bats! Other materials attacked by termites include leather, cloth, rubber, cables, and crops including fruit trees, stem crops such as sugarcane, and a wide variety of underground crops from potatoes to yams.

Damage caused by termites can be very serious indeed. The entire village of Sri Hargobindpur in the Punjab region of India was abandoned in the 1950s because of the pervasive damage by the termite *Heterotermes indicola*. A similar threat may have faced the village of Popayán in Colombia, where the church cross bears the inscription "a Paternoster to Jesus that we may be free of termites."

Yet the same capacity for destroying dead plants that is so troublesome to us is also the reason for termites' unrivaled ecological importance. In any natural ecosystem it is essential that dead plant material should be broken down, incorporated into the soil and once again made available for the growth of living plants. Bacteria and fungi play the largest part in this process of decay, but in tropical savannas and forests termites also have an important role. In the tropics

termites may consume up to a third of the total annual production of dead wood, leaves and grass. Their populations often reach 200–400 in every square foot of soil surface (about 2,000–4,000/sq m), sometimes as high as 1,000 (10,000/sq m), and they dominate over other soil animals. Their biomass, usually in the range 0.04–0.2oz/sq ft (1–5g/sq m) can reach as high as 0.8oz/sq ft (22g/sq m), over twice that of the greatest densities of vertebrates on earth, in the migrating herds of wildebeest and other hoofed mammals on Tanzania's Serengeti Plains.

The Isoptera is the only order of insects with a general ability to digest cellulose, the main chemical constituent of all plants. The secret of the termites' success is their ability to enter into cooperative associations with protozoa, bacteria and fungi that can produce the enzymes needed by termites to digest plant material.

The presence of such protozoa in the gut, as in the primitive Darwin termite, is a feature of all "lower termites," most of whose members feed on dead wood. Nevertheless, much of the material consumed by termites remains undigested; the copious feces are often used in nest building, or are simply ejected onto heaps from the wood or soil in which the termites are living.

The "higher termites," the seventh family, lack special gut protozoa, but have a range of more sophisticated associations that inlcude bacteria and fungi. This certainly accounts in part for the family's enormous evolutionary success, in terms of both diversity of species and adaptations to a wide range of feeding habits. In three of the four subfamilies of the higher termites (Apicotermitinae, Termitinae and Nasutitermitinae), large cultures of bacteria grow in the hindgut, where they help ferment plant material.

Both lower and higher termites (except the fungus-growing subfamily Macrotermitinae) also have gut bacteria that can fix atmospheric nitrogen, that is, they can take nitrogen from the air and ultimately incorporate it into amino acids, the building blocks of proteins. The only other insect known to have this ability is, again, the Brown-hooded cockroach—further evidence of the close relationship between termites and cockroaches.

Most termites prefer to eat dead plant material that has already been attacked by fungi, which help to break up the cells, releasing the nutrients. In the savanna regions of Africa and Asia the long dry seasons greatly slow down the activities of fungi and of the termites that depend upon

Nature's Finest Builders

Most species of termite hide their nests underground or inside dead wood, but a few higher termites build bizarre mounds and tree nests that can be a significant, even familiar, component of the tropical landscape. In the African savannas, high temperatures and low rainfall pose a real threat to termites. Exposed to the midday sun, termites would survive only a few minutes. To protect the colony, the fungus-growing species *Macrotermes bellicosus* builds a towering earth mound up to 25ft (7.5m) high, most of the above-ground portion being hollow to allow circulation of air (1). Its function is to maintain an equable temperature in the nest below ground level, preventing it from overheating during the day, or cooling too far at night. Much of the nest itself is occupied by the fungus combs, which produce substantial amounts of heat.

Around Darwin in arid northern Australia, the remarkable Compass or Magnetic termite (*Amitermes meridionalis*) builds 11.5ft (3.5m) high wedge-shaped nests that run north to south so that in the morning and evening the sun on the flat surface helps to warm up the nest, but at midday the knife-edge, pointed towards the sun, prevents overheating (2). Also in Australia, the snouted termite *Nasutitermes triodae* builds huge nests up to 20ft (6m) high. They can become a

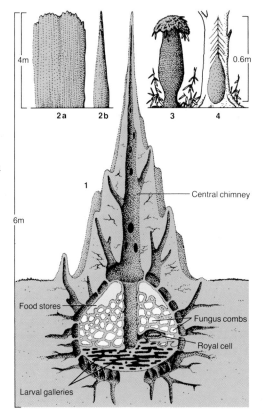

permanent feature of the landscape and some are known to have been occupied continuously for over 60 years. The greatest diversification of the snouted termites has occurred in South America, where at the opposite extreme grass-feeding *Syntermes* species build nests that extend 11ft (3.4m) underground! In the same region, snouted *Cornitermes* species may build either a mound up to 13ft (4m) high (the walls of which may house another termite, *Serritermes serrifer*), or a subterranean nest with a 5ft (1.5m)-tall chimney sticking out of the ground to vent hot air. In northern Kenya *Macrotermes subhyalinus* builds a similar chimney. The wind blowing across the lip of the chimney is said to draw out hot air.

In rain forests, changes in air temperatures are less of a problem than sudden cloudbursts. In African forest, soil-feeding *Cubitermes* species (subfamily Termitinae) build mushroom-shaped nests with a series of caps or tree-side roofs to shed the rain (3). In the same forests, species of *Procubitermes* plaster their nests to a tree and protect them by building up to 40 water-shedding mud barriers in a herringbone pattern above the nest (4). In South America species of the snouted termite genus *Constrictotermes* do precisely the same thing.

them, but one group of termites, the subfamily Macrotermitinae (including the genera *Odontotermes* and *Macrotermes*), has overcome the food shortage in a unique way. They have developed a symbiotic association with fungi of the genus *Termitomyces*, which the termites cultivate inside the nest on "fungus combs" made of their own feces. The fungus, found nowhere else except in the nest of the termites, breaks down the feces which the termites then consume. These fungus-growing termites are of very great ecological importance. Their activities dominate decomposition processes in most seasonally dry areas of the Old World.

A number of mammals are specialist feeders, on termites, including the aardvark and aardwolf of Africa, the pangolins of Africa and Asia, and the anteaters of South America.

However, the termites' greatest enemies are ants. Many ant species specialize in raiding termite foraging parties. Termites are highly variable in their foraging patterns and those that travel furthest tend to be more vulnerable to predators. Some termites, such as the dry wood genera *Kalotermes* and *Neotermes*, never leave the branch in which they are nesting. Others, such as the fungus-growers, may travel over 165ft (50m) from the nest through a semipermanent network of tunnels in order to reach new sources of food. They defend themselves in a number of ways: by building fortified nests, by covering their food in a protective sheet of mud while they feed underneath, and with the specialized caste of soldiers.

Among the soil-feeding higher termite subfamily Apicotermitinae are a number of genera (eg *Ateuchotermes*, *Alyscotermes*) that have no soldiers, but the workers defend the colony by bursting their slimy gut contents over marauding ants, killing themselves in the process. Most termite species have soldier castes with large armored jaws, but in the most advanced form of soldier these have become redundant. The Nasutitermitinae (snouted termites) have a specially developed frontal gland that produces sticky and irritating chemicals from the tip of an extended snout. This strategy is so successful at warding off the attention of ants that most snouted termite soldiers have very reduced jaws, and a number of nasute genera forage in open columns defended at the sides by snouted soldiers (eg grass-gathering "harvester" termites of the genus *Trinervitermes* and also *Longipeditermes*).   NMC

▲ **Column of foraging worker termites** of the snouted termite genus *Hospitalitermes* (Termitidae) in Malaysia. The workers forage on lichens and other vegetation on the forest floor and on tree trunks. Both sides of the column are guarded by nasute soldiers, which, though blind, can accurately discharge through their snouts a sticky, poisonous substance which quickly immobilizes ants, the termites' main enemies.

◄ **Mounds of termites are major features** of the landscape in many tropical countries. This is particularly true of dry savanna country, where the "chimneys" of large nests, such as this one of *Macrotermes* in Namibia, play a vital role in air conditioning the colony (Termitidae).

MANTIDS

Order: Mantodea
Class: Insecta, subclass Pterygota.
Phylum Uniramia.
About 1,800 species in 8 families.
Distribution: all warmer regions; best
represented in tropics.

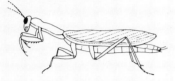

Features: adults medium to large, 0.4–6in
(1–15cm) long; downward-directed triangular
head on flexible neck; large eyes; long first
segment of thorax (prothorax); large grasping
forelegs; form and coloration often cryptic in
imitation of plants. Eggs laid in capsules
(oothecae) whose shape characterizes the
species. Day-active carnivores. Found on
shrubs, tree trunks, tall herbs, taking chiefly
insects for food; other terrestrial species may
take spiders and other terrestrial arthropods.

By far the largest family is the Mantidae which
includes the **European praying mantis** (*Mantis
religiosa*). The Amorphoscelidae, best
represented in Australia, differ in having a
short dorsal plate (pronotum) covering the
prothorax, and no spines in the crook of the
forelegs.

MANTIDS are superbly designed ambush predators. Their triangular head, with its large compound eyes and chewing mouthparts, swivels freely atop a long, narrow prothorax (first section of the thorax), which also carries the highly modified, grasping forelegs with their array of hooks and spines.

In addition to their keen eyesight and formidable armory, mantids are cryptically colored to resemble the plant on which they lie in wait, and projections of the cuticle of the body and legs often enhance their likeness to bark, twigs, leaves or flowers.

While waiting for a prey insect to pass, the mantid remains motionless, or gently rocks from side to side as if swaying in the breeze. Its forelegs are held folded against the prothorax and suggest an attitude of prayer (hence the common name Praying mantis). An insect passes, and the mantid slowly turns its head and prothorax towards it. When the insect strays within range, spined forelegs suddenly shoot forward to seize the creature. Held in a pincer-like grip, the prey is brought to the mantid's jaws and devoured.

All mantids are carnivores, feeding mainly on a variety of insects, including other mantids. They are solitary creatures and it is possible that the observed tendency toward cannibalism is partly responsible.

Depending on the species, female mantids lay from 10 to 400 eggs in a frothy mass produced by glands in the abdomen. This froth hardens on contact with the air, so that the developing eggs are protected by a horny capsule and often a tough, spongy coat. The size and shape of this structure, called the ootheca, depends on the species. Many species, including the European and North African *Mantis religiosa*, attach the ootheca to a flat surface such as a tree trunk or rock. In others it surrounds twigs or stems and in some species it is deposited in the soil.

Despite the protective coat, parasitism of the eggs, particularly by certain wasps, is common and often few if any larval mantids emerge from an ootheca. The young larvae leave the egg case via a series of exit holes which lie along its upper midline. In some species the mother stands guard until the young emerge.

Newly emerged larval mantids disperse, and commence their predatory existence as small, vulnerable versions of their parents. After passing through several molts, during which they increase in size and their developing wing buds become progressively larger, the larvae go through a final molt to become adults. Adult male mantids usually have fully developed wings, while the wings

Risks of Being a Male Mantid

Female mantids are famous for eating their suitors. But, while this behavior does occur, it is not nearly as common as generally thought. In one American species it never occurs at all, not because males are adept at avoiding being eaten or because females are not cannibalistic, but because no males are known to exist. All the offspring are female and produced from unfertilized eggs. This is known as parthenogenesis and is common among the insects, although sexual reproduction usually occurs as well in most species.

Nevertheless, male mantids are sometimes eaten by females, before, during, or after mating. How might eating a mate benefit a female mantid? For a start, she gets a nutritious meal. Also, by only mating with a male which courts her appropriately, and eating those others which do not (as sometimes occurs), a female may ensure that her male offspring will inherit the successful courtship behaviour shown by their father and thus live to sire many offspring of their own.

Another intriguing possibility is that the male actually mates more effectively when partly eaten! It has been shown that removal of the male's head, the bit which the female eats first, releases the male's genitalia from nervous inhibition from the brain and leads to incessant copulatory movements.

There is obviously no advantage to a male in being eaten. If he survives mating, he can mate with other females and sire more offspring. As a result, males have evolved a number of forms of behavior which minimize the risk of being eaten. They approach a female very slowly and cautiously, generally from behind, and, when close, leap onto her back. It is vital that the male sits on the female in a position where he cannot be reached by her grasping forelegs. The fact that he is smaller than the female makes him harder to grab in this position.

During copulation the female goes into a trance-like state, but on completion the male is again in danger. So when he is finished, the male leaps off and runs away very quickly indeed.

◀ **Female African mantid eats mate** BELOW (*Polyspilota* species) during copulation, while a second male sits on her back (Mantidae).

▼ **Gin-trap forelegs poised,** a female mantid (*Acontista* species, family Hymenopodidae) sits motionless on a *Bidens* flower in Trinidad, awaiting a nectar-seeking insect.

of the females of many species are reduced or absent.

The cryptic coloration and behavior which serve mantids so well as hunters also protect them from falling prey themselves to birds, lizards and insectivorous mammals. Once disturbed, mantids utilize a variety of defenses. They may run away very quickly and possibly launch into flight. Some species stand their ground and rear back to display brightly colored marks on the insides of their forelegs. If approached too closely by a predator (or an entomologist!) they will strike out and the spined forelegs can inflict a painful jab.

If picked up, a mantid will bend its mobile forelegs backwards over its prothorax and use the spines to ensure that the insect is either dropped by its tormentor or else held more carefully. Mantids will also sacrifice one or more mid- or hindlegs in order to escape. This shedding of limbs is known as autotomy and results from the contraction of a special muscle at the base of the leg. Very rarely are the grasping front legs autotomized, and a mantid without its front legs soon dies of starvation. Regeneration of lost appendages may occur if the limbs are shed early in the life of the mantid.

The earliest known fossil mantids date from the Oligocene, 36–25 million years ago. Mantids are often confused with stick insects. The two orders, while superficially similar in appearance, are in fact easy to tell apart. Most notably, the prothorax is extremely elongate in mantids but not in phasmids. Also, stick insects, which are herbivores, not carnivores, lack the armored grasping forelegs and the mobile triangular heads of mantids. ssi

EARWIGS AND STONE FLIES

Orders: Dermaptera, Plecoptera
Class: Insecta, subclass Pterygota.
Phylum: Uniramia.

Earwigs

Order Dermaptera
About 1,200 species in 3 suborders.
Distribution: worldwide except polar regions.

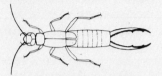

Features: adults of most species medium sized,
0.4–2in (1–5cm) long, generally drab in color,
with elongated, flattened bodies, relatively
short legs; tip of abdomen bears a pair of
prominent pincers or forceps; most have small,
hardened forewings (elytra) covering large, fan-
shaped hindwings. Larvae like wingless adult.

The **true earwigs** (suborder Forficulina) include
the **Common earwig** (*Forficula auricularia*) and
other mostly free-living species. The wingless
Arixeniina (2 known species) and Hemimerina
(10 species) are specialized parasites.

Stone flies

Order Plecoptera
About 3,000 species known, in 2 suborders.
Distribution: worldwide except polar regions.

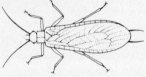

Features: adults medium sized, about 0.4–5in
(1–5cm) long, with flattened, soft body, and
usually two pairs of wings (hindwings broader)
held flat across body at rest; antennae long,
threadlike, and cerci often thread-like; lower
leg (tarsus) has 3 segments. Chiefly terrestrial
along riverbanks; herbivorous or do not feed.
Larvae aquatic, like wingless adults;
herbivorous, sometimes carnivorous.

Suborder Filipalpia comprises small to
medium-sized species found mainly in cold
waters; nymphs and adults usually vegetarian.
Includes the large family Nemouridae. The
family Leuctridae includes the **needle flies** or
rolled-wing flies, which bend the wings round
the sides of the body when at rest, and the
angler's **February red** (*Taeniopteryx nebulosa*).
Suborder Setipalpa comprises small to large
species, commoner in warmer waters; nymphs
usually carnivorous, adults generally do not
feed. The family Perlidae includes anglers'
Large stone fly (*Dinocras cephalotes* and *Perla
bipunctata*). Other families include the
Isoperlidae (**Yellow Sally**, *Isoperla grammatica*)
and the Chloroperlidae.

▶ **Yellow Sally stone flies** ABOVE mate on
waterside vegetation (Isoperlidae).

▶ **The Common earwig,** contrary to folklore,
has no desire to enter people's ears (Forficulidae).

EARWIGS are designed to inhabit narrow
crevices. Their body is smooth and compressed, their legs are short, and the chewing mouthparts are directed forward on a
flattened, mobile head. The abdomen can
"telescope" and bend freely. A pair of long
pincers projects from the tip of the abdomen.
These are a highly modified form of the
antenna-like cerci which many insects possess. In earwigs they are straight in females,
curved in males. They are used to capture
prey, in offense and defense, and in courtship and mating. They may also help to fold
the hindwings after flight.

Beneath the very short, hardened forewings lies a pair of large, intricately folded
membranous hindwings (hence Dermaptera, skin-winged). Without this protection
the delicate wings would be torn and damaged as the earwig crawled beneath the bark
of a tree or into crevices in a rock. Earwigs
are nocturnal. They are omnivorous, using
their biting and chewing mouthparts to eat
small insects, decaying plant and animal
material, and also living plant tissue. The
cosmopolitan Common earwig can be a pest
in large numbers, as it eats flowers and fruit.

When an earwig comes to rest, it touches
as much of its body as possible against an
object. This contact has the effect of inhibit-
ing locomotory activity by the earwig and
is known as thigmotaxis. Earwigs also tend
to move against gravity. Gardeners and
entomologists can make use of such
tendencies to catch earwigs. A very effective
earwig trap is an inverted flowerpot stuffed
with cotton wool and placed over a short

length of dowel which is stuck into the ground. Passing earwigs climb up the dowel, as they would a flower stem, and crawl into the cotton wool, where the inactive insect can be found next morning.

The female digs a short burrow in the soil in which she lays 20–50 (depending on the species) creamy white, oval eggs. She stays in the burrow for 2–3 weeks until the eggs hatch, regularly cleaning and turning the eggs. Presumably this prevents fungal infections from setting in. She also guards her batch against predators. Such parental care is unusual among insects. For a week or two the female continues to guard her young. After this time she encourages them to leave by developing a marked tendency to eat them. The larvae molt 4–5 times before adulthood, reached in late summer by the Common earwig in temperate zones.

Today's **stone flies** differ little from their Permian period ancestors of 280–225 million years ago. Adults are poor fliers. They spend most of the time sitting on waterside rocks or vegetation, their membranous wings folded flat across the body. In some species there are reduced wings, or none. During their 2–3 weeks of adult life, the delicate brownish or yellowish stone flies generally do not feed, although some species scrape algae from rocks and trees or take pollen.

The female usually lays her eggs, of which there may be over 1,000, by dipping her abdomen, while in flight, under the surface of the water. The eggs of many species are spherical and become sticky on contacting water. They then adhere to rocks and gravel in the stream. Other species have flat, disk-like eggs with one adhesive surface.

Stone fly larvae live underwater and either breathe simply by diffusion or else have external tufted gills on the mouthparts, thorax, legs, abdomen or, often, extruded from the anus. A very few species have terrestrial larvae which live in cool, moist areas away from water, but one bizarre wingless species of the family Nemouridae lives its entire life some 200ft (60m) beneath the surface of a lake in North America.

Larval stone flies survive best in cool, well-aerated, unpolluted water with a gravel bottom. Stone flies pass through a large number of molts before becoming adult. Over a period of usually one, but up to 3–4 years, they may molt more than 30 times, the exact number depending on the species. The Large stone fly (*Dinocras cephalotes*) goes through 33 molts. Larval stone flies are an important part of the freshwater food web, providing food for many insects and fish.   ssi

Bizarre Earwigs

There are just two known species in the earwig suborder Arixeniina (**1**). They live in association with two species of Southeast Asian bats, on the bats themselves or in their roosts. As adults they are about 1in (2.5cm) in length. Rather than being long, smooth and flattened as are most earwigs, they are robust and hairy. Not being free living, they have no wings. They live in almost perpetual darkness and have very poor eyesight. Except for the males of one species, they do not have abdominal forceps, just two short pegs.

Arixeniids feed on dead skin, excreta and other waste products associated with the bats and their roosts. They are also unusual among earwigs in that they give birth to live young.

The Hemimerina (**2**) are even more remarkable. They are true parasites and the 10 known species are associated specifically with various species of the giant South African pouched rats (genus *Cricetomys*). Hemimerines live under the fur of the rats, where they probably feed on dead skin and the

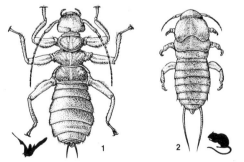

sebaceous secretions of their host. Their lifestyle is similar to that of the mallophagan lice.

Hemimerines are small for earwigs, being less than 0.4in (1cm) long as adults. They are oval, highly flattened, and smooth. They move freely through the host's fur on short legs which are hooked with pads on the feet for gripping the hair. Hemimerines are blind and flightless, having no need for either eyes or wings. Their cerci are long and cylindrical, rather than pincer-like; presumably forceps would be redundant for their parasitic existence.

CRICKETS AND GRASSHOPPERS

Order: Orthoptera
Class: Insecta, subclass Pterygota.
Phylum Uniramia.
Over 20,000 species in 2 suborders and 15
families.
Distribution: all but coldest parts of the world.

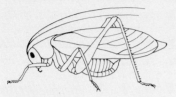

Suborder Ensifera

Suborder Caelifera

Features: mainly medium to large, 0.4–6in
(1–15cm), stout or elongate insects with
chewing mouthparts; hindlegs usually
modified for jumping; shield or "saddle" covers
first segment of thorax; forewings (when
present) hardened, protect hindwings (when
present) that fold fan-like; ears, and sound
producing (stridulatory) organs (usually only in
males) often present. Larvae (nymphs) more or
less resemble wingless adults.

CRICKETS and grasshoppers are noted for jumping (to escape predators) and singing (to potential mates). The associated powerful hindlegs, special noise-producing equipment, and ears to receive the sounds so produced, are characteristic of most members of the large order Orthoptera.

The grasshoppers and crickets also demonstrate a huge range of life styles, some times even within one species ranging from solitary to massive swarms, and from free-living species with camouflage or warning coloration, to near-blind burrowers with shovel-like legs.

The earliest fossils of the order date from the Triassic period (225–190 million years ago). Broadly speaking, the Orthoptera have evolved into two ecological types: those species which are adapted to a life in the open and those which live a largely concealed existence, often below ground.

Insects which live in the open are in constant danger of being eaten by all manner of predators, invertebrate (eg spiders, other insects) and vertebrate (eg lizards, frogs, birds). Orthopterans with such a life style have evolved many ways of minimizing this risk. A common strategy is to blend with the surroundings. Many members of the order bear a striking resemblance to living, dead or even diseased leaves, and to bark, burnt tree trunks, twigs, lichens, stones or sand. Other species have become highly distasteful to predators, often by incorporating toxins from food plants into their bodies. Such insects are usually brightly colored so that predators learn to recognize that they make hazardous eating. Some orthopterans have evolved to resemble other insects. By mimicking unpalatable or dangerous species they reduce the chance of being eaten. Certain species of long-horned grasshoppers or bush crickets mimic other insects as larvae (nymphs) but subsequently develop into cryptically colored adults.

Most crickets and grasshoppers which live above ground have keen eyesight and hearing. They are very wary and are quick to leap away if disturbed, using their highly developed hindlegs. The adults of many species also fly. In escaping, brightly colored areas of the body, which are normally kept hidden, may be exposed. Such flashes of color may serve to startle or to mislead predators.

A variation of this behavior is the distracting flash display of certain grasshoppers, for example the Yellow-winged locust. When disturbed, the grasshopper leaps into the air and flies a short distance. It has brightly colored hindwings which are only visible during flight. Its wings also produce a clicking sound. During the escape flight the grasshopper suddenly shuts its wings and drops to the ground. The bird or entomologist in pursuit, having suddenly lost sight and sound of the quarry, follows its brightly colored trajectory. In fact, the well-camouflaged grasshopper is sitting very still some feet back from this point, and lives to eat grass another day.

Should the predator manage to seize it, an orthopteran will kick out with its powerful and often spiny hindlegs and regurgitate the contents of its foregut. Many of the distasteful species also release offensive secretions from glands which open onto their body surface. If held by a hindleg, a grasshopper will sacrifice the limb by the contraction of a special muscle at the base. A small diaphragm immediately closes the wound and prevents infection or massive blood loss.

Orthopterans which spend most of their time concealed fall into one of three types. The first includes crickets and grasshoppers which burrow in the soil, live in rotting wood or beneath bark or stones, but also spend some time in the open, usually at night. However, they are generally modified for digging and not for avoiding vertebrate predators. Their legs are often short and shovel-like, their wings reduced or modified and their bodies are generally cylindrical and smooth.

Cave-dwelling species are dull-colored,

The Cooloola Monster

In 1976, a strange creature was collected from a pitfall trap set on the rain forest floor of the Cooloola National Park in Queensland, Australia. The Cooloola monster, as it came to be known, created a sensation among entomologists.

This adult male was about 1.2in (3cm) long and extremely robust in appearance, with its broad body and shovel-like legs and head. It had very short antennae and was almost blind. The wings were very short and non-functional (females are completely wingless). Such features strongly suggested that the insect was a burrower; as indeed it is.

The beast was clearly an orthopteran but did not fit into any of the known families. In fact, it did not clearly fit into either of the two suborders. Taxonomists finally agreed that the monster should be placed in the suborder Ensifera, along with the crickets and long-horned grasshoppers, but that it represented a new family, the Cooloolidae. The discovery of a new species, or even genus, of insects is common. A new family is very rare indeed.

The Cooloola monster burrows in the sandy, moist soil of coastal rain forests and

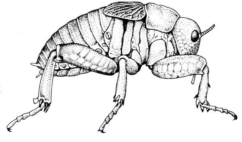

open eucalypt forest in central Queensland. Adult males appear above ground only at night, apparently after rain, as this is the time when they are most commonly collected. Females, on the other hand, seem to live their entire lives underground. They can barely walk on the surface, having a large, swollen abdomen and very small feet and claws.

The shape of its mouthparts suggests that the Cooloola monster is a predator. Possibly it feeds on beetle larvae and other insects which live among the tangled roots of plants near the surface of the forest soil.

Recently several new species of Cooloolidae have been discovered in Australia.

▲ **Protective resemblance to an inedible object** is a survival strategy evolved by a wide range of insects. Here, a male of the South American grasshopper *Apioscelis bulbosa* (Proscopidae) mimics a stick in rain forest in Peru. Many stick mimics heighten their resemblance by swaying gently, as though caught in a light breeze.

delicate insects. Their eyesight is poor, but extremely long legs and antennae endow them with excellent senses of touch, smell and temperature detection.

Finally, a few orthopterans live their entire lives underground, never coming into the open. Some live in the soil and are soft, blind, unpigmented creatures whose legs are highly modified for digging. The bizarre ant-loving crickets are very small, flattened, wingless insects which live in ants' nests. They feed on secretions produced by their hosts and behave very much as members of the colony.

Most crickets and grasshoppers feed on the foliage of plants, some being restricted to a small number of plant species, while others are less choosy. Soil-dwelling species feed on the roots of plants or on algae and other microorganisms which they ingest along with mud. Many orthopterans are

omnivorous and will eat living plants or dead plant and animal material. Certain groups are even predacious, catching other insects with their grasping forelegs in a manner similar to mantids. All orthopterans have chewing mouthparts, modified according to the species' diet. For example, the structure of the mandibles of different short-horned grasshopper species varies with the toughness of their chosen food plants.

The production of sound (stridulation) is a notable feature of orthopteran behavior. Stridulation, normally by males, plays an important role in the courtship of many species. The song differs between species, thus ensuring that only females of the correct species are attracted for mating. (The song may also be important for males in distancing one from another.) Many orthopterans have courtship dances involving intricate patterns and leg and body movements.

There are two basic mechanisms used to produce courtship songs. In one, specialized veins on the bases of the forewings are rubbed together. This tooth-and-comb technique is found mainly in species of the suborder Ensifera (crickets, and katydids or long-horned grasshoppers). The other mechanism used largely by the suborder Caelifera (short-horned grasshoppers and locusts), could be termed a washboard technique as it involves friction between a ridge or row of pegs on the inside of the hindleg and one or more pronounced veins on the forewing. Many other techniques are employed but these are the most characteristic of the order.

The ears of the orthopteran are found on the abdomen or legs and consist of a thin membrane to the back of which are attached specialized receptors. Sounds cause the membrane to vibrate and so stimulate its receptors.

The sounds produced by orthopterans may be surprisingly loud. Normally this is simply because of the design of the sound-producing apparatus itself. However one family, the mole crickets, actually build their own amplifiers. The shape of the male mole cricket's burrow is such that it magnifies his song so that on a still evening it may be heard up to 1.2mi (2km) away! The most sophisticated and recent advances in loudspeaker design have recently produced, by the use of computers, something which appears to copy almost exactly the burrow of a mole cricket.

Most orthopterans lay their eggs either in the soil or in plant tissue. Species in the suborder Ensifera have a well-developed, sword-shaped or cylindrical ovipositor which is introduced into the appropriate site for egg-laying. Normally ensiferans lay their

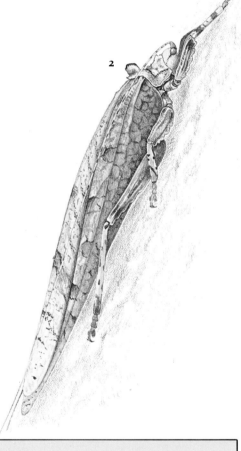

eggs singly. Members of the suborder Caelifera, however, lay eggs in batches or "pods" of 10–200 surrounded by a protective foam, often quite deep in the soil. The female digs down with her short, pronged ovipositor and specialized muscles between segments allow her to extend her abdomen down to more than twice its normal length before depositing her eggs.

The larval orthopterans (nymphs) which emerge are usually similar in appearance and behavior to adults. They may pass through 3–5 molts before becoming adults. The number of molts and the time they take depends on the species and on environmental conditions.

As a whole, the orthopterans are not notably gregarious or destructive, but some species of the family Acrididae occur in two phases; one solitary and one gregarious. In the latter form they may mass in swarms of many millions and devastate huge areas of crops. Such acridids are called locusts (see overleaf).   ssi

The 2 Suborders and Key Families of Crickets and Grasshoppers

Ensifera

Nine families. Antennae sometimes very long, with more than 30 segments; ears (where present) on forelegs; stridulate usually by rubbing together bases of forewings; egg-guide or ovipositor (when present) sword or stylet shaped; eggs laid singly.

Long-horned grasshoppers (bush crickets) and **katydids** (family Tettigoniidae, some 5,000 species) are medium-sized to large, active insects living on plants or on the ground; most are foliage feeders but some are predators.

True crickets (family Gryllidae) number some 2,000 species, most of which are medium-sized, pale brown, some black; active at night and sheltering during day under logs, stones or in soil burrows; sing or chirp loudly; herbivorous and/or carnivorous. Species include the **American field cricket** (*Acheta assimilis*), **European house cricket** (*A. domestica*) and **Field cricket** (*Gryllus campestris*).

Other families include: the burrowing **mole crickets** (Gryllotalpidae); the small **ant-loving crickets** (Myrmecophilidae) which live entirely in ants' nests; the **cave crickets** (Raphidophoridae); the large, terrestrial and sometimes predacious **king crickets** (Stenolpelmatidae); and the bizarre **Cooloola monster** (*Cooloola propator*, Cooloolidae).

Caelifera

Six families. Antennae with less than 30 segments, sometimes short and thick; ears (when present) on first segment of abdomen; stridulate usually by rubbing inside of hindlegs against side of forewings; ovipositor or egg-guide (when present) consists of 4 separate prongs; eggs laid in "pods." Some species migratory in swarms.

Short-horned grasshoppers and locusts (family Acrididae), with 10,000 or more species, is the largest family of the order; all are active, foliage feeders usually living on the ground or among herbs and grasses; includes the **Migratory locust** (*Locusta migratoria*), **Desert locust** (*Schistocerca gregaria*), and **Yellow-winged locust** (*Gastrimargus musicus*).

Other families include: the **ground locusts** (Tetrigidae), small ground dwellers that feed on algae or eat mud; the **pygmy mole crickets** (Tridactylidae), very small, shiny black insects that live in burrows by fresh water; and the Cylindrachetidae, small, pale, living entirely underground.

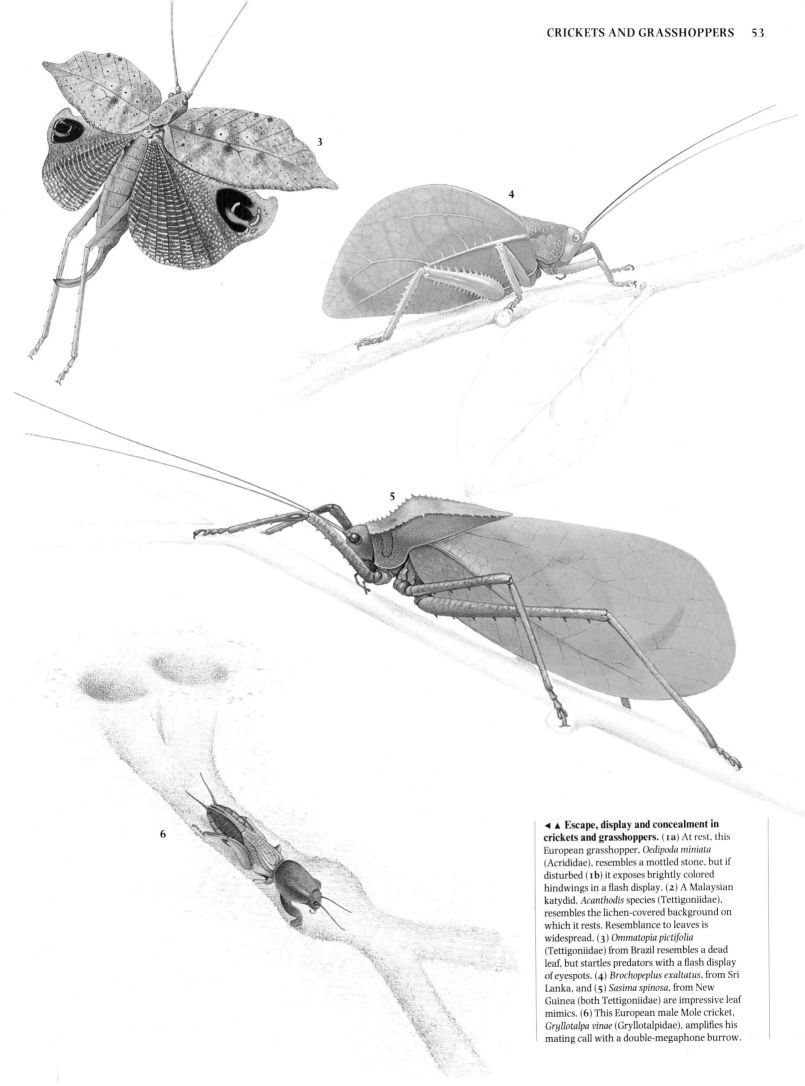

◄ ▲ **Escape, display and concealment in crickets and grasshoppers.** (1a) At rest, this European grasshopper, *Oedipoda miniata* (Acrididae), resembles a mottled stone, but if disturbed (1b) it exposes brightly colored hindwings in a flash display. (2) A Malaysian katydid, *Acanthodis* species (Tettigoniidae), resembles the lichen-covered background on which it rests. Resemblance to leaves is widespread. (3) *Ommatopia pictifolia* (Tettigoniidae) from Brazil resembles a dead leaf, but startles predators with a flash display of eyespots. (4) *Brochopeplus exaltatus*, from Sri Lanka, and (5) *Sasima spinosa*, from New Guinea (both Tettigoniidae) are impressive leaf mimics. (6) This European male Mole cricket, *Gryllotalpa vinae* (Gryllotalpidae), amplifies his mating call with a double-megaphone burrow.

Origin of a Locust Swarm
From solitary individual to a swarm of millions

Sparse vegetation covers the floor of a shallow valley between the barren hills of the North African desert. Sitting alone here and there in the dried grass, or perched on the branches of shrubs, are grasshoppers. They are secretive, solitary creatures, blending with their background and tolerating the presence of others only to mate. Every now and then a grasshopper moves, grasps a piece of grass between its forelegs and begins to feed. A female can be seen laying eggs on the hard, dry earth below a bush; elsewhere young larvae struggle from the soil and immediately disperse into the vegetation.

But an unusual event is disturbing the desert scene. Clouds have gathered, and within a short time it begins to rain, the first decent rain to fall for five years.

Within a week, the valley has become overrun with vegetation. Tender, green grass and herbs grow where there was only bare ground. The grasshoppers are taking advantage of the abundant food. Females can be seen laying more frequently in the soft, moist ground, and more larvae are emerging successfully. Encounters between grasshoppers are becoming more frequent as the population builds up in the valley.

A remarkable change begins to occur. Rather than avoiding each other, the grasshoppers begin actively to seek each other's company. More surprisingly still, the appearance of the young grasshoppers begins to change as they develop. No longer do they blend perfectly with their background. Many have acquired striking colors—stripes of black, yellow and orange.

The rains continue. A month later, large bands of brightly colored larvae, or nymphs, can be seen feeding or marching across bare ground. The bands begin to join together and soon the valley is filled with hundreds of thousands of these marching hoppers.

After molting for the fifth time, the larvae have become fully fledged adults. During the hottest part of the day they roost on the upper branches of trees and shrubs where it is cool. In the mornings and evenings they feed, flying from one part of the valley to another. Soon, however, the food supply has been exhausted and the insects take to the air as a massive swarm.

The density of a locust swarm can be at least 100 million insects per square mile (260 million/sq km) and sometimes over 200 million per square mile (500 million/sq km). Since swarms often cover over 400 sq mi (1,000 sq km), a locust swarm may easily number 50 thousand million individuals!

Within the swarm, insects fly as members of small groups. When such a group reaches the boundary of the swarm, the insects turn back toward the center, so that the enormous cloud remains a cohesive unit. The cloud itself, however, is at the mercy of prevailing winds, and moves downwind until a patch of green is spied far below. The swarm descends to feed. The crop (probably millet) is soon stripped bare and the swarm takes to the wind again. It continues in this way for hundreds of miles, generally southward behind weather fronts, until after several weeks the insects remain at a suitable food site to mate and lay eggs. If the weather is kind, these eggs will give rise to another swarm. If not, millions of grasshoppers will starve or die of disease. Sometimes the weather cheats the swarm in another way, by blowing it out to sea, where eventually the insects drown.

Meanwhile, back in the valley where it all began, the rains have stopped. The sun, unchallenged once again, has dried the grass and baked the ground. Only a few grasshoppers are struggling from their desiccated egg pods. They grow up in isolation, rarely contacting others, and develop not into brightly colored gregarious locusts, but into camouflaged, solitary grasshoppers.

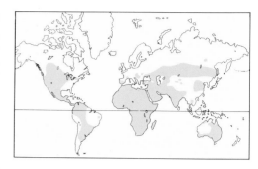

▲ **Areas vulnerable to infestation** by locusts or grasshoppers that severely damage crops.

▶ **Desert locusts** (*Schistocerca gregaria*). Even in the tropics, insects may have to absorb radiant heat from the morning sun before being warm enough to fly (Acrididae).

▶ **Swarm of locusts** BELOW. Locusts achieve pest status not only in Africa, but also in many other parts of the world. Here, a swarm of the Australian Plague locust *Chortoicetes terminifera* (family Acrididae) flies over a field of alfalfa (lucerne) in New South Wales.

▼ **Feeding on grass,** Australian Plague locusts. More conspicuous markings and brighter coloration of the gregarious phase in some locusts contrasts with the duller, camouflage coloration in solitary insects.

These are no ordinary grasshoppers; they are, of course, locusts, most likely Migratory locusts or Desert locusts. Members of the family Acrididae, they are no different from any other short-horned grasshopper, except that they exist in two different forms: solitary and gregarious. These two phases differ in color, form, behavior, physiology and ecology. In fact they are so different that, not long ago, they were thought to be different species. Many intermediate stages are found between one phase and the other, and if a change begins it may be reversed during the development of an individual locust.

Phase change is an extremely complex phenomenon which is not fully understood. Certainly it is a function of locust population density and environmental conditions and is regulated, at least partly, by hormones and pheromones. The function of the changing phase would seem to be to reduce predation pressure. For the individual insect in a low-density population, it is best to be well camouflaged and not draw the attention of predators. If, however, because of favorable environmental conditions, the population density increases, it is a better strategy to flock into as large a group as possible. The change to brighter coloration makes this easier. A large group may be conspicuous to predators, but if it is large enough the chances for any one individual of being eaten are reduced.

There are a number of species of locusts and the cycle of events described above may occur in Africa, the Middle East, India, Southeast or Central Asia, Australia or America (see map).

A swarm can defoliate large areas and cause great human suffering through crop loss. In 1957 a swarm of Desert locusts destroyed 167,000 tons of grain crop, enough to feed 1 million people for a year. However, the individual insect is a restrained eater, feeding for a couple of minutes and then not for an hour or so. Different species are more or less particular about the plants they will eat. Some, such as the Migratory locust, have a diet restricted almost solely to grasses, while others, such as the Desert locust, are more catholic in their tastes.

Locust swarms have become less frequent during recent years, due largely to constant monitoring of weather conditions and locust densities in potential outbreak areas, most of which are in the Sahel belt of Africa. If locusts do form hopper bands, they are controlled while on the ground and not allowed to become winged swarms.　　ssi

LEAF AND STICK INSECTS

Order: Phasmatoidea (or Phasmida)
Class: Insecta, subclass Pterygota.
Phylum: Uniramia.
Over 2,500 species in 2 families.
Distribution: chiefly warmer regions,
particularly tropics.

Features: large to very large, some species over
12in (30cm) long; body elongated and usually
closely resembles twig or (with wings
expanded) leaves; head conspicuously domed;
long legs; forewings (if present—usually
reduced in females) hardened and often smaller
than membranous hindwings that fold fan-like;
eggs seed-like with a conspicuous lid. Larvae
more or less resemble adults; no pupal stage.
All foliage feeders, found in shrubs, tall herbs,
trees. Most active at night.

Leaf insects
Family Phyllidae
About 50 species of SE Asia, Australia and New
Guinea; many belong to the genus *Phyllium*.

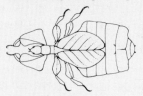

Stick insects
Family Phasmatidae
About 2,500 species. Very large species include
Extatosoma tiaratum, *Acrophylla titan*; European
species include the **Mediterranean stick insect**
(*Bacillus rossii*), *Clonopsis gallicus*, *Leptynia
hispanica*, and the wingless "**Laboratory stick
insect**" (*Carausius morosus*).

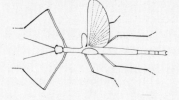

THE stick and leaf insects are one of the most spectacular of all insect groups. They are large, and their striking mimicry of plants depends on a unique range of adaptations in color, shape, and behavior.

Most phasmids are mottled green or brown. Within a population of a species at one site there may be a wide variation in coloration, some insects being green and others brown, for example. Coloration also varies in the same species at different locations.

Population density may influence the color of developing phasmids. While most species are relatively solitary creatures, some reach plague densities. In Australia species including *Didymaria violescens*, *Padocanthus wilkinsoni* and *Ctenomorphodes tessulatus* can when swarming become pests as defoliators of eucalypt forest. As density increases, developing insects become, like locusts, more brightly colored. For the solitary insect it is probably better to be inconspicuous, while as one of a group it is advantageous to see the others clearly and stay together.

Some stick and leaf insects also change color with temperature, humidity and light intensity. The cells of the epidermis beneath the cuticle contain granules of pigment which migrate within the cells in response to environmental conditions. On hot, sunny days the pigment granules clump together, forming larger light-colored areas, with the result that the insect reflects more heat. When the environment is cool and humid and light intensity is low, the granules disperse within the epidermal cells and the insect darkens in color. It then is able to absorb more heat and keep warm.

Stick insects are long and slender, with cuticular knobs and bumps that give the insect the same shape and texture as the twigs of the species' host plant. The head, body and legs of other species also bear leaf-like flanges and extensions, which are most extremely developed in the leaf insects, whose body is also flattened laterally; the whole insect takes on an extraordinary likeness to a leaf, complete with midrib and veins.

A perfectly camouflaged phasmid would not last long if it drew attention to itself by moving rapidly about its host plant. In fact, leaf and stick insects are incapable of running quickly; they spend most of their time sitting motionless, their long forelegs extended in front of them. However, they would not remain inconspicuous if they remained stationary while their surroundings were moving, as happens when a breeze ruffles the foliage of a tree. The rhythmic side-to-side swaying movements of stick and leaf insects may have evolved for just this reason.

The resemblance of phasmids to parts of plants goes beyond the adult insects themselves. Their eggs look very similar indeed to plant seeds. They are usually oval and have a thick shell which may be smooth or else intricately sculptured and patterned. The exact shape and ornamentation of the egg depends on the species.

The female normally lays her eggs one at a time. She either just lets them drop to the ground below, or else catapults them away by suddenly flicking her abdomen. She may lay from 100 to 1,300 eggs in this way, depending on the species.

▶ **Spending its life on lichen-covered tree trunks,** this Venezuelan stick insect resembles its background very closely, with green, lichen-like outgrowths from its body. The outgrowths serve also to blur the insect's outline, making it very difficult to detect (Phasmatidae).

▶ **This leaf insect** OPPOSITE a *Phyllium* species in New Guinea, is a remarkable mimic of a dead, crinkled leaf. Other species of *Phyllium* are green, resembling living leaves, while some mimic diseased leaves with blotches and symptoms of insect damage. The whole effect is enhanced by the insect swinging slightly from side to side, like a leaf caught in a light breeze (Phyllidae).

On the ground, eggs are protected by their seed-like appearance, and may lie for one, two or even three years. There is a short hatching period of several weeks every spring. Young phasmids are miniature versions of their parents. They hatch by pushing the specialized lid off the egg and, because they tend to move against gravity and towards light, they then climb up the nearest vertical object. Since eggs are deposited beneath the mother's host plant, there is a good chance that the young larvae will find appropriate food to eat. Phasmids feed solely on foliage, using their chewing mouthparts. Many species will only feed on a small number of plant species and are normally most choosy when young.

The larvae pass through a number of molts before becoming adult. Adult females are ready to mate soon after the last molt, while adult males require longer to become sexually mature. Normally males go through five molts, one less than females, and this ensures that males from eggs laid at the same time are ready to mate when the females become adult.

The production of offspring from unfertilized eggs is common among the phasmids. This is known as parthenogenesis and in most species seems to operate as a fail-safe device. Adults are often widely dispersed and, despite the fact that males are usually able to fly and females possibly emit a sex-attractant pheromone, there is a risk that mating might not occur. In a few species, such as the "Laboratory stick insect," however, parthenogenesis is obligatory— males have never been found. Normally unfertilized eggs develop to become females, but in at least one Australian species (*Ctenomorphodes tessulatus*) males may be produced as well.

Despite their fantastic disguises, the eggs, larvae and adults of phasmids often fall prey to others. Eggs are most frequently carried away by ants, while birds are the main predators of the young and adults.

If disturbed, many species take avoiding action; they become momentarily cataleptic and fall from their perch. During the fall the legs are thrown back and the insect becomes, in effect, a shuttlecock. This ensures that they land on their feet and can at once crawl to safety. Other phasmids attempt to deter; they may rustle and expose brightly colored hindwings from beneath the horny, camouflaged forewings. Some species regurgitate gut contents or squirt irritating chemicals from glands in the prothorax. Many species will jab their attacker with the spines on their legs.   ssi

BOOKLICE, WEB SPINNERS, THRIPS, ZORAPTERANS

Orders: Psocoptera, Embioptera,
Thysanoptera, Zoraptera
Class: Insecta, subclass Pterygota.
Phylum: Uniramia

▶ **Network of silken tunnels** ABOVE on a tree trunk in Trinidad betrays the presence of a colony of web spinners (order Embioptera). The funnels usually radiate from a central retreat, extending over the moss and leaf litter on which the insects feed.

▶ **Adult barklice** BELOW of an unidentified species (order Psocoptera) cluster on bark in a Peruvian rain forest. In this species, the males are winged, the females wingless. There may be several generations in a year.

P SOCOPTERANS or **booklice** are fast active runners that scavenge on lichens, fungal hyphae, single-celled algae, spores and other plants and insect tissue fragments. Most of the winged psocopterans live on foliage of trees and shrubs, and under bark, leaf litter and stones. Some (family Archipsocidae) live communally in large silken sheets, produced by labial silk glands, which may cover entire trees. Most prefer damp, but not wet, conditions, and some are associated with bracket fungi and the litter and nests of mammals, birds, wasps and ants. Psocopterans are frequently gregarious. Some feed on the stored products of humans in homes, barns and grain stores, eg flour products, paper, book-bindings—hence the common name booklice.

The psocopterans probably descend from early bugs (Hemiptera) and their nearest relatives appear to be the chewing lice. The earliest known psocopteran fossils date from the upper levels of the Cretaceous (135–65 million years ago).

After a nuptial dance, the male psocopteran transfers his sperm to the female in a sperm packet (spermatophore). The female lays ovoid or oblong eggs singly or in clumps

on leaves, under bark or in crevices, and may conceal them with silk and debris. In some species there may be asexual, as well as sexual races, in which males are rare or absent. The nymphs have fewer antennal segments and ocelli than the adults, and undeveloped wings. They may camouflage themselves by attaching debris to their glandular body hairs. In outdoor species there are commonly 2–3 generations in a year, the insects overwintering as eggs. Those frequenting buildings have more or less continuous generations.

When feeding, the strong, rod-like lacinia of the maxilla is apparently braced against the substrate while the mandibles scrape up food material. Although outbreaks of psocopterans can occur in poorly maintained or undisturbed stored products, the order is not of great economic importance. Psocopterans are preyed upon by pseudoscorpions, spiders, ants, larvae of neuropterans, as well as falling victim to parasitic nematode worms and fungi.   GCM

Web spinners are dull-colored, soft-bodied insects which live gregariously in tunnels made of silk. The silk is secreted by glands

---

Booklice and barklice
Order Psocoptera

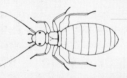

About 1,700 species in 21 families. Distribution: very common in all world regions. Features: mostly 0.2in (0.5cm) long (range 0.04–0.4in/1–10mm), head characteristically round with bulbous shield-like clypeus, long thread-like usually 13-segmented antennae, large compound eyes, 3 simple eyes (winged forms only), and biting mouthparts; body squat, soft, commonly with 2 pairs of membranous wings held roof-like at rest, forewings slightly larger, venation simple; many species have short-winged or wingless forms; slender legs adapted for running. 9-segmented abdomen without cerci at tip; reproduction sexual or asexual; some give birth to live young (viviparous); wings develop externally through the usually 6 adult-like nymph stages (hemimetabolous development).

Three main suborders: Troctomorpha, Trogiomorpha, Psocomorpha; family Liposcelidae includes the cosmopolitan **booklouse** (*Liposcelis divinatorius*).

Web spinners
Order Embioptera

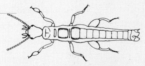

One hundred and seventy species in 8 families. Distribution: pantropical, a few in warm temperate zones. Features: small to medium-sized, with elongated 0.2–0.5in (5–12mm) cylindrical body adapted for living in tubular silk tunnels; antennae with 12–32 segments; eyes kidney-shaped; no simple eyes (ocelli); biting mouthparts; males have 2 pairs of long, narrow wings; all females, and males of some species wingless; legs short, thick, with 3-segmented tarsi; swollen basal tarsal segment of forelegs bears silk gland; hind femora enlarged; abdomen 10-segmented, with 2-segmented cerci at tip; nymphs adult-like, without wings or genitalia; wings develop externally.

Most numerous and widespread family is in the Embiidae; the Australembiidae are endemic to Australia. About 1,800 species estimated yet to be discovered.

Thrips
Order Thysanoptera

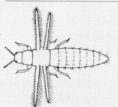

About 4,500 species in 2 suborders and 8 families. Distribution: worldwide. Features: tiny adults 0.02–0.06in (0.5–1.5mm) long; only the left mandible is developed; maxillae in form of stylets forming a sucking tube; wings have fringe of hair-like cilia; tarsi tipped with extrusible bladder used to cling to smooth surfaces; 2 nymphal and 2–3 pupa-like pre-adult stages; some reproduce without mating.

Suborder Terebrantia
Seven families, including the Thripidae: 1,500 species worldwide feeding in flowers or on leaves, a few on fungi, some predatory, eg **Greenhouse thrips** (*Heliothrips haemorrhoidalis*), **Onion thrips** (*T. tabaci*), **Pine tree thrips** (*Oxythrips bicolor*), **thunderfly** or **Grain thrips** (*Limothrips cerealium*).

Suborder Tubulifera
One family, the worldwide Phlaeothripidae, comprising the subfamilies Idolothripinae—400 species feeding on fungal spores on

twigs, eg **Gustavia thrips** (*Anactinothrips gustaviae*)—and Phlaeothripinae—2,300 species mostly feeding on fungal hyphae. many on green leaves, some in flowers, a few predatory. eg **Laurel thrips** (*Gynaikothrips ficorum*), **Wheat thrips** (*Haplothrips tritici*).

Zorapterans
Order Zoraptera

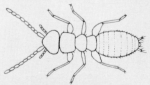

Twenty-two species in 1 family (Zorotypidae). Distribution: most regions but not Palaearctic or Australia. Features: small, under 0.1in (3mm) long, with unspecialized chewing mouthparts, 9-segmented "beaded" (moniliform) antennae and either winged, pigmented, with compound eyes and 3 simple eyes, or wingless, unpigmented, eyeless; prothorax large, 2 pairs of wings, if present, membranous, with pigmented area at tip, reduced venation, develop externally, may be shed, leaving stumps; legs adapted for walking; abdomen 11-segmented with short unjointed cerci at tip.
Single genus: *Zorotypus*.

in the swollen basal segment of the fore tarsi. The tunnels protect the insects from predators and desiccation.

Although the short-lived males have well-developed jaws, they do not feed, but use jaws to grasp the female during mating. Newly emerged males leave their colony of origin for a short dispersal flight and later enter a new colony, where they seek mates. Females may eat the males after mating.

Both sexes can run rapidly, backward as well as forward. The males' wings are adapted for this, being highly flexible, and can be bent forward over the head. For flying, wings are stiffened by the inflation of a blood sinus formed by the radial vein. Because the Embioptera show so many specialized characters, it is difficult to assess their affinity with other insect groups. However, they are now thought to share ancestry with the orthopteroid orders.   CO'T

Among the several groups of minute insects which have wings fringed with hair-like cilia, the **thrips** (Thysanoptera = fringe-winged) are unique for their sucking mouthparts. Thrips feed by punching a hole in their food (often a leaf, flower or pollen grain) with their single mandible, inserting the syringe-like stylets, and sucking out a cell's contents. The Idolothripinae, found under bark sometimes in groups ranged in concentric circles, take in whole fungal spores through stylets that are $5-10\mu$m across instead of the usual $1-3\mu$m. Some thrips prey on small arthropods such as scales, whitefly and mites.

Thrips probably evolved along with booklice as fungus or detritus feeders in plant litter; they are related to the bugs and parasitic lice. Some (suborder Terebrantia) retain a primitive saw-like egg guide, but in the Tubulifera the ovipositor is soft and eversible. The life cycle, with two nymphal and 2–3 "pupal" stages, is intermediate between those of primitive and advanced insects.

Thrips abound in warm dry weather; they may feed and grow, but usually do not fly, in cooler conditions. In warm sultry weather following a cool spell, great numbers may crawl to the top of the object they are resting on, spread their wings, and jump. Wingless thrips may do likewise and be distributed by the wind.

The common Greenhouse thrips that cause such damage to plants are nearly all females—only two dozen males have ever been identified. Like the equally abundant pest Onion thrips and other species with few males, they can reproduce rapidly without

mating. Most thrips are bisexual, but while fertilized eggs develop into females, unfertilized eggs become males with only half the number of chromosomes in females.

From egg to adult thrips may take just three weeks. Some species produce several generations a year, but the Pine tree thrips, for example, only has one. Since its pine pollen food is available for barely three weeks, it spends the rest of the year dormant. The Gustavia thrips of Panama, like other large spore-eating species, guards its eggs and young, a noxious droplet exuding from the abdomen raised over its head.

Given the wide range of food plants used by some species, and the ability to disperse rapidly, travel unseen in transported plants and breed rapidly, thrips are pests of many crops. The loss of cell sap disfigures and debilitates the plant, reducing crop yields. Five thrips species are known to carry plant diseases, notably tomato spotted wilt virus, which affects pineapples as well as tomato plants.   LAM, JMP

The small, winged or wingless **zorapterans** have antennae shaped like a string of beads. They are gregarious, but without any real social organization, living colonially under rotting wood, sawdust, bark, moist litter and in and around termite nests.

The Zoraptera have sometimes been grouped with the booklice due to some similarities of the head, mouthparts, wing venation and overall appearance. Similarities in the presence of cerci, unspecialized chewing mouthparts and certain features of the male genitalia associate the Zoraptera with some crickets and grasshoppers. The large number of Malpighian tubules, the concentrated nervous system and the fore-wings slightly larger than the hindwings are features of the bugs (order Hemiptera) but these similarities could be due to convergence. Some primitive characters are common also to web spinners (Embioptera) and termites (Isoptera) but are not thought to indicate any close relationship. No fossils have been found representing the stem group of this order. Zorapterans are generally thought to feed on fungi but fragments of arthropod tissue have been found in gut-content analyses. The male genitalia are often asymmetric and the female ovipositor is greatly reduced or lacking. Eggs are ovoid and the young hatch by means of an egg burster. The nymphs produced are of two forms, with or without wing buds. It is thought that the winged adults are dispersal forms which arise when the habitat becomes unsuitable.   GCM

PARASITIC LICE

Order: Phthiraptera
Class: Insecta, subclass Pterygota.
Phylum: Uniramia.
About 3,150 species in 27 families.
Distribution: cosmopolitan.

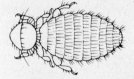

Features: 0.2–0.4in (0.5–11mm) long
permanent external parasites of birds and
mammals; wingless, do not jump; flattened
body with inconspicuous coloration; short
antennae with usually 5 segments; 1 pair of
spiracles (breathing holes) on thorax; abdomen
may be distinctly segmented; larvae resemble
adults in shape (incomplete metamorphosis).

Sucking lice
Suborder Anoplura
500 species in 43 genera and 15 families.
Piercing mouthparts with 3 stylets; all 3
segments of thorax fused. Hosts: placental
mammals. Food: blood. Include **Human crab
louse** (*Pthirus pubis*), **Human body louse**
(*Pediculus humanus*), **Human head louse**
(*Pediculus capitis*), and **seal lice** (family
Echinophthiriidae).

Elephant lice
Suborder Rhyncophtherina
2 species in 1 genus. Front of head prolonged
into rigid cylindrical snout (rostrum) with
biting mouthparts at tip. Hosts: elephants,
warthog. Include **Elephant louse**
(*Haematomyzus elephantis*), **Warthog louse**
(*H. hopkinsi*).

Chewing lice
Suborder Ischnocera
1,800 species in 120 genera and 5 families.
Unique spongy pad (pulvinus) between front of
head and biting mouthparts. Hosts: birds,
placental mammals. Food: feathers, skin, skin
secretions, blood. Include **Dog louse**
(*Trichodectes canis*), **Sheep chewing louse**
(*Bovicola ovis*).

Suborder Amblycera
850 species in 75 genera and 7 families.
Maxillary palps present; biting mouthparts;
third segment of antennae cup-shaped. Hosts:
birds, mammals. Food: feathers, skin, skin
secretions, blood. Include **guinea pig lice**
(eg *Gliricola porcelli*), **hummingbird lice**
(eg *Trochiloecetes* species), **Curlew quill louse**
(*Actornithophilus patellatus*), **pelican lice**
(*Piagetiella* species) and **rodent lice** (family
Gyropidae).

PARASITIC lice spend their entire lives in the "dermecos"—the environment provided by the skin and fur or feathers of the host—and they change hosts only when two host individuals are in contact. No louse has any free-living stage—all are obligate parasites. Most species of lice have only one or two host species, and are thus very "host-specific."

The ancestor of the parasitic lice probably lived in the Cretaceous period (136–65 million years ago) and was very like modern book lice (Psocoptera). It lived in the nests of early mammals or birds, feeding on fungus and pieces of feather or skin shed by the nest builder. Because wings are a hindrance to a nest-dwelling insect, the ancestor had probably lost them (no lice have wings), so to reach other nests the insects "hitched rides" on the nest builders, a habit called phoresy. Whilst being carried by the host, the insect would have been able to feed on scurf or feathers just as it had in the nest, but with less competition from other arthropods, and thus the opportunity of a parasitic association arose.

Parasitic lice are divided by some authorities into two orders, the Anoplura (sucking lice) and the Mallophaga including all others. Here parasitic lice are separated on the basis of anatomy into four suborders of a single order, the Phthiraptera.

Use of the dermecos or "skin world" as a permanent home has resulted in modern lice quite different from their ancestors. Among the novel selective pressures on the evolving parasites have been the food available, the grooming or preening activities of the host, and the composition of the feathers or fur. Although the initial diet of skin flakes or feathers is still taken by most lice, others feed on sebaceous exudates and blood. One of the guinea pig lice of South America (*Gliricola porcelli*) has serrated mouthparts with which it cuts into hair follicles to extract the oils and waxes. Many chewing lice, such as the Dog louse, have sharp pointed mandibles with which they make small wounds and thus extract blood. Some hummingbird lice also feed on blood, but they have developed long stylets to pierce the skin of the host. All members of the suborder Anoplura (sucking lice) have stylets that work in a similar way, and they are even more adapted to blood feeding. Many lice have an association with bacteria, which live in specialized cells or tissues next to their gut and enable the insects to digest blood and skin protein (keratin).

The "skin" of lice is tough and flexible, the body and head dorso-ventrally flattened (unlike fleas, which are laterally flattened) and their legs and antennae have become much shorter than those of their ancestors. These adaptations help minimize the risk of destruction by the grooming or preening activity of the host and facilitate easy movement through the feathers or fur. The grooming activity of the host may vary according to the part of its body to be groomed, and some lice have adapted to this. Most birds use their beaks a great deal, but naturally are unable to do this on their heads and necks. Some lice live only on these parts of the bird, and are slow moving with broad heads and round abdomens that are only slightly flattened. Birds can preen their wings very easily, however, and lice living here are fast moving, long and slender, and can slip sideways through the feathers with ease. Some lice are even more secure from preening thanks to their extraordinary habitats. The Curlew quill louse lives inside the quills of the wing primaries, and the pelican lice live inside the throat pouches of pelicans and cormorants, coming out through the nasal holes of the bill to lay eggs on the head and neck feathers.

In the dermecos, sight is unimportant, and in lice the eyes have become small or absent. Other senses are more valuable, however, and most species are thickly covered in sensory hairs. Most lice species use their claws and the broadened end of the tibia or tarsus to hold onto the hair or feathers of their host, although members of the family Gyropidae (amblyceran rodent lice found in South America) hold onto the hair by wrapping their strongly ridged legs around it. Many chewing lice of the suborder Ischnocera, when at rest, hold onto the hair or feather barbules of their hosts with their mouthparts and let go with their legs. For unknown reasons most mammal lice have only one claw on each leg, while bird lice (like most other insects) have two.

Female lice cement their eggs directly onto the hairs or feathers of the host. They do not require a developed egg-guide (ovipositor), and the ovipositor lobes are therefore reduced or absent. The Sheep chewing louse uses the lobes of its ovipositor to "catch" the hair upon which the egg will be laid and it is likely that many other mammal lice do the same. Others use the lobes to mold the cement that is extruded with the eggs. This cement dries very hard and is quick-setting; the female lice sometimes become caught in it and are cemented to the hair themselves. The eggs are laid in protected positions in clumps on birds' heads and necks, in the grooves between the barbs of

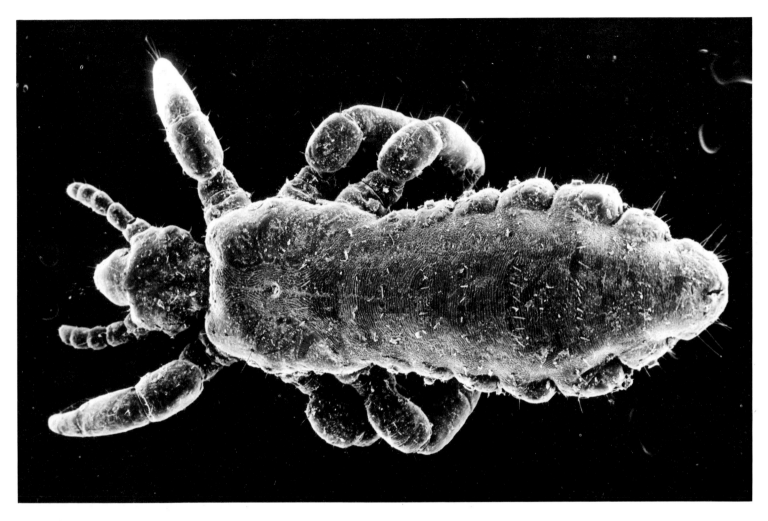

▲ **An adult Human head louse** photographed with a scanning electron microscope at a magnification of 80 ×. Louse infestations are often heavy among school children and the insects have developed resistance to some insecticides (Pediculidae).

▶ **A recent blood meal** shows up as a dark central streak in the transparent body of this nymph of a Human head louse. Lice grip the hairs of their host with modified claws, just visible here.

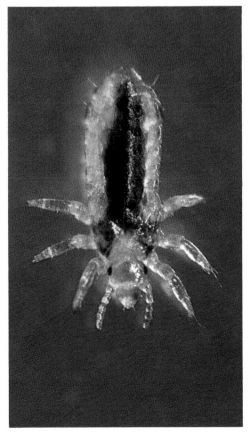

flight feathers, or at the base of mammalian hairs. Moisture is taken up by the eggs via the cement and numerous small holes at the base. Many species have complex outgrowths from the egg, but the function of these is not known.

The young louse breaks out from the egg by swallowing air which it passes through its alimentary canal, so that pressure is built up in the egg behind the larva. This forces off the cap of the egg and, in some species, causes the nymph to be "fired" from the egg like a cork from a bottle. After hatching, the nymph sheds its skin three times before becoming adult; there is no pupal stage. The Human body louse can become adult eight days from hatching, whilst some of the seal lice take almost a year. The adult lifetime is probably less variable, and lasts from 2–3 weeks to several months.

The Human body louse spreads typhus and relapsing fever and thereby has caused the death of many millions of people; the Human head louse and crab louse are not known to spread disease. In domestic animals disease and, more importantly, weight loss due to irritation, are caused by lice.   CHCL

BUGS

Order: Hemiptera
Class: Insecta, subclass Pterygota.
Phylum: Uniramia.
Over 67,500 known species in two suborders.
Distribution: worldwide.

Features: both adults and larvae (nymphs) have piercing and sucking mouthparts in form of long "beak" (rostrum) bearing thread-like stylets; this large group includes a vast range of forms, habitats, life styles and behavior; many pests of plant crops, some carriers of disease.

▶ ▼ **Bugs—camouflage, warning colors and aquatic bugs.** (1) These treehoppers, *Umbonia spinosa* (Membracidae), escape detection by resembling thorns. (2) Bright colors signal that this shield bug, *Catacanthus anchorago* (Pentatomidae), is protected by a foul smell. (3) An assassin bug, *Acanthaspis* species (Reduviidae), feeds on a caterpillar. (4) A fulgorid, *Phenax variegata* (Fulgoridae), roosts on lichen-covered bark which it resembles. The water's surface provides a living for (5) this water strider, *Hydrometra stagnorum* (Hydrometridae), and (6) pond skater, *Gerris lacustris* (Gerridae). Active predation is the life-style of (7) the saucer bug, *Ilyocoris cimicioides* (Naucoridae), (9) the lesser water boatman, *Corixa punctata* (Corixidae), and (10) the back swimmer, *Notonecta glauca* (Notonectidae). (8) The water scorpion, *Nepa cinerea*, and (11) the water stick insect, *Ranatra linearis* (both Nepidae), hang from the surface film by their respiratory siphons and wait to grasp passing prey with their raptorial front legs.

ONE feature distinguishes all bugs from other insect orders—the presence of piercing and sucking mouthparts housed in a long beak-like rostrum. Most bugs tap plant juices, but some suck blood from insects or higher animals. The resulting damage to crop plants and transmission of diseases have serious implications for man.

The **true bugs** (suborder Heteroptera) are distinguished from others by their ability to swing the "beak" forward from its resting position on the underside of the body. Precise direction of the mouthparts makes it possible for heteropteran bugs to exploit sources of food other than the living plant tissues to which other bugs are restricted. Many heteropterans are predatory and some specialize in feeding on seeds. All of the aquatic bugs are true bugs. This diversity of biology is reflected in a great variety of body forms, and the 25,000 known species of true

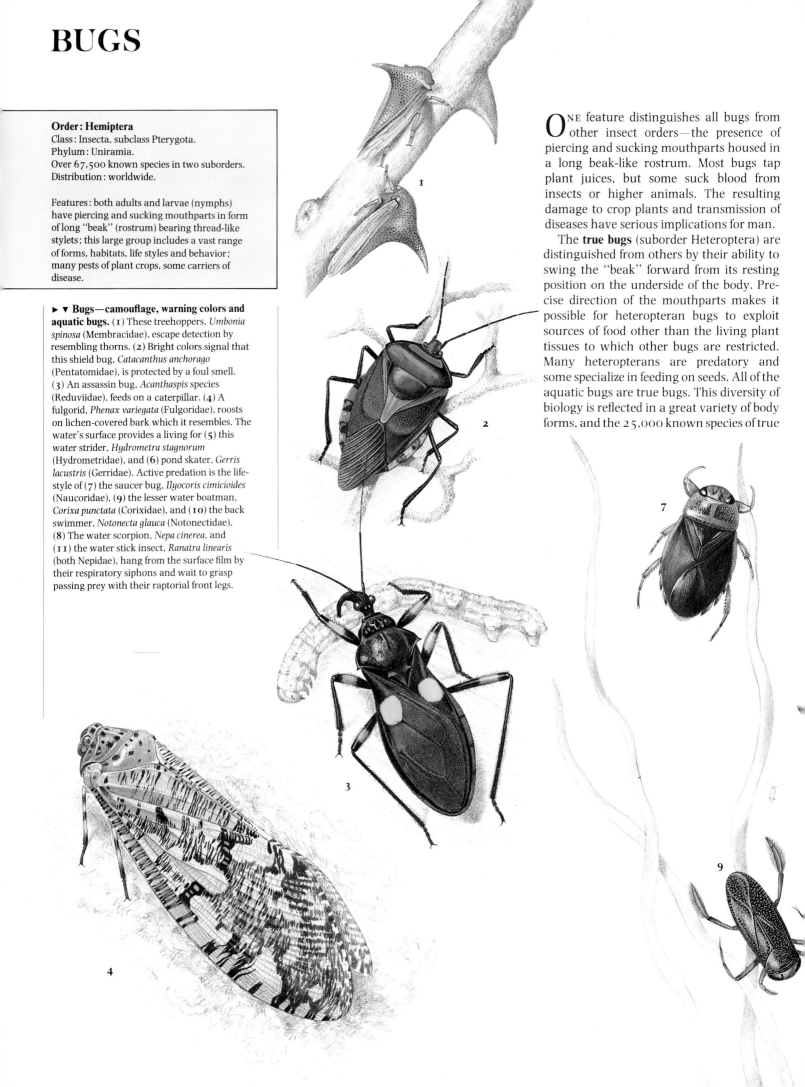

bugs are distributed among more than 60 families. True bugs are so called because they have the non-uniform forewing, with both membranous and hardened portions, which give the order Hemiptera its name.

Stink glands are a characteristic feature of true bugs. In the juvenile stages they are located on the back of the abdomen. In adults, the abdomen is roofed by the wings, and a different gland or pair of glands comes into use, opening on the sides or underside of the thorax. The product of both types of gland is believed to smell repugnant to many insectivorous animals. Because of this protection, many bugs advertise themselves by bright colors and striking patterns; others are cryptically colored and use stink glands only as a second line of defense.

The surface of ponds, lakes, slow-flowing rivers and streams, and even the sea, literally supports the pond skaters, water striders or water skippers. These insects exploit the phenomenon of surface tension, standing on the surface film with water-repellant feet. In all parts of the world, there is a constant "rain" of insects falling from the air. The struggles of those that fall onto the water surface send out tiny ripples which water skaters can detect from a distance of a few inches. Their large, prominent eyes also help to detect prey and avoid predators. All of the 1,300 or so species of water surface-dwelling bugs are predators.

Beneath the surface of fresh waters live a variety of predatory bugs. Unlike the water striders these bugs have to solve the problem of underwater respiration. The water scorpions are named for the long respiratory siphon at the hind end of the body through which they maintain contact with the air above the surface. They are poor swimmers and remain motionless until a potential prey item comes within striking distance of their grasping (raptorial), mantis-like forelegs. The related giant water bugs are active swimmers and visit the surface from time to time to replenish their air supplies through a retractable siphon. Like the water scorpions, they seize their prey with raptorial forelegs. Other active aquatic predators, the saucer bugs and the back swimmers or water boatmen, have silvery air bubbles on the underside of their bodies, which are replenished at the surface without the use of a siphon. The lesser water boatmen resemble the water boatmen in general appearance but differ from all other water bugs in their method of feeding. They use their scoop-like, hair-fringed forelegs to sift through silt and detritus for possible food

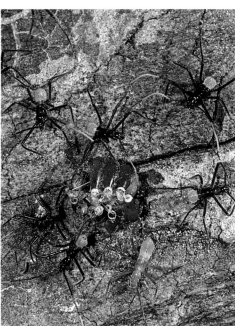

▶ ▼ **Birth of an assassin.** Female assassin bugs lay eggs in batches. Here FAR LEFT a nymph of the Australian "bee-killer" assassin bug, *Pristhesanchus papuensis* (Reduviidae), breaks out of its egg. Like the nymphs of many bugs, it uses an "egg burster" consisting of detachable spines to break out of the egg. The burster is left behind in the "lid" of the egg. On first hatching, the nymphs are pale colored but soon LEFT begin to darken. The nymphs feed in the same way as the adults, using the rostrum to inject a paralyzing saliva into small insect prey. The saliva pre-digests and liquefies the victim's tissues, which are then sucked up by the rostrum. BELOW An adult female *P. papuensis* feeds on a fly, though often the species preys on bees visiting flowers.

items, which may be small aquatic animals, algae or decaying organic matter. There are over 1,100 species of water bugs.

On land, the main predatory bugs are the assassin bugs. These mainly tropical and often brightly colored bugs seize their prey with the forelegs like the aquatic predators. Some of the 4,000 or so species are delicate, mantid-like forms that feed on mosquitoes and other small flies, while others are robust insects capable of overcoming large beetles and millipedes. Some lie concealed in flowers and attack visiting insects, some exude odors attractive to bees which are lured to their deaths, but the majority are active hunters. Some assassin bugs can inflict a painful "bite" on people, and in South America assassin bugs transmit Chagas' disease to humans.

There are two groups of bugs to which the term "timid predators" has been applied. These are the small flowerbugs and the larger predatory shieldbugs. They attack slow-moving, defenseless prey like caterpillars and aphids and do not use their legs to overpower or manipulate their prey. Bedbugs, which feed on the blood of their sleeping human or other warm-blooded victims, are closely related to the flowerbugs.

Shieldbugs, of which there are over 5,000 species, and squash bugs are the best known of the plant-feeding bugs because of their comparatively large size and often bright colors or bizarre form. The younger stages of many species of these two families feed only on the shoots or unripe seeds of a limited range of plants, but the older immatures and adults can be found feeding on a wide variety of fruits unrelated to these

Piercers and Suckers

Bugs are specialized to feed by piercing the outer surface of their food source and to suck up liquid and liquefied products. The majority of bugs are plant feeders, using all parts of a diverse array of plants, but many are predators on other insects and some may suck blood from mammals and birds. While many bugs feed on liquid food products, those that utilize seeds may secrete enzymes to liquefy or semi-digest the seed before ingestion.

The most obvious feature of a bug's head is its segmented, movable rostrum or labium (**a**, of a squash bug). The tip of the rostrum contains sensory cells which may aid the insect in choosing its preferred food source and avoiding unsuitable or unpalatable food. Along its length the rostrum carries four thin threads or stylets in a groove (**b**, cross section). The outer pair (mandibles) each have sharp teeth near the tip which enable a hole to be

cut in the plant or animal surface. The inner pair of stylets (maxillae) are grooved along their length and fit closely together so that their inner grooved surfaces form the food canal and the salivary canal.

In bugs that feed from small plants in which the plant vascular system is close to the surface the rostrum may be shorter than in those feeding from large plants whose vascular tissue is further from the surface. When not in use, the rostrum is held pointing backward close to the body and between the front legs. In plant-feeding forms the rostrum is brought downward to the surface of the plant. In many predatory bugs the rostrum may be held forward in front of the head in order to be able to attack the prey.

When feeding, the outer labium is pulled away from the feeding stylets (**c**). Salivary fluid, including enzymes such as amylase and

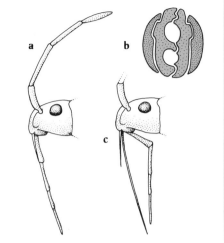

pectinase, is pumped down the salivary canal and semi-digested food pumped back up the food canal. The pump comprises a series of plates at the base of the stylets. MRW

host plants. For example, when young, the Dock bug of Europe seems to depend on plants of the family Polygonaceae but adults are frequently to be found feeding on the fruits of bramble and other rosaceous plants. The name stinkbug derives from the odor produced from the stink glands (as happens especially if the insect is roughly handled), which the bugs leave on the plant where they feed, often contaminating fruit (eg blackberries).

The lace bugs are a less well known family of plant feeders. Their small size and muted colors are responsible for this neglect, but close examination reveals an intricate raised network covering the thorax and forewings. The infinite variety of patterns in this reticulation, which is the origin of the family's common name, makes these the most exquisitely beautiful of all bugs.

The majority of the 2,500 species of ground bugs feed on ripe seeds, though some, like the American Chinch bug, feed on green plant tissues, some are predators and a very few suck the blood of birds and mammals.

The most numerous of all the families of true bugs are the leaf bugs, a group of some 6,000 species of generally rather delicate bugs found on plants throughout the world. There are both plant-feeding and predatory leaf bugs. Some are serious pests of crops, while others play an important role in keeping potential pests in check by preying on them. In North America the lygus bugs (genus *Lygus*) are important pests. European species include the Apple capsid. In the tropics members of the genus *Helopeltis* are pests of tea and coffee. WRD

Cicadas and hoppers (series Auchenorrhyncha), aphids and scales comprise the suborder Homoptera. Homopterans direct their piercing and sucking rostrum down, never forward, feed exclusively on plants, and have membranous wings that at rest lie sloping over the body and lack hardened portions on the forewings. Cicadas and hoppers are a large and diverse grouping of entirely plant-feeding insects that range in size from leafhoppers of 0.1in (2 mm) in length to some cicadas with a wing span of 8in (20cm). Economically they are less important than aphids, especially in temperate regions, but they are becoming increasingly known as vectors of plant virus disease. A few species are important for the direct effect their feeding may have on plants.

There are 20 families of plant hoppers and 10,000 species, often placed in the superfamily Fulgoroidea. Among these the largest, up to 3.2in (8cm) in length, are found among the predominantly tropical lantern flies. These are often brightly colored insects, while others may have cryptic forewings and brightly colored hindwings. Many have large extensions to their heads, and a Brazilian species (*Fulgora laternaria*) has a head resembling a crocodile! The popular name for the group stems from old, unsubstantiated, accounts that the head glows in the dark.

The plant hopper family contains over 2,000 species, mostly small in size, up to 0.2in (5mm) in length. Most are grass feeders and some are important pest species. The Asian rice brown plant hopper is the most important rice pest in Asia at present, and can destroy a crop through its direct

The 2 Suborders of Bugs

True bugs
Suborder Heteroptera

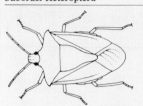

"Beak" can be swung down or forward from body; many species predatory; base of forewings often hardened, remainder and hindwings membranous; at rest wings overlap, lie flat over body; stink glands present.

25,000 known species in over 60 families, including **assassin bugs** (Reduviidae), **back swimmers** or **water boatmen** (Notonectidae); **bedbugs** (Cimicidae); **flower-bugs** (Anthocoridae); **giant water bugs** (Belostomatidae); **ground and seed bugs** (Lygaeidae), including the

Chinch bug (*Blissus leucopterus*); **lace bugs** (Tingidae); **leaf, plant** or **capsid bugs** (Miridae), including the **Apple capsid** (*Plesiocoris rugicollis*); **lesser water boatmen** (Corixidae); **saucer bugs** (Naucoridae); **shieldbugs** or **stinkbugs** (eg Pentatomidae); **squash bugs** (Coreidae), including the **Dock bug** (*Coreus marginatus*); **water scorpions** (Nepidae); **water striders** (Hydrometridae); and **pond skaters** (Gerridae).

Cicadas, hoppers; aphids and scales
Suborder Homoptera

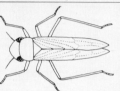

Over 42,500 known species. Beak brought down, never forward, to feed on plants; wings membranous, at rest lie sloping over body; many species produce honeydew.

Series: Auchenorryncha
Beak appears to arise from "neck"; antennae very short, ending in a bristle; sound-producing structures present. Almost 33,000 species in over 30 families, among them: **cicadas** (Cicadidae), including the **Periodical** or **Seventeen-year cicada** (*Magicicada septendecim*); **froghoppers** and **spittlebugs** (Cercopidae), including the **Meadow spittlebug** (*Philaenus spumarius*); **lantern flies** (Fulgoridae); **leafhoppers** (Cicadellidae), including the **Green rice leafhopper** (*Nephotettix virescens*) and **Rose leafhopper** (*Edwardsiana rosae*); **plant hoppers** (Delphacidae), including the **Asian rice brown plant hopper** (*Nilaparvata lugens*) and **Sugarcane plant hopper** (*Perkinsiella saccharicida*); and **treehoppers** (Membracidae).

Series: Sternorrhyncha
Beak appears to arise from thorax between bases of forelegs; antennae usually well developed; usually very small, many species form large colonies. 12,500 species known, among them the **aphids, greenfly** and **blackfly** (families Aphididae, Pemphigidae, Adelgidae, Phylloxeridae), including the **Black bean aphid** (*Aphis fabae*) and the **Vine phylloxera** (*Phylloxera vastatrix* or *Viteus vitifolii*); **armored scales** (Diaspididae); **jumping plant lice** (Psyllidae), including the **Apple sucker** (*Psylla mali*); **mealy bugs** (Pseudococcidae); **scale insects** (families include the Coccidae and Diaspidae), including the **Soft brown scale** (*Coccus hesperidum*); and **whiteflies** (Aleyrodidae), including **Cabbage whitefly** (*Aleyrodes proletella*) and **Glasshouse whitefly** (*Trialeurodes vaporarium*).

---

feeding as well as by transmitting virus disease. Many species of the genus *Perkinsiella* are found on sugarcane. One (*Perkinsiella saccharicida*) introduced from Australia almost destroyed the Hawaiian sugar industry early this century, before it was controlled by introducing a capsid bug of the family Miridae that preys on the eggs.

Among the cicada-like families the 2,500 species of froghoppers and spittlebugs are most familiar because of the frothy masses in which the nymphs live on the plants. This "cuckoo spit" is formed by blowing air from an abdominal channel on the underside, through a film of anal excretions, to form bubbles. The bubbles may protect the developing nymph from both parasites and predators, as well as from desiccation. The group feed from the mineral-bearing xylem sap of plants. The adults (froghoppers) do not live in a spittle mass. The most common and widespread species in Europe, and in the USA where it has been introduced, is the Meadow spittlebug *Philaenus spumarius*. This feeds on a very wide range of plants, unlike the majority of cicadas and hoppers which are restricted to a narrow range of plants. Meadow spittlebugs also occur in a range of distinct color forms (color polymorphism) from entirely dark individuals to very pale varieties. Many adult froghoppers have black and red markings, like the British *Cercopis vulnerata*.

The 2,300-odd species of treehoppers contain some of the most bizarre forms in

the entire group. The back plate (pronotum) of the thorax is extended and developed into a whole range of shapes and processes. The thorn-like appearance of some species may protect them by mimicry. Some species closely resemble ants in the form of pronotal extensions. Many treehoppers are found in small groups of individuals and some degree of social behavior has been recorded. Ant attendance is common throughout the group and this appears to be of mutual benefit to both ant and treehopper. The treehoppers produce honeydew which is taken by the ants, who in turn may protect the membracids against predators such as spiders.

Some of the 3,000 species of cicadas are abundant in tropical and subtropical parts of the world. Their most notable feature is the ability to produce loud sound. Although the Malaysian species *Pomponia imperatoria* has a wingspan of up to 8in (20cm), some cicadas may be only 0.4in (1cm) in length. One species (*Cicadetta montana*) is found in Britain, confined to the New Forest.

Cicada larvae live entirely underground, where they feed from the xylem sap of plant roots. As a result of the low nutrient content of this watery diet many species take several years to attain full size. The American Periodical cicada lives 17 years (all but a few weeks as a subterranean larva), giving rise to the alternative name "Seventeen-year cicada." Eggs are laid in the woody stems of trees and shrubs, and on hatching the young nymphs drop to the ground and enter

▶ **A newly hatched adult cicada,** *Venustria superba*, from Australia, emerges from its nymphal skin. The pale colors and soft cuticle make this a dangerous time in the life of any cicada, for it is conspicuous to birds and lizards. However, the wings soon expand, the cuticle hardens and assumes the mottled markings which make many cicada species such superb examples of camouflage.

▶ **Resplendent livery** OVERLEAF of these Australian shield bug nymphs, *Lyramorpha* species (Tessaratomidae), is a warning to would-be predators that they produce a foul-smelling and bitter liquid from glands in the abdomen. The four gland openings are clearly visible.

The Song of the Cicada

In tropical, subtropical and warm Mediterranean regions, the song of the cicada is among the most familiar of sounds. The sound production mechanism in cicadas is entirely different from the friction methods used by grasshoppers (eg the drawing of pegs over a file).

In cicadas the sound-producing organ consists of a pair of thin membranes in the cuticle, the tymbals (**a**) situated on each side of the first segment of the abdomen. Each tymbal is distorted, or buckled, by a large muscle (**b**) rather in the manner of a tin-lid being clicked in and out. Contraction of this muscle causes the tymbal, via the connecting strut (**c**), to buckle, and relaxation returns the tymbal to rest. Each such movement produces a pulse or "click," and the songs of cicadas consist of trains of pulses. Air sacs (**d**) may be present in the abdomen which greatly amplify the sound. The "clicks" may also vary greatly

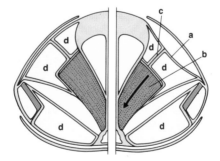

in amplitude, depending on the form of buckling of the tymbal.

Cicada calls are often very loud, some being audible to the human ear over distances of well over $\frac{1}{2}$mi in tropical forests. Only the males produce sound, and their calls serve to attract females of the same species.

Variations in the structure of the tymbal and its associated plates are an essential basis for the classification of cicadas. However,

some species may be more readily separated by their songs in the field than by examination of dried specimens, which may appear identical.

While the airborne sounds produced by cicadas have been known for centuries, it was only 50 years ago that it became known that the small leafhoppers and plant hoppers also produced sound for communication. Adult males, and also many females, were found to contain structures which appear comparable to the tymbals of cicadas. It now appears that all cicadas and hoppers (series Auchenorrhyncha) use sound for communication. The low-intensity sounds produced by these small insects are transmitted via the plants on which they live. In some species females may attract males by a simple series of pulses; the male then produces a more complex "courtship song" before mating takes place.   MRW

the soil. The forelegs, large and developed for digging, resemble those of a mole.

The leafhoppers comprise the largest family of the entire order of bugs, with over 15,000 species described and many new ones described each year. A large number of plant families are represented among the host plants, but most leafhoppers feed only on a narrow range, and many on just one genus or group of related genera.

The leafhopper subfamily Delto-cephalinae contains many chiefly "grass" feeding species, some of which are carriers of serious virus disease. The Green rice leafhopper (*Nephotettix virescens*) was once so abundant in India that when attracted to street lamps it could be swept up and sold as bird food. It remains important as a vector of rice virus disease in Asia.

Most leafhoppers feed from phloem sap, the organic nutrient-bearing medium of plants, but members of the subfamily Cicadellinae feed from xylem sap (as do also cicadas, froghoppers and spittlebugs). Copious amounts of dilute honeydew are produced because the sap is low in nutrients and large quantities of it need to be ingested. The dilute honeydew may be voided almost continuously, giving rise to the name "sharpshooters" in some. Cicadas may void liquid on disturbance, perhaps discouraging predators. Another leafhopper subfamily, the Typhlocybinae, consists of small frail species. Many of these feed from the upper cell layer beneath the cuticle of leaves. When the cells are ruptured and the contents removed, air enters the empty cells, groups of which form easily visible whitish patches. MRW

Aphids and scales (series Sternorrhyncha) are usually very small insects, made conspicuous only because many species form large colonies. These colonies may seriously weaken or kill the plants on which they feed and the damage caused is recognized by farmers and agriculturalists as "blight" or "wilt." Some species disfigure fruit or flowers to such an extent as to render them unsaleable. Some transmit virus diseases from plant to plant. The effect of feeding by some species is to cause deformations of the host plants, ranging from simple pits in the stem or curled edges of the leaves to large and elaborate galls.

Aphids and scales produce feces in the form of honeydew; gall-inhabiting species also produce quantities of wax which prevent the honeydew from wetting and drowning them. Voided honeydew is attractive to many insects, including bees; some

species of ants tend aphid and scale insect colonies, driving away predators and carrying the honeydew producers to the most nutritious parts of the plants.

Jumping plant lice (1,300 species including the family Psyllidae) are the only members of this series that can leap, an ability confined to adults. The immature stages are almost immobile. Jumping plant lice disperse on the wing, and the females are very discriminating in the choice of plant species on which to lay their eggs, so that almost all the 1,300 psyllid species are restricted to a single host, or at most to a few closely related species. The Apple sucker of European orchards belongs to this group.

Whiteflies (1,200 species, including the family Aleyrodidae) have similar life histories to those of jumping plant lice; the adults are delicate insects, covered in white wax, and the immature stages are immobile and scale-like. The Cabbage whitefly can often be disturbed in clouds from cabbages and related crops but it seems to do little damage to them. Its relative the Glasshouse whitefly is often troublesome on houseplants and in greenhouses.

Scale insects (6,000 species, including the families Coccidae and Diaspididae) are important pests of many tropical crops, and the Soft brown scale and some species of mealy bugs (Pseudococcidae) are injurious to houseplants and glasshouse crops. A few produce substances useful to man; both shellac and cochineal are produced by scale insects. Adult females are always wingless and either slow-moving or totally immobile; males are short-lived and do not feed, devoting their brief lives to reproduction. The newly hatched larvae are very active little creatures called "crawlers" and these are the stage in which dispersal usually occurs; crawlers of some species can survive being blown about by the wind and thus travel a considerable distance before settling down on a plant to commence feeding.

The 4,000 species of aphids are generally less modified in structure than scale insects. Their main economic impact is as pests of crops in temperate parts of the globe. In extensive areas of conifer forests the honeydew of tree-dwelling aphids may be the main ingredient of the honey produced by hive bees. This "forest honey" is greatly prized by connoisseurs. A close relative of the true aphids is the Vine phylloxera which almost destroyed the European wine industry in the late 19th century, when it was introduced from North America. Many of the true aphids (family Aphididae) have complex life histories. WRD

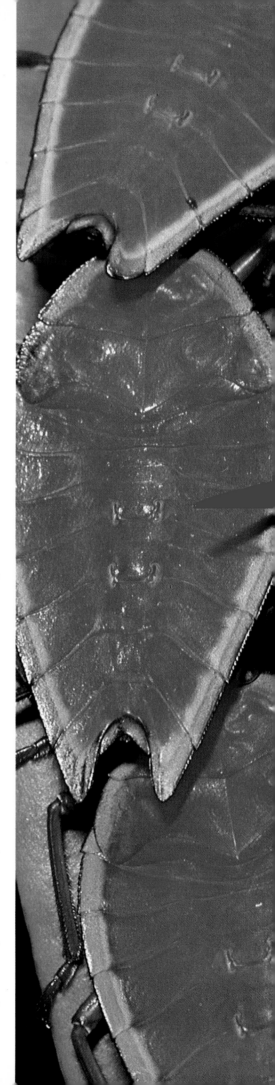

SNAKE FLIES, ALDERFLIES, LACEWINGS

Orders: Raphidioptera, Megaloptera, Neuroptera
Class: Insecta, subclass Pterygota.
Phylum: Uniramia.

Snake flies
Order Raphidioptera
Eighty species in 1 family (Raphidiidae).
Distribution: all continents except Australia, commonest in Europe and America.

Features: small, 0.4–0.8in (1–2cm) long, wingspan 0.4–1.6in (1–4cm); antennae bristle-like, rather short; prothorax or "neck" very long; 4 wings have pigmented patch, some veins fork at ends; female has long egg-laying tube; cerci at tip of abdomen are very short; larvae terrestrial, carnivorous.
Includes: *Erma, Glavia, Inocellia, Raphidia.*

Alderflies, dobson flies, fish flies
Order Megaloptera
About 300 species in 2 families.
Distribution: chiefly in temperate regions.

Features: wingspan up to 6in (15cm); antennae usually long; prothorax short; wings without pigmented patch, hindwings fold fanwise in basal region and are coupled to forewings by jugal lobe; veins rarely fork at tip; female lacks ovipositor; male has 1-jointed cerci; carnivorous larvae are all aquatic.
Families: the **dobson flies** and **fish flies** (Corydalidae) and **alderflies** (Sialidae).

Lacewings, mantispids and ant lions
Order Neuroptera
About 4,500 species in 16 families.
Distribution: worldwide, mainly tropics.

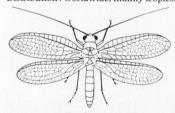

Features: small to large, 0.2–3in (0.5–7.5cm) long, wingspan 1.2–6.4in (3–16cm); sometimes rather hairy; antennae thread-like or clubbed; 4 wings without pterostigma, have inefficient coupling mechanism, veins nearly all fork at tip; no ovipositor or cerci; larvae mainly terrestrial predators, 3 larval, 1 pre-pupal stage (hyper-metamorphosis); syringe-like mouthparts.

Includes Sisyridae, Hemerobiidae (**brown lacewings**), Chrysopidae (**green lacewings**), Osmylidae, Mantispidae (**mantispids**), Nemopteridae, Ascalaphidae, Myrmeleontidae (**ant lions**).

THE alderflies, lacewings and snake flies are three fascinating orders of insects, though of little economic importance. First appearing in the Permian 280–225 million years ago (snake flies possibly earlier in the Carboniferous), they were the first insects to have wings developing internally and represent the earliest occurrence of a pupal stage, and therefore of complete metamorphosis. Their larvae, some of which may be active for several years, have well-developed legs and a head with powerful biting jaws, and they give rise to an exarate pupa (ie with the appendages not stuck down on the body) which can crawl about. All have four wings in the adult stage which can be folded along the body like a pitched roof. The wings are large and richly veined. Flight is fluttery and weak in most species. Adults are short-lived and in a few species do not feed.

The **snake flies** (order Raphidioptera) owe their name to the long prothorax on which the adult holds up its head to look for prey. Females lay eggs under bark with a long egg-laying tube. The predatory larvae are terrestrial, often living under loose bark.

The **alderflies**, **dobson flies** and **fish flies** (order Megaloptera) include some very large insects, some American dobson fly adults attaining a wingspan of 6in (15cm). The aquatic larvae of dobson flies bear seven pairs of unjointed tracheal gills on the abdomen and additional ventrally placed gill tufts. The gills are regularly protracted and retracted, causing water to be swished past them. The body ends with a pair of prolegs bearing large claws which help it to move about. Adult females lay eggs near water in large masses sometimes of several thousands. Different generations of some Australian species lay eggs on the same tree stump year after year. After hatching, the larvae fall into the water, where they catch prey (small insect larvae etc) with their large jaws. They may take several years to mature before pupating in soil nearby. The adults of some species do not feed, but the males have huge tusks which are probably used in sexual competition with other males. The brownish, rather stout alderflies (*Sialis* species) are abundant near water in the early summer. The larvae have seven pairs of gills each with five joints rather like limbs, and there is an additional gill on the last segment. They feed on aquatic insects, worms and other small invertebrates.

The larvae of most **lacewings**, **mantispids** and **ant lions** (Neuroptera) are terrestrial predators. They feed with mouthparts formed from the maxillae and mandibles, which act as a sucking tube through which

food can be imbibed under the action of a pump-like mechanism in the pharynx. The gut ends blindly and any solid indigestible material is stored. Excluding a few families of mainly small, aphid-like species, neuropterans can be divided into the superfamilies Hemerobioidea and Myrmeleontoidea.

The Hemerobioidea comprise the lacewings, mantispids and some related forms. Among these, the family Sisyridae have aquatic larvae which are specialized to feed on freshwater sponges. The eggs are laid on branches overhanging the water and the larvae hatch and fall in. They are equipped with seven pairs of gills. The brown lacewings (Hemerobiidae) are an important family whose terrestrial larvae feed on aphids and other plant suckers. The nocturnally active adults prey on the same food as the larvae, and some are adept at feigning death when caught. In the more familiar green lacewings (Chrysopidae) the larvae are important aphid predators. Some have developed the trick of hiding from predators under the empty skins of their prey. The females protect their eggs from parasites and predators by attaching them to long stalks. They form the stalks by sticking blobs of "glue" onto a leaf and then rapidly moving the abdomen upward, which draws the rapidly hardening glue out into a long

▼ **A roosting ant lion fly** BELOW, *Ascalaphus macaronius* (Ascalaphidae), in the French Alps. These day-flying insects hawk up and down in search of prey, in the manner of dragonflies.

▼ **Aquatic larva of the alderfly,** *Sialis lutaria* (Sialidae), showing the seven pairs of tracheal gills, each of which has its own blood supply. The larvae are predators of other aquatic invertebrates.

thread, to which the egg is attached, clusters of eggs giving a "pin-cushion" effect. The adults fly at night and they possess hearing organs in large wing veins which can respond to the short, high-frequency pips emitted by bats, so helping them to avoid being eaten.

The lacewing-like Osmylidae have larvae which, although they prey on larvae of chironomid midges and other aquatic forms, lack gills. The adults of some species have beautifully marked wings. Finally, the intriguing Mantispidae resemble small mantids with their raptorial forelegs, extended prothorax and mobile head with large compound eyes, well suited to catching prey. Mantispids are mainly tropical but quite common also in temperate climates.

The other superfamily, the Myrmeleontoidea, includes some very striking species mainly confined to warmer climates. Their larvae are voracious predators with large serrated jaws through which they inject enzymes into their prey and then suck out their juices. Adults of the family Nemopteridae are well known for their extraordinary streamer-like hindwings which do not contribute to flight but trail behind and probably have a sexual function. The males dance up and down like mayflies, forming swarms which attract females. The larvae

of some species are equally strange, having the prothorax greatly elongated to form a long neck which helps them to seize prey.

The Ascalaphidae hunt prey on the wing by day. They have much better powers of flight than most other neuropterans, and they can be mistaken for dragonflies at a distance but, close to, their long clubbed antennae immediately distinguish them. The males of some species are attractive insects with brightly colored wing markings. When caught, some tropical species not only feign death but also release the foul smell of rotting meat—enough to deter any predator. The eggs are placed on grass or twigs and in some species are surrounded by a stockade of rod-like bodies (repagula) which probably help to protect them from predators and parasites. The ant lion-like predatory larvae live in debris on the ground.

Ant lions are larvae of the family Myrmeleontidae which dig pits in sand and lie concealed at the bottom with their large jaws just protruding. Any small insect which stumbles into the pit has the sand pulled away from under its feet by the ant lion, and, as it slithers down, is seized in the lion's jaws. Other species have larvae which live on tree trunks or burrow into the soil without forming pits.   PLM

BEETLES

Order: Coleoptera
Class: Insecta, subclass Pterygota.
Phylum: Uniramia.
About 300,000 known species in 4 suborders.
Distribution: cosmopolitan, almost everywhere except the sea.

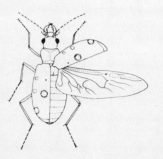

Features: front pair of wings modified to form hardened cases (elytra) for rear wings; forward-projecting, biting mouth-parts; development includes larva and pupa (with complete metamorphosis, or holometabolous).

Beetles are the most successful group of animals on Earth, forming almost one-third of all described animal species and about two-fifths of all insects. They are found in virtually every habitat, exploiting the most extreme conditions, and they occur in all shapes and colors and in sizes from less than 0.01 to 8in (0.25mm–20cm).

Beetles are characterized by a thickened pair of forewings called elytra, which meet at the midline to cover the membranous hindwings (Coleoptera = sheathwings). The elytra are held away from the body when the insect is airborne, and in repose, the wings are folded to fit beneath them. Some beetles have adopted a flightless existence, and may, like the oil beetles, have fused elytra, or rudimentary wings and flight muscles.

The typical jointed insect legs may be modified for various life styles: long and slender for speed (ground beetles), broad and toothed for digging (dung beetles, dor-beetles), curved and paddle-like for swimming (true water beetles) or expanded hindlegs for hopping (flea beetles).

The feeding habits of beetles range from predation to dung feeding and parasitism, though none is parasitic on man. Most of the predators attack other insects, but the large water beetles will take small fish and tadpoles. The European *Phosphuga atrata* (Silphidae) feeds on snails, predigesting the body with enzymes and sucking out the juices.

The mouthparts have four main components, the mandibles, the maxillae and palps, an upper lip or labrum, and a lower lip or labium. The mandibles are the cutting, piercing and crushing organs, while the other mouthparts deal with tasting and preparing the food and pushing it into the mouth. The large, sharp jaws of tiger beetles are an adaptation to a highly predatory way

▲ **About to take flight,** this South American click beetle (Elateridae) raises its horny forewings (elytra), exposing the membranous hindwings. Although mainly protective in function, elytra also provide some lift during flight.

◄ **All weevils have a snout or rostrum,** which bears the biting jaws at its tip. The rostrum is massively developed in this denizen of Peruvian rain forest, *Rhinastus latesternus* (Curculionidae).

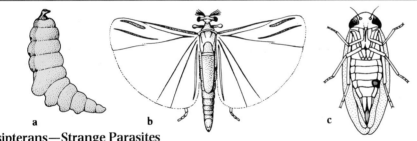

Strepsipterans—Strange Parasites

Strepsipterans are highly specialized internal parasites of other arthropods. In the past, they have been included in the Coleoptera, or thought to be closely allied. Today, characters once thought to show close relationship to other insect groups (beetles, hymenopterans, scorpion flies) are believed rather to derive from strepsipterans, special life-style. The 300 or so species are placed in a separate order, the Strepsiptera, comprising five families.

Adult females (**a**) are typically grub-like, wingless, and never leave their host. Only the fused head and thorax project from the host's body. An exception is the family Mengeidae, in which females are active, free living and found usually under stones but sometimes parasitic on bristletails.

The active, short-lived adult males (**b**) are 0.02–0.16in (0.5–4mm) long, black or brown, with a large transverse head, bulging eyes and fan- or comb-shaped antennae. The club- or plait-like forewings gave rise to the name "twisted-winged parasites." Borne on large, fan-like hind wings with reduced

venation, their body held vertically with the abdomen turned horizontally, males seek out virgin females, which emit a sex pheromone.

Insemination takes place through a "brood passage" between the female's cephalothorax and last larval cuticle. Up to 1,000 eggs mature in the female's inflated abdomen, to hatch, via the brood passage, as six-legged triungulin larvae. In late summer this free-living "infective" stage enters its host, usually an immature stage. After winter, and five or more grub-like stages, the mature larva extrudes its front end between the host's segments and pupates. The adult male emerges by pushing a cap off the pupa, but the adult female remains in the puparium formed by her last larval cuticle. Her position on the host helps to identify the species (**c**, female *Halictophagus* on jassine leafhopper). Strepsipterans are very host-specific: the Elenchidae on grasshoppers; Halticophagidae on tree- and leafhoppers, spittle bugs and mole crickets; stylopids (eg *Stylops*) on andrenid and halticid bees, sphecid and vespid wasps.   GCM

of life; the small, hard mandibles carried by weevils (snout beetles) at the tip of an elongated snout or rostrum are for crushing plant material. Specialized nectar feeders like species of the New World genus *Nemognatha* have tube-like mouthparts formed from elongated sections of the maxillae.

A beetle's sense organs are concentrated on its head, but tiny vibration-sensitive hairs are present on the thorax, abdomen and legs. Most (except a few cave beetles and many larvae) have compound eyes and probably see in color. Those relying on vision for hunting (eg ground beetles) or mating (fireflies) have larger, more efficient eyes. Whirligig beetles, which swim on the surface of ponds, have divided eyes, one half for vision under water, the other in air.

The antennae, which carry receptors sensitive to vibrations and airborne scents, are highly variable. Reduced in the larvae, in the adults the antennae may be abruptly bent or elbowed (eg Curculionidae weevils), thread-like or filiform (eg longhorn beetles), toothed (eg cardinal beetles), or plate-like or lamellate (chafers).

Beetles undergo complete metamorphosis from egg to adult with an intervening resting pupal stage (ie they are holometabolous). The wings develop internally and only appear after pupation. The insects may change their diets when they become adult. The eggs may be laid in the soil (rove beetles) or inserted into plant tissues (Curculionidae weevils), deposited singly (chafers) or in batches of several thousand (oil beetles). The larvae break through the eggshell using their mandibles and body spines or "egg-bursters." They feed and grow, passing through several more stages (instars) each of which ends with a molt or change of skin. They do not resemble the adults, except female fireflies, whose adults retain a larval form (glowworms), and may be legless grubs (furniture beetles), C-shaped (chafers), similar to sawfly larvae (leaf and flea beetles), or long-bodied and long-legged (rove beetles). Most aquatic larvae are air breathers, rising to the surface to take in oxygen through spiracles; screech beetles remove oxygen directly from the water using a gill system.

To reproduce successfully, a beetle, like any other animal, must ensure that its chosen mate belongs to the correct species, so before copulation or courtship can take place, specific signals must be given and received. This mate location may involve sight, sound, scent or a combination of all three.

The Deathwatch beetle uses sound. Deep inside old timbers where it has developed as a larva, the beetle braces its front legs against the wooden tunnel then taps rapidly on the tunnel floor with the top of its head. Occurring in spring, and most obvious at night, the mating call is made by both sexes. The high-pitched squeaks of screech beetles, caused by rubbing the tip of the abdomen against the underside of the elytra, are also

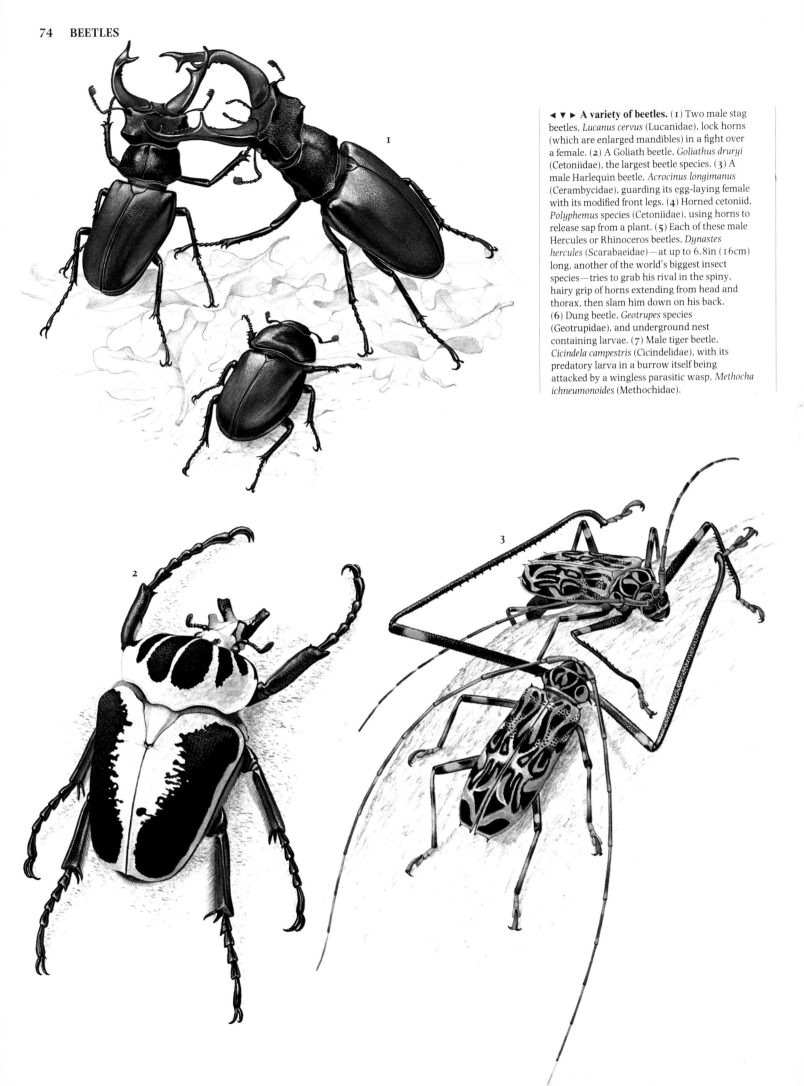

◄ ▼ ► **A variety of beetles.** (1) Two male stag beetles, *Lucanus cervus* (Lucanidae), lock horns (which are enlarged mandibles) in a fight over a female. (2) A Goliath beetle, *Goliathus druryi* (Cetoniidae), the largest beetle species. (3) A male Harlequin beetle, *Acrocinus longimanus* (Cerambycidae), guarding its egg-laying female with its modified front legs. (4) Horned cetoniid, *Polyphemus* species (Cetoniidae), using horns to release sap from a plant. (5) Each of these male Hercules or Rhinoceros beetles, *Dynastes hercules* (Scarabaeidae)—at up to 6.8in (16cm) long, another of the world's biggest insect species—tries to grab his rival in the spiny, hairy grip of horns extending from head and thorax, then slam him down on his back. (6) Dung beetle, *Geotrupes* species (Geotrupidae), and underground nest containing larvae. (7) Male tiger beetle, *Cicindela campestris* (Cicindelidae), with its predatory larva in a burrow itself being attacked by a wingless parasitic wasp, *Methocha ichneumonoides* (Methochidae).

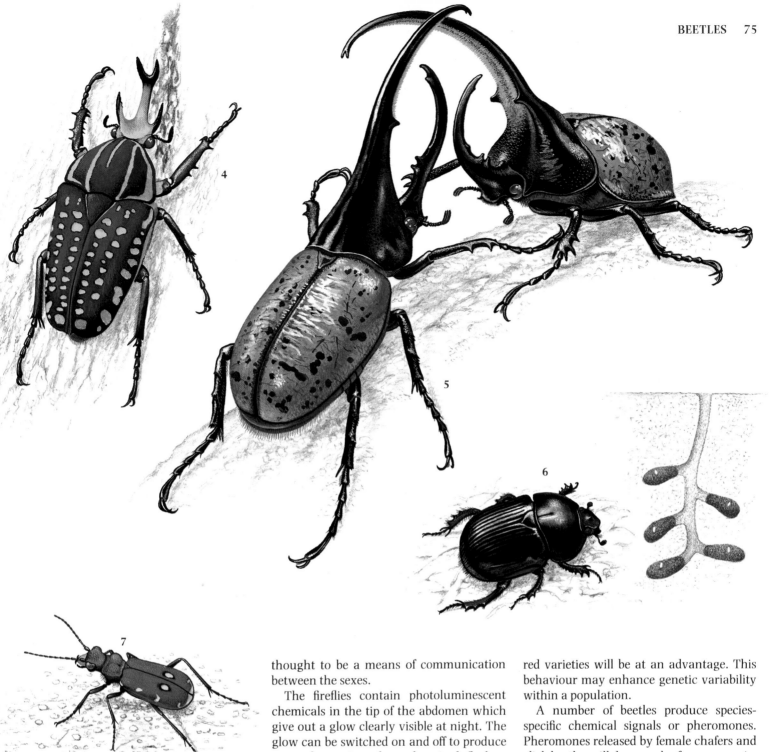

thought to be a means of communication between the sexes.

The fireflies contain photoluminescent chemicals in the tip of the abdomen which give out a glow clearly visible at night. The glow can be switched on and off to produce a regular series of synchronized flashes, each species having its own distinct pattern. The male fireflies display the light signal, and the wingless larva-like females (glow-worms) signal back when they see the appropriate flash sequence; size and brightness of the flash may be as important as sequence. The males drop down to the females with remarkable accuracy. Predatory glowworms of the genus *Photuris* can mimic the signals of *Photinus* females, and lure searching *Photinus* males to their death.

Females of the Two-spot ladybird, which is very variable in color pattern, seem to select their mates on the basis of color. In a largely red population, a female is more likely to accept the attentions of the black forms, while in a dark population, the rarer

red varieties will be at an advantage. This behaviour may enhance genetic variability within a population.

A number of beetles produce species-specific chemical signals or pheromones. Pheromones released by female chafers and click beetles will draw males from a surprisingly large area. The expanded, comb- or leaf-like male antennae are beautifully adapted for receiving these messages. Both the skin beetles and bark beetles release aggregation pheromones, which attract both males and females to a site suitable for burrowing and egg laying; this increases the chances of successful mating. In bark beetles, once females are mated and start burrowing, they emit a deterrent which inhibits further arrivals. The male usually remains with the female, helping with burrowing and guarding.

Once contact has been established, a courtship ritual usually takes place before the male is accepted. This may involve the male tapping the female with his legs or antennae. Among the oil beetles a complex

stroking ritual is necessary to make the female receptive. *Malachius* (Melyridae) males produce chemical secretions which the female chews; she is presumably reassured by the presence of a species-specific chemical. Other males similarly "taste" the female by nibbling her elytra.

Mating occurs when both insects are sure about their partner's identity, and if the female is sexually receptive. The frequently smaller male mounts the larger female and grips her elytra and thorax with his feet; male feet are usually larger for this purpose, and some males may even grip with specially adapted antennae. He inserts his copulatory organ (aedegus) into her vagina and deposits either a package of sperm (spermatophore) or free sperm; these will be stored in a special sac, the spermatheca, until the female is ready to lay her eggs. The female now ceases, either permanently or temporarily, to be sexually receptive. In some species she may mate more than once and possibly have some control over which male's sperm fertilize her eggs.

Many chafers and members of the family Passalidae form a monogamous pair and

Chemical Warfare

Bombardier beetles, such as *Brachinus* species, deter would-be predators by spraying them with boiling hot quinones, noxious chemicals which have a blistering effect on the skin and will frighten off both ants and toads.

The beetle itself suffers no ill effects because the quinones are present only briefly in its body. The quinones' precursors, hydroquinone and hydrogen peroxide, are produced by special glands and stored in a cuticle-lined abdominal chamber. They are

discharged as required into a second "combustion" chamber, where they are acted upon by the enzyme peroxidase. The reaction that follows produces quinones, water and oxygen, and also considerable heat. The oxygen allows the quinones to be expelled with some force, and an audible "pop," from the nozzle at the tip of the abdomen. The heat, an added deterrent, causes much of the liquid to be converted to an irritating gaseous cloud, resembling a tiny puff of smoke.

By swiveling the mobile abdominal tip, the beetle can aim its spray to either side, both forward and backward, with remarkable accuracy. The spray is released in tiny pulses, and the insect can continue spraying for some time before its reservoir is exhausted.

Many darkling beetles also use quinone sprays. Some *Eleodes* species, less mobile than bombardier beetles, lower the head and raise the abdomen to direct the spray at the face of a vertebrate attacker. Since the rest of the beetle is not distasteful, certain mice have adopted a method for getting around the defense mechanism. The beetle is snatched up and its abdomen rapidly inserted into sand where the quinones discharge harmlessly; the mice eat it from the head downward.

▶ **With their warning colors** OVERLEAF, these toxic oil beetles, *Mylabris oculata*, mate in the open in South Africa. *Mylabris* species (Meloidae) contain cantharidin, a powerful drug, which is extracted from the elytra by the pharmaceutical industry. Cantharidin is the basis of "Spanish fly," the alleged aphrodisiac normally associated with the European beetle *Lytta vesicatoria*.

◀ **The boiling hot quinone spray** BELOW of this bombardier beetle (*Brachinus* species) serves to frighten off a would-be predator.

◀ ▼ ▶ **Concealed or conspicuous.** Many insects escape detection by resembling lichen-covered bark, like this longicorn beetle LEFT, *Onychocerus crassus* (Cerambycidae) in Peru. Others resemble crinkled, dead leaves. In both such cases, posture is as important as appearance in maintaining the deception. Here BELOW another longicorn, *Capholymma stygia*, hangs from a leaf in a Malaysian forest.

By contrast, poisonous and distasteful insects blatantly advertise their noxious natures with conspicuous warning color patterns, like this mating pair RIGHT of leaf beetles, *Doryphora testudo* (Chrysomelidae), in a Peruvian rain forest.

cooperate in providing for their young; typically the sexes resemble one another. More usually, the males are polygamous and play no part in raising their offspring; the sexes are more likely to be dimorphic, ie different in size, form or color.

To protect themselves from a wide range of predators, beetles have developed an impressive armory of defenses. The hard, shiny elytra may form the first line of defense against other insects. When threatened, many dome-shaped leaf beetles and ladybirds retract their legs and antennae under this protective shield, clamp down to the surface on which they are standing, and wait until it is safe to re-emerge; even the sharp mandibles of predatory tiger beetles cannot establish a grip on the slippery surface. A number of beetles, particularly the larvae, have spiny or hairy surfaces which make them more difficult to attack; skin beetle larvae (eg genus *Trogoderma*) have hairs designed to penetrate a predator's skin and set up a local irritation.

Some ladybird larvae have hollow spines which, when ruptured, release sticky yellow blood (hemolymph) containing distasteful chemicals (reflex bleeding). The adults produce the same substance from "knee-joints" if, for example, a leg is seized in the jaws of an ant. It gums up the antennae and mouthparts of the attacker, which rapidly backs away in distress.

Use of repellent chemicals is widespread and very effective. Flightless ground beetles of the genus *Anthia* squirt out jets of formic acid which will burn the skin and cause serious eye damage. The juices of crushed *Paederus sabaeus*, a rove beetle, will, if accidentally brushed onto the cornea, set up the painful condition known as "Nairobi eye" and deter further attacks on the species. The body fluids and elytra of oil or blister beetles contain cantharidin, a blistering agent which can be fatal if ingested in sufficient quantity, while the larvae of the leaf beetle genus *Polyclada* are so poisonous that Kalahari bushmen use them to tip their hunting arrows. The forked tail of the larva of the leaf beetle *Cassida rubiginosa* allows it to carry a protective umbrella made of cast skins and feces. This is waved at an attacking ant, smearing it with feces; the ant retreats and cleans itself assiduously.

Beetles which are distasteful advertise the fact with bright, distinctive color patterns, usually black with red, yellow or white. This warning coloration exploits the ability of vertebrate predators to learn by their mistakes. The inexperienced insectivore will try anything that looks potentially edible, but soon learns to associate unpleasant experiences with particular colors. The use of a limited number of colors means that the number of fatal experimental attacks on these insects is much less than if the predators had to learn a different color pattern for each species.

Sound may be used as a deterrent. A sudden unexpected squeak could be enough to make a predator drop the beetle on its first experience—the effect is reinforced if the beetle is also distasteful. Like many other ground beetles, *Cychrus caraboides*, which makes a protest sound if handled, also ejects butyric acid from glands opening near the anus on the tip of the abdomen (pygidium). The sound produced when a click beetle is disturbed is caused by a spring mechanism lying between the thorax and abdomen. A peg on the thorax is forced into a groove on the abdomen, where it causes a release of muscular tension which throws the insect (also called a skipjack or snapping beetle) for some distance with an audible "click."

Concealment is perhaps the commonest form of defense against vertebrate predators, with immobility playing a very important part—once the beetle moves it may reveal itself. Those that live under stones, under bark and in soil are generally plain black or brown, and remarkably easy to overlook. Those living in more exposed habitats often come to resemble their backgrounds (crypsis). The concealed head and expanded thorax and elytra of members of the darkling beetle genus *Endustomus* make the insect look less like a beetle than the winged seeds among which it lives. Weevils of the genus *Gymnophilus* have taken crypsis a stage further by encouraging the growth of fungi and algae on their elytra.

Mimicry, resemblance to a poisonous or potentially unpleasant animal, may also give a measure of protection. Many myrmecophiles look like their ant hosts, possibly avoiding predation by animals which might not want to risk a painful bite. One tropical longhorn shows reverse head mimicry, with its deceptive eyespots at the end of the abdomen—at a random glance it looks more like a poisonous frog than a beetle.

Beetles have been associated with people and their dwellings since humans first began to establish a settled way of life. Insect remains from archaeological sites indicate that many of the species we consider pests today have long been with us. A pest species is simply a beetle that is going about its normal business in a place that has been annexed by humans; the same activities may be considered beneficial if people gain, or at least do not lose, by them.

Wood-boring beetles break down dead trees, so that the nutrients locked up in the wood can be recycled and support new life. People use wood for structural timbers and furniture, and both are subject to internal attack by beetles. Longhorn beetle larvae will feed on roof timbers, often taking several years before emerging as adults; the Old house borer or beetle is commonly found in pine. Old oak timbers are more likely to

be infected by the Deathwatch beetle. Furniture and floors will be attacked by the woodworm beetles *Anobium punctatum* and *A. inexspectatum*, which can be detected by the presence of tiny round holes in the wood. These are the adults' flight holes, from which they emerge after spending their lives as legless larvae chewing tunnels through the wood.

Bark beetles are more of a problem with living trees. The Elm bark beetle has had a drastic effect on the character of the British countryside, once dominated by tall elms. In itself, the beetle does little harm, the larvae chewing out tunnels in surface wood directly beneath the bark, but it transports a virulent fungus (*Ceratostomella ulmi*) that spreads into the tree's transport vessels, causing a blockage so that the tree dies.

Other beetles attack crops, causing heavy losses. A wide range of weevils (Curculionidae, Bruchidae) feed on the seeds, flowers and leaves of legumes, fruit and root crops. Larvae of the Boll weevil feed inside the flowers of the cotton plant so that the valuable cotton fiber, which normally surrounds the seeds, fails to form. Another species of the same genus, *Anthonomus pomorum*, lays its eggs in apple blossom, preventing proper development of the fruit. Indian corn (maize) may be badly affected by the larvae of several species of click beetles, which feed

on its roots; among weevils, Maize billbug larvae attack the soft pith of corn stems.

Among the leaf-feeding Chrysomelidae is the well-known Colorado beetle much feared by potato growers. The brightly colored adults and larvae feed on the potato haulms, so preventing the production of tubers, and a heavy infestation will devastate a whole crop. Other villains include the Mexican bean beetle and its close relatives, which attack legumes such as the soybean, the forage plant cowpea, and solanaceous plants such as the tomato and aubergine.

Some crop damage may be accelerated by the transmission of a pathogenic microorganism. Among leaf beetles, the cucumber beetles carry the bacterium which causes wilt disease—it is deposited in the insects' feces, from where it is washed into a fresh plant wound. Any insect subsequently feeding on the infected plant will

▲ **The safety-in-numbers principle** and mechanical protection by branched spines are adopted by the larvae and shiny black pupae of this leaf beetle in Mexico (Chrysomelidae).

▶ **Maternal care** is shown by some beetles. Here a fungus beetle, *Pselaphicus giganteus* (Erotylidae), shepherds her larvae on fungus in forest in Trinidad.

▶ **This latter-day tribolite** BELOW is in reality the larva of a net-veined beetle, *Dulticola* species (Lycidae), grazing on mossy bark on Mount Kinabalu, Borneo. The orange markings signal to would-be predators that this is a highly distasteful insect.

◀ **Larvae** of (1) ground beetle (active, predatory); (2) leaf beetle; (3) chafer (lives in soil, rotten wood); (4) weevil (in plant material).

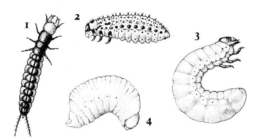

The 4 Suborders and Key Families of Beetles

Archostemata

A very ancient group comprising 2 families, the Cupedidae (25 species, chiefly fossils from the Lower Permian, beginning 280 million years ago) and Micromalthidae (1 species, *Micromalthus debilis*, with 5 larval forms).

Adephaga

30,200 species in 10 families, most of which are predatory as both adults and larvae except Haliplidae (**crawling water beetles**) feeding on algae and Rhysodidae (**wrinkled bark beetles**), found in rotting wood; many Paussidae live in ants' nests; Carabidae are all ground dwellers, including **ground beetles, bombardier beetles, tiger beetles**; aquatic families include Amphizoidae, Hygrobiidae (**screech beetles**), Noteridae, Gyrinidae (**whirligig beetles**) and Dytiscidae (**predacious diving beetles** or **true water beetles**); Trachypachidae inhabit wet regions and larvae may be aquatic.

Myxophaga

22 species in families Sphaeriidae, Lepiceridae, Hydroscaphidae, Torrincolidae. Tiny beetles with aquatic larvae; mostly found in hotter regions.

Polyphaga

About 248,000 species in 150 families. Feed on a variety of plants and animals. Distinguished by absence of 6th segment in leg of larvae. Families include:
Hydrophilidae (**water scavenger beetles**), divers, in wet places.
Erotylidae, Corylophidae, Cisidae, Lathridiidae are fungus feeders.
Lucanidae (**stag beetles**), Cerambycidae (**longhorn beetles**, including **Old house borer** or beetle *Hylotrupes bajulus*), Anobiidae (**furniture beetles** and **woodworm**, including **Cigarette** or **Tobacco beetle** *Lasioderma serricorne*, **Deathwatch beetle** *Xestobium rufovillosum*), Bostrychidae (eg **Bamboo borer** *Dinoderus minutus*), Lyctidae (**powderpost beetles**), Pyrochroidae (**cardinal**

beetles) and Passalidae (**Betsy beetles, patent leather beetles**), wood feeders.
Histeridae (**hister beetles**), Staphylinidae (**rove beetles**), Cleridae (**checkered beetles**, including the **Redlegged ham beetle** *Necrobia rufipes*), Lampyridae (**fireflies, glowworms**) and some Coccinellidae (**ladybugs** or **ladybirds** or **lady beetles**, including the **Two-spot ladybird** *Adalia bipunctata* and **Seven-spot ladybird** *Coccinella septempunctata*) are predators. **Soft-winged flower beetles** (Melyridae), are predators that also feed on pollen.
Rhipiphoridae, and Meloidae (**oil** or **blister beetles**) are parasitic as larvae.
Geotrupidae (**dung beetles, dorbeetles**), Trogidae (**hide beetles**) and Scarabaeidae (**chafers** and **scarab beetles**, including **Hercules beetle** *Dynastes hercules*, **Sugarcane chafer** *Podischnus agenor*), all live on dung.
Most Silphidae (**burying** or **sexton** or **carrion beetles**) feed on carrion.
Apionidae, Curculionidae (including the **Boll weevil** *Anthonomus grandis*, **Biscuit** or **Drugstore weevil** *Stegobium paniceum*, **Maize billbug** *Sitophilus maidis*)—with over 50,000

species one of the largest families in the animal kingdom, and Bruchidae are all plant-feeding **weevils** or **snout beetles**.
Elateridae (**click beetles, skipjacks** or **snapping beetles, wireworms**), Dascillidae and many Buprestidae (**jewel beetles**) attack roots.
Chrysomelidae (**leaf beetles**), including the **Colorado beetle** *Leptinotarsa decemlineata*, **cucumber beetles** (*Diabrotica* species), **Mexican bean beetle** *Epilachna varivestis* and **Corn flea beetle** *Chaetocnema pulicaria*) eat foliage.
Scolytidae (including **Elm bark beetle** *Scolytus scolytus*), under bark.
Nitidulidae (**pollen beetles**), Cantharidae (**soldier beetles**) and Oedemeridae adults are commonly found on flowers.
Scydmaenidae (**stone beetles**) and Pselaphidae, found in soil, leaf litter, Byrrhidae (**pill beetles**) in moss.
Dermestidae (**skin beetles, carpet beetles, "woolly bears"**) and Ptinidae (**spider beetles**) are household pests.
Many Tenebrionidae (**darkling beetles, meal worms**) are adapted for desert conditions.

help to transmit it further. The Corn flea beetle similarly transmits the bacterial wilt disease of Indian corn.

Not all beetles found on crops are harmful. Predatory ladybirds feed, as adults and larvae, on aphids and scale insects, and can, in large enough numbers, save a crop from destruction. Several, such as *Aphidecta obliterata*, which feeds on fir tree aphids, have been deliberately introduced into new areas and become permanently established. Others may be periodically applied in large numbers as eggs, larvae or adults to particular crops—the Seven-spot ladybird is used to control potato aphid in parts of the United States. Dung beetles are being used in Australia to solve a different farming problem. The existing insect fauna cannot deal with the large amounts of dung produced by the non-native cattle, so dung beetles were imported from Africa and South America. Those imported into Hawaii and Puerto Rico have been very successful in controlling the numbers of dung-feeding horn flies (*Haematobia*, family Muscidae) which, as adults, suck the blood of cattle.

Many beetles have highly specialized, often bizarre, life histories, particularly those that are parasitic. Eight families are known to contain species that live only as parasites (obligate), or are facultative (optional) parasites which mainly attack the eggs or pupae of other insects—the larvae of oil beetles of the genus *Mylabris* burrow into the soil to feed on grasshopper eggs.

All members of the Rhiphiphoridae are parasitic as larvae, although the adults feed at flowers. *Metoecus paradoxus* larvae are found in nests of common wasps (*Vespula* species). The female beetle oviposits on flowers, and the eggs hatch into minute, bristly planidium larvae, a non-feeding stage, specialized for transport by the host adult to its nest, with a thick, spiny cuticle and suckers. These await the arrival of a wasp and hitch a lift back to the nest; few will be successful, so large numbers are produced. Each larva goes through several different larval forms (hypermetamorphosis). First it penetrates a wasp grub and feeds internally as an endoparasite. Later it emerges, molts to become a legless grub, and wraps itself around the body of the wasp larva where it continues to feed as an ectoparasite. After pupation it becomes a fully winged adult.

Adults of some species of the chafer family have adopted a semi-parasitic way of life, clinging to the fur of mammals in the anal region. This allows the female to drop her eggs in a ready food source. The African

Zonocopris gibbicollis lives inside the shell of the large *Bulimus* snail, where it feeds on fecal material.

Well over a thousand species of beetle are known to live in close association with ants, as predators or parasites, or obtaining food from but neither damaging nor benefiting the ants (commensalism). Some are actively welcomed, while others avoid attack by mimicking the chemical odor and behavior of their hosts. A number of rove beetles share the nests of ants, both as larvae and adults, and many species produce attractive secretions that the ants lick from special glands.

Larvae of the rove beetle *Lochmechusa pubicollis* are so attractive to *Formica polyctana* ants that they are adopted and carried into the brood chamber. They probably give off a pheromone which stimulates brood-rearing behavior in the ants. The larvae mimic the begging behavior of the young ants by rearing up and tapping the mouth-parts of the ant "nurse": she responds by regurgitating a droplet of digested prey juices. The beetle larvae will also prey upon any nearby ant or other beetle larvae. In the fall the adult beetle, not yet sexually mature, once more begs food from its *Formica* hosts, then flies off in search of the nest of *Myrmica*, a different ant genus which carries on raising its own brood throughout the winter. The beetle offers the *Myrmica* ant a secretion from the tip of its abdomen, which forestalls any aggressive behavior. The ant then samples secretions produced by glands just behind the elytra; these contain chemicals which cause it to adopt the beetle and carry it into the brood chamber where the beetle finishes its development. Mating and egg-laying take place near a *Formica* nest in the spring.

Few adult beetles show any concern for their offspring other than positioning the eggs close to a potential food source. Among the dung beetles are a number of exceptions. A mated pair of the scarab beetle *Copris lunaris* cooperate to construct an underground nest, which they provision with dung. The male works in the upper part of the entrance tunnel, driving off intruders and other males. The female shapes about five brood balls out of the dung mass and inserts a single egg into each one. Eventually the entrance tunnel is sealed off with only the female remaining in the brood chamber. Here she stays for three months, repairing brood balls, preventing the growth of fungi and repelling intruders. She only leaves the chamber when the first adults begin to emerge.   LJL

▶ **Flowers are vital refuelling stations** for many beetles. Here, a chafer, *Diphucephala* species (Scarabaeidae), feasts on pollen at an *Acacia* flower in Australia.

◀ **A mêlée of mating soldier beetles** on thistle flowers in England. A common sight in summer, *Rhagonycha fulva* (Cantharidae) has been called the "soldier beetle" since the days red uniforms were worn by the British army.

▼ **Lesser grain borer beetles,** *Rhizopertha dominica* (Bostrychidae), infesting stored wheat. Both larvae and adults feed on the wheat grains. They also attack cork and wooden and paper boxes.

Partners in Destruction

Inside the gut of a number of beetles which feed on very dry foodstuffs such as hair, skin, wood or feathers, live symbiotic organisms, usually bacteria or protozoa. These secrete enzymes which enable the beetle to digest such unpromising material. The symbionts allow beetles to attack material which is too dry to support bacterial or fungal growth, so the beetles form a major threat to stored products—many are common household pests.

The young beetles are infected with the symbionts by their parents. In the wood-feeding powder-post beetles the symbionts migrate into the egg before it is laid, while in *Rhizopertha dominica* (family Bostrychidae), a grain weevil which also feeds on wood and paper, they are transmitted by the sperms. In the furniture beetles, the outer egg surface is infected via the female's anus; on hatching, the young eat the empty egg cases.

The tiny, hairy larvae of *Anthrenus verbasci* and *A. flavipes* (family Dermestidae) are the notorious "woolly bears" or carpet beetles, which attack woollen fibers and chew holes in expensive carpets. *Anthrenus museorum* will

gradually reduce dried museum specimens of animals to dust. When about to pupate, *Anthrenus* larvae will enter firmer material, such as wood or cork, on which they do not feed. The adults are pollen feeders and cause no damage.

Among the furniture beetles there are several pests of materials other than wood. The Cigarette or Tobacco beetle can cause serious economic loss by attacking all types of tobacco products. Among weevils, the Biscuit or Drugstore weevil was the bane of early sailors, feeding on the hard tack which formed their staple food.

Many pests of stored products take a varied diet, and are consequently difficult to control. The Bamboo borer seems to eat almost anything of plant origin; it specializes in bamboo products, particularly furniture, but has also been found in dried fruit, avocados, ginger, cinnamon and various types of wood. The quaintly named Red-legged ham beetle prefers materials with a high fat or oil content, such as smoked bacon, cheese, nuts and copra, but will attack other insects and their eggs, bone meal and even guano.

SCORPION FLIES

Order: Mecoptera
Class: Insecta, subclass Pterygota.
Phylum Uniramia.
Fewer than 400 species in 8 families.
Distribution: worldwide; generally in cool,
moist conditions.

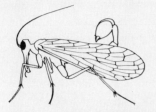

Features: slender, small to medium-sized, with
downward-projecting "beak." Adults mostly
0.5–1in (12–26mm) long, usually with two
pairs of similar long, membranous wings with
span up to 2in (5cm), thread-like antennae,
and male genitalia upcurved (family
Panorpidae) like scorpion's tail. Larvae
caterpillar-like, usually with prolegs, and
characteristic compound eyes. Pupae have
movable mandibles and appendages free from
the body. Development with complete
metamorphosis (holometabolous), and wings
develop internally (endopterygote).

Families include: **true** or **common scorpion flies**
(Panorpidae), including the **Common scorpion
fly** (*Panorpis communis*); **snow scorpion flies**
(Boreidae); and **hanging scorpion flies**
(Bittacidae).

▶ **Mating pair of hanging scorpion flies,**
Harpobittacus species in Australia, the female
feeding on a fly caught by the male as a nuptial
gift (Bittacidae).

▼ **Scavenging on a dead insect,** a male
Common scorpion fly (Panorpidae) eats a dead
damsel fly.

THE name "scorpion fly" properly applies only to males of one family (Panorpidae) of the order Mecoptera, which have an upturned and enlarged tip to the abdomen, reminiscent of a scorpion's tail.

Members of the order are slender, small to medium-sized carnivorous insects with primitive biting mouthparts that project down at right angles to the body to form a beak-like rostrum. The beak is formed by elongation of parts of the head capsule, the clypeus, labium and maxillae. The adults have long, thread-like antennae with many segments (40–50 in *Panorpa*, 16–20 in the hanging scorpion fly genus *Bittacus*), well-developed compound eyes and usually three simple eyes or ocelli.

Adult scorpion flies generally have two pairs of similar, long, membranous wings (Greek *mekoptera*, long wing) with many cross-veins. The wings may be carried horizontally or longitudinally at rest, and are usually transparent or semitransparent, but often conspicuously spotted or banded. The Californian genus *Apterobittacus* lacks wings, while males of the family Boreidae have a pair of slender, bristle-like vestiges instead of wings, and the females have scale-like lobes on the middle segment of the thorax.

The legs are long and slender and generally adapted for walking, with the claws usually paired. In *Bittacus*, however, the claws are single and the fourth and fifth segments of the tarsus have fine teeth along their inner margins, serving to grip prey items by means of the fifth segment closing onto the fourth. The abdomen is elongated, with short cerci and prominent genitalia (in the male), and it usually comprises 10 segments.

The larvae are caterpillar-like (eruciform) with a well-developed head, short, three-segmented antennae, compound eyes and sharp mandibles. The larva's compound eyes on either side of the head are formed by groups of simple eyes and are a distinguishing feature of the order. Some larvae are very similar to sawfly larvae, while others are covered with branched projections arising from the body segments.

The larvae all live on plant remains (are saprophagous) or on dead insects (necrophagous). The number of molts (ecdyses) is not known, but some members of the family Panorpidae have seven. Pupation occurs in the soil and the pupae are able to escape from the cocoon by means of mandibles (dectitious).

The scorpion flies first appear in the fossil record before the end of the Permian period (280–225 million years ago). The order is one of the most primitive having a pupal stage (complete metamorphosis).

Of the eight recognized families, five live almost exclusively in the Southern Hemisphere—the Choristidae, Nannochoristidae, Notiothaumidae, Austromeropeidae and Meropeidae—and they are represented by a total of only 11 species possessing very archaic features, seemingly unchanged since the Jurassic (190–136 million years ago). The other families (Boreidae, Bittacidae and Panorpidae) are much mure common and abundant, nearly half of all mecopteran species belonging to the third of these. Of the order's fewer than 400 species, some 85 occur in the United

Courtship and Nuptial Gifts

The complex courtship of scorpion flies involves exchange of "nuptial gifts" and the production by the male of pheromones to attract females, which mate more than once and are receptive in cycles.

Courtship in hanging scorpion flies of the genus *Harpobittacus*, for example, depends on temperature, the majority of matings occurring around midday. The male grasps a prey item with his hind legs, then punctures it with his beak before flying to a resting place where he holds the nuptial gift of prey in his mouthparts. Females of the species are attracted by a secretion produced from a special glandular area behind the seventh and eighth dorsal plates (tergites) of the male's abdomen. An approaching female is seized and the male juxtaposes his genitalia with the female's aperture by means of a twist of the abdomen. The male transfers the nuptial gift to the female, who feeds on it while mating

takes place. After several minutes they separate and the male may finish eating the nuptial gift, then leave to forage once more.

Only males with nuptial gifts are attractive to females. Several females may be attracted to the same male, which may use the same prey item as a nuptial gift for several mates.

Female hanging scorpion flies are not often observed to feed and it is thought that the prey offered by the male as a nuptial gift is important as a valuable food source enabling the female to produce mature eggs.

Some males will try to seek out other males in order to steal their nuptial gifts, a factor giving rise to often dense aggregations of males. The males of some scorpion flies have been observed forcibly to oust rival mating males before sperm transfer has been completed, but the terminal structures of most species are adapted for maintaining a grip on the female, thus reducing this possibility.

States, 20 in Australia and four in the United Kingdom.

Scorpion fly adults, like their larvae, feed on plant or insect remains or hunt live prey, although some occasionally feed on pollen, nectar and flowers. Both sexes of the Common scorpion fly have been seen raiding spiders' webs for insect prey, when they seem able to walk safely over the web, which they do without attracting the spider's attention.

Most adults prefer moist, cool situations and some are never found far from swamps, pools or small streams. After mating, eggs which are ovoid (*Panorpa*) or cuboidal (*Bittacus*) are dropped or laid in batches in soil crevices or on the ground. In *Panorpa* species the larvae emerge in a week or so and forage over the ground for food which may be consumed from below or dragged down into a burrow.

The true, or common, scorpion flies are common and widely distributed. They are about 0.6–0.8in (15–20mm) long, with brownish bands and spots on the wings. They are usually yellowish-brown. *Panorpa communis* is a very common species throughout Europe, with a wing span of 1.2in (30mm). The digestive system is unusual in having a pumping oesophagus, a proventriculus equipped with long setae, and a large midgut.

The snow scorpion flies, characterized by their vestigial wings, are found in Europe and North America and live and feed on moss. These unusual insects are often found on the surface of the snow in winter and are 0.08–0.2in (2–5mm) long and dark colored. Male snow scorpion flies have bristle-like wings which are used for grasping the female during mating.

The hanging scorpion flies are so called for their method of capturing prey with their hind legs while hanging from twigs or vegetation by their forelegs, although some species do actually catch prey on the wing. Most adults are yellowish-brown with long legs and look superficially like crane flies. The majority of species hang with their legs folded back but *Bittacus apicalis* holds its dark-tipped wings out. The last (fifth) segment of the tarsus in this group is grasping (raptorial), folding back on the fourth segment to catch small flying prey items such as flies and aphids.

Some species can be cannibalistic, while large robber flies have been found feeding on adult scorpion flies. Scorpion flies do not bite or sting humans, and they are considered to be of no economic importance.

GCM

FLEAS

Order: **Siphonaptera** (Aphaniptera, Suctoria, Rophoteira).
Class: Insecta, subclass Pterygota.
Phylum Uniramia.
About 1,800 species in 200 genera and 16 families.
Distribution: worldwide as parasites of mammals and birds.

Features: adults small, 0.04–0.33in (1–9mm) long, wingless, laterally flattened and streamlined, with piercing and sucking mouthparts for diet exclusively of blood; eyes when present simple (ocelli), antennae short and lie in grooves (foveae) each side of head; body covered in shiny, tough integument colored yellowish-brown to black, bearing backward-pointing bristles and combs; abdomen composed of 7 typical segments, the remaining terminal 3 segments modified as uniquely complex reproductive organs; extensive adaptations for jumping include powerful rear legs, pleural arch; skeletal locking mechanisms; development holometabolous (complete metamorphosis), with egg, larva (3 stages or instars), pupa (enclosed in a silk cocoon) and adult. Larvae free living, legless, eyeless but with well-developed head; feed on organic debris and dried host blood derived with mouthparts and head muscles modified for grinding and sucking.

Superfamily Pulicoidea.
One family, 181 species, including the **Arctic hare flea** (*Euhoplopsyllus glacialis*), **Cat flea** (*Ctenocephalides felis*), **hedgehog fleas** (*Archaeopsylla* species), **Human flea** (*Pulex irritans*), **Oriental rat flea** or **Plague flea** (*Xenopsylla cheopis*), **porcupine fleas** (*Periodontis* species), **Rabbit flea** (*Spilopsyllus cuniculi*) and **Sand flea, chigoe** or **jigger** (*Tunga penetrans*).

Superfamily Malacopsylloidea
Three families, 172 species, including the **alakurt** (*Vermipsylla alakurt*) and **penguin fleas** (*Parapsyllus* species).

Superfamily Ceratophylloidea
Twelve families, 1,578 species, including the **Beaver flea** (*Hystrichopsylla schefferi*), the largest known flea, **bird fleas** (*Ceratophyllus, Callopsylla, Frontopsylla* species), **European rat flea** (*Nosopsyllus fasciatus*), *Palaeopsylla* species, **Tasmanian devil flea** (*Uropsylla tasmanica*).

▶ **A Rabbit flea** (Pulicidae) sucking blood through the thin skin of a rabbit's ear. A major vector of myxomatosis, the rabbit flea sometimes strays onto birds which nest in burrows or on the ground, such as shelduck, puffins, shearwaters and partridge.

FLEAS are distinctive blood-sucking insects, highly specialized for their ectoparasitic life on warm-blooded hosts. They are laterally flattened and streamlined with a keel-shaped head for "swimming" rapidly through the fur or feathers of their host.

Most fleas possess, in addition to many backward-pointing bristles all over the body, two sets of spines which form combs (ctenidia); there is a genal comb on the head and pronotal comb on the first thoracic segment. Combs and bristles play a dual role in protecting delicate joints and the eyes, and in anchoring fleas in the host's fur. Hedgehog fleas and porcupine fleas, both living on spine-covered hosts, have short, stout, widely spaced spines in the combs which are thought to catch around the host's spines to prevent the fleas being dislodged. This is an excellent example of convergent evolution in unrelated groups. Fleas of birds, bats and flying squirrels which must remain on the host at all costs or be lost completely have well-developed combs with many spines; some even have evolved extra combs.

The nearest relatives of the fleas are the scorpion flies, with which they share similarities in skeletal structure, muscle arrangements and chromosome complements. Probably, mecopteran ancestors gave rise to fleas, butterflies, moths and flies (together known as the panorpoid group) about 160 million years ago, with the newly evolving mammals as flea hosts.

Fleas undoubtedly evolved as mammalian parasites since only about 10 percent of species are found on birds (mostly seabirds and small perching birds). Only aquatic mammals (whales, seals, muskrats, platypuses) and certain land mammals including flying lemurs, primates, zebra, elephants, rhino and aardvarks are normally untroubled by fleas. Generally, fleas need hosts which build nests or live in burrows or dens. Many flea larvae feed on host blood that has dried, having been passed out by the adult flea as feces while the host is in its lair. The larva of the European rat flea will beg for food by grasping an adult by a bristle on its posterior, thus stimulating it to release a drop of blood from its anus which the larva then drinks. Flea larvae are very vulnerable to climatic change, especially extremes of humidity: a flea larva is so small that it is easily trapped and drowned in a droplet of water, and in dry conditions it may become desiccated and die. This may explain why, for example, the characteristically secure nests of swallows and martins are very popular with fleas. As many as 19

flea species are commonly associated with these birds worldwide.

The adult flea's range may be limited by the tolerance of its larva and may fall short of the host's range, so that widespread host species may support several different flea species separately in different areas. Conversely, some fleas are notoriously adaptable and infest a wide variety of hosts. Cat fleas will feed on nearly every kind of host, even lizards, and only rodents appear to be unacceptable to them. In India and Africa they may even become a pest on livestock. However, this flexibility in host choice may cost the flea dear in loss of fertility. When Cat fleas in a pet owner's house turn to feed on him or her it is almost accidental, since the thirsty fleas are really in search of a cat or a dog: humans are a poor second best.

Although the bite and resulting skin irritation is a most unpleasant aspect of the insect, the flea's method of reaching blood is fascinating. Inside the flea's head is a special membrane made of resilin, the same material as in the flea's pleural arch (see box). Embedded in the head next to the resilin is a hammer-like bar attached to the flea's piercing stylets. As soon as the hungry flea reaches a particularly appetizing patch of host skin the stylet muscles press the hammer hard against the resilin. The flea prepares to feed by tilting its head down and backside up, and suddenly it relaxes the muscles, the resilin membrane springs back, plunges the hammer down and drives the stylets into the victim's skin. This is repeated rapidly and blood capillaries in the skin are reached, usually painlessly unless the flea touches a skin nerve-ending.

The basic life cycle of fleas is simple: the adults are ectoparasites while eggs, larvae and pupae develop freely in either the nest or habitat of the host. There are exceptional species, among them the Arctic hare flea whose larvae live alongside adults in the fur of the Arctic hare host and, even more extreme, the Tasmanian devil flea, the female of which sticks her eggs to the fur of the host and hatching larvae burrow into and develop in the host's skin. On the other hand the eggs and larvae of the alakurt parasitic on deer, yaks, goats and horses throughout central Asia, are scattered far and wide wherever the hosts have roamed.

Fleas which as adults live mostly on the host are termed fur fleas (eg cat and dog fleas), while those found mostly in the nest, jumping on to the host for brief periods of feeding, are termed nest fleas. Fur fleas lay shiny, smooth eggs which fall out of the host's fur into its lair or other parts of its

Flying With Their Legs

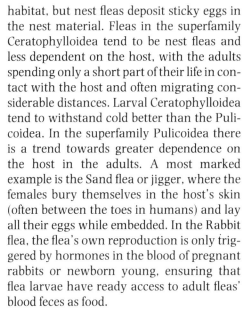

Fleas have been described by Miriam Rothschild as "insects which fly with their legs." This is because, despite their being wingless, fleas possess a special structure, the pleural arch, which is a modification of the wing-hinge of the fleas' winged ancestors. The pleural arch, made of the elastic protein resilin, is the powerhouse for the flea's remarkable jump. To jump effectively in a wide range of temperatures from arctic cold to equatorial heat, fleas cannot rely exclusively on muscle since it has a slow twitch and becomes less efficient at low temperatures. They achieve their extraordinary acceleration during the jump by using a triggered click mechanism.

The helmet-shaped pleural arch (**a**) when compressed, generates and stores energy needed for jumping: resilin is extremely efficient and may release as much as 97 per cent of its stored energy when required. As the flea gathers itself to jump, muscles associated with the second segment of the rear leg (**b**) (trochanter depressor muscles) distort the cuticle, and "flight" muscles (**c**) compress the pleural arch. A series of link-plates on the flea's hard exoskeleton interlock to clamp the three segments of the thorax together. The rear legs are raised and the flea, now resting on its trochanters (**d**), is poised for take-off.

As soon as a poised flea is stimulated by, for example, the carbon dioxide breathed out by a potential host, the muscles relax to release the pleural arch and a sudden burst of energy is sent down a cuticular ridge (**e**) and into the trochanters. The recoil of this force, which arrives with an easily heard "click," accelerates the flea away from the substrate faster than the eye can follow, at about 60 gravities, and the descending rear legs hit the substrate to provide an extra boost up to 140 gravities acceleration. Hungry fleas may jump 600 times an hour for three days in their attempts to find a host. Cat fleas readily achieve a height of 13.4in (34cm) when they jump.

habitat, but nest fleas deposit sticky eggs in the nest material. Fleas in the superfamily Ceratophylloidea tend to be nest fleas and less dependent on the host, with the adults spending only a short part of their life in contact with the host and often migrating considerable distances. Larval Ceratophylloidea tend to withstand cold better than the Pulicoidea. In the superfamily Pulicoidea there is a trend towards greater dependence on the host in the adults. A most marked example is the Sand flea or jigger, where the females bury themselves in the host's skin (often between the toes in humans) and lay all their eggs while embedded. In the Rabbit flea, the flea's own reproduction is only triggered by hormones in the blood of pregnant rabbits or newborn young, ensuring that flea larvae have ready access to adult fleas' blood feces as food.

Plague caused by the bacterium *Yersinia pestis* is primarily a rodent disease, but it is spread from rats to man by fleas such as the Oriental rat flea. Throughout history, plague, or the "Black Death," has been a virulent and dramatic disease: in 14th-century Italy the great cities lost every second citizen to plague. Even now plague is still with us and breaks out periodically in human populations in the USSR, Southeast Asia and the United States of America.

As a flea feeds on the blood of a plague-infected host the bacteria stick to the spines of the blood filter chamber (proventriculus) which leads into the flea's stomach. Here the plague organisms multiply until they block the gut completely. The hungry flea subsequently bites a new host repeatedly but the blood sucked up by the powerful oesophagus muscles cannot pass the blockage and shoots back into the wound, carrying with it some of the plague bacteria, and so the disease is transmitted to the next victim. The most virulent strains of plague bacteria are very sticky and form a block easily. Blocking is reduced as temperatures rise above 82.4°F (28°C), so incidence of plague corresponds closely to seasonal temperatures.

A potentially dangerous situation arises when flea-infested rats live in towns, feeding on rubbish tips and refuse scattered near dwellings. During the Vietnam War, after disturbance of the environment, flooding drove rats into villages and plague epidemics promptly began among the rural people. Nowadays, pesticides are used to control the reservoirs of disease (rodents and fleas) while vaccinations and modern drugs reduce its virulence. Nevertheless the World Health Organization describes plague as "an enemy in ambush."   BWi

FLIES

Order: Diptera
Class: Insecta, subclass Pterygota.
Phylum: Uniramia.
About 90,000 known species in 3 suborders and 114 families.

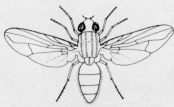

Distribution: worldwide in all possible habitats. Distinguishing features: adults 0.02–2in (0.5–50mm) long, with one pair of membranous wings (maximum span 3.2in/80mm); hindwings modified as club-like balancers (halteres); 2nd segment of the thorax much enlarged, 1st and 3rd reduced; mouthparts for liquid feeding but highly adaptable for piercing, sucking, lapping. Larvae (maggots) legless. Development with complete metamorphosis (holometabolous); pupal stage between larvae and adult.

▶ **Male crane fly**, *Tipula lunata* (Tipulidae), resting in marshy vegetation in England. The modified hindwings or halteres are clearly visible as a pair of clubbed appendages behind the forewings. Halteres are characteristic of all true two-winged (dipteran) flies. They act as gyroscopic stabilizers, providing the feedback necessary for precise flight control.

TRUE flies are not popular—they lack the showy beauty of butterflies, or the intricate societies of some social ants and bees. Yet flies (Diptera) are one of the most diverse and fascinating orders of insects. The beneficial effects of the many flies which visit and pollinate our flowers or which recycle organic nutrients should certainly outweigh our distaste for the relatively few flies which irritate us by biting or by paddling their dirty feet on our foodstuffs. In warmer parts of the world flies can be a genuine scourge, carrying some of the most dangerous diseases of man and livestock, and spreading their pathogens in areas of poor hygiene. In these cases, study of the flies' biology has revealed much about co-evolution between different types of animal, and about the ecology of insects as a whole.

Flies make up about a quarter of all insects in many temperate countries, though in numbers worldwide they are second to the beetles, which abound in the tropics. The known 90,000 species of fly make their living in almost every imaginable manner, in all climatic zones right through to the polar fringes. Among the different life-styles found in flies are those of the flower feeders, of predators and blood suckers, parasites, scavengers and feeders on living plant tissue. Much of their diversity is based upon three main features: their mouthparts, flight machinery, and larval forms.

The mouthparts are essentially suited to liquid feeding but have proved highly adaptable for piercing, sucking and lapping. Borne on a large and mobile head, they can extract fluids from almost any living or decaying source, with the aid of one (or sometimes two) highly muscular pumps within the head.

The flight machinery consists of just two (hence Di-ptera), usually quite short but strong wings. The second pair is reduced to small halteres (as is proved by the fruit fly genus *Drosophila*, in one mutant form of which the halteres revert to a wing-like structure). Having a single pair of wings allows the structure of the thorax to be simpler: the fore and hind segments are virtually lost, and the middle segment is huge and entirely packed with wing muscles. It also means a high degree of maneuverability, with very high speeds and wingbeat frequencies (up to 1,000 beats per second in tiny midges), and a control of direction and position which permits access to every possible landing site, even upside down on ceilings! Many flies can hover, rotate on their own axis and even fly backward. All these habits are aided by the sensory information from the halteres, which act like tiny gyroscopes. The sense organs in their base tell a fly how fast it is flying and turning, and whether it is being blown off course. Associated with maneuverability are flies' relatively large eyes, with acute vision due to a unique separation of the individual sensitive elements of the rhabdome in the nervous supply to the eye facets, and the elaborate claws and pads on the feet which can grip on any surface.

There is a typical endopterygote or holometabolous pattern of development in true flies. Larvae can be quite different from adults in form and habits. Fly larvae are legless, they can survive in a vast range of moisture-providing microhabitats, and they have an extraordinary diversity of appearance, far surpassing that of any other order. By contrast, the pupa (contained in higher flies within the last larval skin, as a "puparium") is generally well protected and

The 3 Suborders of Flies

Thread-horned flies
Suborder Nematocera

Twenty-two families. Delicate, often with long, thin body, long legs and wings. Antennae also long and slender, like body often bearing long fine hairs. Larvae (usually 4 instars) have hardened head capsules and biting jaws; often aquatic, as are pupae. Families include: **blackflies** or **buffalo gnats** (Simuliidae), **crane flies**, **leather-jackets** (Tipulidae), **fungus gnats** (Mycetophilidae), **gall midges** (Cecidomyiidae), **midges** (Chironomidae and Ceratopogonidae), **mosquitoes**, **gnats** (Culicidae) and **winter gnats** (Trichoceridae).

Short-horned flies
Suborder Brachycera

Eighteen families. Well built, rarely very small. Short, stout antennae and often brightly colored body. Larvae (5–8 instars) with partially hardened head capsules, sometimes aquatic. Families include: **bee flies** (Bombyliidae), **dance flies** (Empididae), **horseflies and clegs** (Tabanidae), **long-legged flies** (Dolichopodidae), **robber flies** (Asilidae), and **soldier flies** (Stratiomyidae).

Higher flies
Suborder Cyclorrhapha

Pupate inside the last larva skin (puparium). Usually with short, 3-segmented antennae; larvae are simple maggots feeding with "mouth-hooks." Divided into two series.

Series Aschiza (6 families)
Includes **hover flies** or **flowerflies** (Syrphidae) and **scuttle** and **coffin flies** (Phoridae).

Series Schizophora (68 families in 3 sections)
The acalyptrates (56 families) are small, undistinguished flies, including **carrot** or **rust flies** (Psilidae), **frit flies** (Chloropidae), **fruit flies** (Drosophilidae, Tephritidae), **leaf-mining flies** (Agromyzidae), **shore** and **seaweed flies** (Ephydridae, Coelopidae), **stalk-eyed flies** (Diopsidae), **wasp flies** (Conopidae).

The more familiar calyptrates (9 families), stouter and generally more heavily bristled, include the **blowflies** and **bluebottles** (Calliphoridae), **bulb-** and **root-eating flies** (Anthomyiidae), **dung flies** (Scathophagidae), **flesh flies** (Sarcophagidae), **houseflies** and **stable flies** (Muscidae), **parasite flies** (Tachinidae) and **warble flies** and **botflies** (Oestridae and Gasterophilidae).

The Pupipara (3 families) have flattened bodies, are parasites on birds and mammals, and the female bears live young. They include **bat flies** (Nycteribiidae), **deer flies**, **keds** and **louse flies** (Hippoboscidae).

impermeable, able to resist inclement conditions in unpredictable climates; and it may require precise cues, such as the correct temperature, day length or humidity, to trigger it into further development and thus allow the adult to emerge.

As flower visitors, pollinators of wild flowers and crops, flies are second only to the bees, wasps and ants (order Hymenoptera). Flies are most commonly "generalist" flower visitors, taking nectar or pollen from many different species of flowers as a supplement to their main diet, or using floral products as the main "top-up" fuels for their rather brief adult lives after food stored in the body from the larval stage has been exhausted. Representatives of almost all dipteran groups can thus be found at flowers—especially those with shallow corollas, like umbellifers (hogweed or cow parsley), composites (daisies) and rosaceous plants such as hawthorn and bramble. For those unspecialized flowers, often white or yellow and with nectar and pollen readily available even to a short-tongued visitor, flies may be the principal pollinator. Some rather surprising flies are very frequent visitors: mosquitoes and midges, whose males feed on nectar (only the females, needing protein for their eggs to mature, irritate us by blood-

▶ **Larvae of bristly flies** of the family Tachinidae develop as internal parasites of other insects. As such, several parasite fly species have been used as biological control agents against pests. This African species, *Billaea rutilans*, develops as a parasite of caterpillars.

▼ **A mimic in self-defense,** the hover fly *Eristalis tenax* (Syrphidae) is sometimes called the Drone fly because of its resemblance to a honeybee. Although it is worker honeybees rather than the drones which have a sting, the generalized resemblance to a honeybee is a good example of mimicry—predatory birds are deceived into thinking that the harmless fly has a sting in its tail.

feeding); or dung flies and blowflies, which we normally associate with less aesthetic food sources!

But the flies also include some more specialist flower visitors which make their adult living from pollen and nectar, and these are amongst the most attractive of all insects. They include the hover flies (Syrphidae), also known as flowerflies. Most of these are medium- to large-sized flies, brightly decked in yellows, bronzes and golds in a variety of striped patterns which mimic bees and wasps. Many are also furry or hairy, and their bodies pick up a dense dusting of pollen. Hover flies are often abundant in gardens, where their hovering and darting flights between flowers are characteristic. Even in behavior patterns they seem to mimic the bees, and the drone flies (*Eristalis* species) are excellent and cosmopolitan honeybee mimics which must have often evaded capture for fear of their (non-existent) sting!

Some hover flies also exhibit intricate mating behavior; males may hold solitary territories around a plant, or along a woodland ride, chasing off other flies and even hovering inquisitively in front of an encroaching human. They have developed a clever "computing" system which allows them to set an interception course for an approaching intruder, flying at exactly the right speed and angle to meet and repel the invader. In this way they are able to protect their territory as a mating ground.

Other hover flies have mating "leks," where many males gather as a hovering swarm and compete for females attracted to the conspicuous group. Many "thread-horned" (Nematoceran) flies also have mating swarms, a familiar sight on summer evenings over meadows and along riverbanks. In such mating swarms and on flowers, syrphids and other flies often use humming noises or patterns of changing wing beat frequency as sexual signaling devices.

Some flies are particularly specialized as flower feeders, with long tongues to penetrate tubular corollas. A few hover flies come in this specialist category, as do the bee flies (Bombyliidae); temperate bee flies have long tongues to visit primroses and periwinkles, and are adept hoverers, while some tropical examples have enormously elongated tongues and resemble miniature delta-wing jet planes. Such flies may have a critical role in pollinating flowers inaccessible to more conventionally proportioned insects.

Flies may visit flowers for reasons other than nectar collection. Many of those to be seen on umbellifers have more sinister motives—they await the pollinating insects, and use them for their own ends. The brightly striped wasp flies frequent flowers to await the wasps and bees on which they deposit their eggs; and dance flies and dung

When Flies Fly

Nearly all insects depend on sunny conditions for flight, since (unlike many vertebrates) they cannot themselves generate sufficient body heat to operate the wing muscles. But larger insects can absorb more radiant heat from limited sunlight than smaller ones, and dark-bodied insects absorb heat quicker than pale or shiny forms. So small, bright flies are rarely seen around dawn or dusk, when they are too chilled for effective flight; whereas larger dark-bodied drone flies, flesh flies or muscids can be abundant at these hours. However, in hot summer conditions larger flies may risk overheating, and the small colorful hover flies, soldier flies and long-legged (dolichopodid) flies come into their own.

At sites frequented by many flies (eg the flower head of an umbellifer such as hogweed), or convenient resting perches like sunlit twigs or large leaves, the sequence of fly visitors through a day correlates neatly with their body temperatures resulting from microclimatic conditions at the site.

Watching such activity patterns also highlights interesting anomalies—some flies appear when, on the basis of their size and color, one would predict they should be either

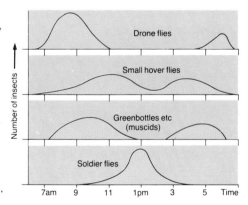

chilled into inactivity or dangerously overheated. For example, some hover flies and botflies can warm up, and therefore be active, without significant radiant heat from the sun, by "shivering' their thoracic muscles; other flies can control the distribution of heat between the hairy thorax and the uninsulated radiator-like abdomen, by special blood-shunting mechanisms. However, we still do not understand how the tiny winter gnats manage to fly efficiently even on days when snow is lying!

flies may also use flowers as fruitful patrolling stations when seeking prey. A few flies lay their eggs in flower heads. Yet others use flowers for sunbathing, as a cup-shaped corolla can be considerably warmer than its surroundings, especially in rather cool climates. Arctic mosquitoes use white flowers which track the sun as a standard way to warm up, sitting at the "hot spot" in the center of a corolla until their wing muscles have heated up enough for flight.

All these flower-visiting activities involve benefit to the fly: but sometimes the plants benefit and flies are exploited instead. Some flowers, like cuckoo pints (*Arum*), attract flies by producing odors like carrion or dung, then trap the flies until pollination has been ensured. Some of the largest and most curious flowers in the world, such as species of *Stapelia* and *Aristolochia*, are carrion-scented and rely on pollinating flies for their continuing success. Other flowers trap small flies with sticky exudations, and devour them slowly to extract nitrogenous food, familiar examples being sundews and butterworts.

Predators and blood suckers are not common among adult flies (though larvae are often predacious). Several families of "short-horned" flies (suborder Brachycera) come in this category—dance flies, long-legged flies and robber flies are noteworthy—and a few of the "higher flies" related to dung flies and house flies are also predacious. The robber flies have proved to be highly opportunist, taking almost any small creature that is available—often another fly! A few more specialist examples are known—some flies prey on insects trapped in the surface film on ponds, swooping low to "net" the victim in their trailing feet; and other flies are specialist at stealing trapped prey from spiders' webs. Some predacious flies extend their habits to help them in courtship. One example occurs in dance flies, where males catch a small prey item, wrap it up in silk and present it to a female to pacify her or divert her interest while he mates with her. (Similar "nuptial gifts" are given by male scorpion flies.)

Predation in flies is closely allied to the blood-sucking habit and requires similar mouthparts and behavior. But bloodsuckers usually use larger animals for their food source and take only a little of their juices, exploiting vertebrates in particular. Many families have evolved this habit: midges, mosquitoes and gnats, blackflies, horseflies, deerflies and stable flies are the best known, and in most cases only the female fly bites. Midges and mosquitoes have elongate

needle-like mouthparts, while horseflies and the bulkier muscid biters (eg stable flies and tsetse flies) have shorter blade-like mouthparts. Many of these flies carry diseases to animals and even to man.

Predation in flies is very much more important as a larval way of life, and the larvae of many fly species are extremely useful in controlling crop pests. Some fly larvae consume the young stages of beetles, including bark beetles, several types of pest weevil and carpet beetles. More important are their attacks on homopterans, the hoppers and aphids which can plague farmers and horticulturalists. In this role the larvae of many types of house fly and a few gall midges are especially beneficial. Hoverfly larvae are regularly recorded as scourges of aphids in market gardens—these mobile, cryptically colored, and flattened creatures work their way through aphid colonies at rates of up to 80 aphids per hour each. Some syrphids specialize on root aphids, or on the woolly aphids found on conifers: in all these cases they must have an important effect (along with ladybirds) in controlling aphid populations.

A few larval flies have even stranger predatory habits. One family (Sciomyzidae) specializes in eating slugs and snails, while a few species of seashore long-legged flies (dolichopodids) have larval stages which eat barnacles!

Parasitic flies are, with the exception of the parasitic hymenopterans, the most abundant and influential of all insect parasites, laying their eggs in or on a vast range

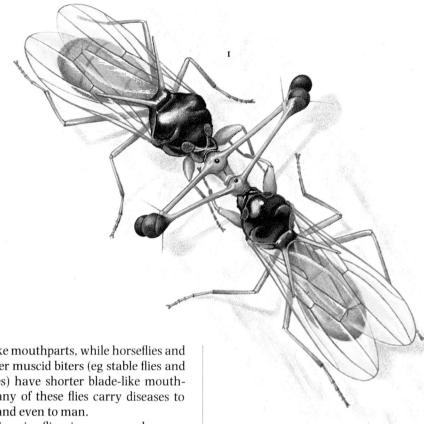

▲ ▶ **Stalk-eyes and bee parasites.** (1) Two male stalk-eyed flies, *Diopsis* species (Diopsidae), use their eye-stalks as yardsticks to assess their relative sizes in a territorial contest. (2) Robber fly mimic and predator, *Hyperechia bifasciata* (Asilidae) RIGHT of an African carpenter bee, *Xylocopa inconstans* (Anthophoridae). (3) A pupa of the same fly RIGHT emerges from the bee's nest after its larval life spent feeding on bee larvae, two of which have escaped its attentions. (4) Remarkable predatory mimic, another robber fly, *Mallophora fascipennis* (Asilidae) BELOW shadows a female orchid bee, *Eulaema fasciata* (Apidae), from South America.

of other animals, but especially on other insects and on vertebrates. The Tachinidae are the most important family of internal parasites (endoparasites); along with some flesh flies they form a group of rather bulky, bristly, adult flies, having larvae which live especially off the flesh of beetles, bugs, wasps, caterpillars and grasshoppers.

Various other groups of flies have specialized associations with vertebrates. Some Pupipara families, like louseflies and keds (hippoboscids) and bat flies (Nycteribiidae) are strict external parasites (ectoparasites) of birds and mammals, and have remarkable structural adaptations as a result. Hippoboscids live on birds and some large mammals, feeding on the host's blood; their wings are often tiny, while their claws are greatly enlarged and used in moving sideways in a crab-like fashion. Nycteribiids are even more peculiar—tiny wingless insects living exclusively on bats, with their heads so reduced that they can be tucked back into a groove on the thorax, and with feet again much enlarged. Both these families have dispensed with the egg stage and give birth to larvae directly, often so late that the larvae are immediately ready to pupate.

The warble flies and botflies are somewhat intermediate between external and internal parasites. Eggs (or sometimes live larvae) are laid on the outside of a large mammalian host, and larvae then burrow into the flesh, or enter the host's body via openings such as the nostrils. Maggots then live for some time either just within the skin, breathing via a tube, or in the nasal passages or mouth area. They drop off (or are sneezed out) when ready to pupate and complete their life cycle. Such parasitic flies can be irritating, and are often a source of secondary infections, but they rarely do much harm directly (except by soiling the fleeces and hides of some livestock) unless infestation is heavy.

Flies are pre-eminently scavengers. Since they are essentially liquid feeders, with mouthparts appropriate to sucking and lapping, it is not surprising that decaying matter of all kinds provides perhaps the most important foodstuff of all for them. As a result, flies are immensely important in the processes of decomposition, and in recycling nutrients through an ecosystem; their habits may not endear them to us, but without the fly maggots the world would be a much less clean and pleasant place!

Flies have complex associations with all kinds of decaying matter. Some are linked with fungi, especially in woodlands; one group lives on fresh fungal material (which itself is hastening the breakdown of green plants), while another group invades the fungus after it has fruited and begun to

decay in its turn. The larvae of fungus gnats grow on a wide range of fungal species and often fly up as clouds from rotting wood when disturbed. A great many other flies feed on naturally decaying plants, once the dead matter has begun to liquefy; many of the acalyptrate families are of this type, and the fruit flies (*Drosophila* species and their allies) are classic examples, being able to sense the vinegar-like substances produced when green plants decay. Perhaps most conspicuous of all are the flies which live on either the excreta of animals (dung flies and others) or their dead bodies. These flies get ideal nutritious liquid food, and by laying their eggs in such places they also ensure a moist and relatively safe microhabitat for their youngsters to grow up in.

Among flies which feed on and recycle the dead and decaying remains of other organisms there is a characteristic sequence of interrelated species which has been studied on vertebrate corpses. Generally the first arrivals are blowflies, especially the familiar "greenbottles" which can detect a corpse when flying more than 115ft (35m) above it. Once decay has begun, members of certain muscid genera and of some acalyptrate families arrive; and once decay is well advanced, and the dead tissue is liquefying, many more flies begin to appear and lap up

the juices, including fruit flies and other generalists. The corpse then becomes ammoniacal, and finally, as it dries out, the coffin flies (Phoridae) are characteristic visitors. Similar successions of insects occur on dung, where there may be considerable competition between dung flies, beetles and others to lay eggs on a fresh dungpat while it still warm and soft, so that larvae can develop below the protective crust which soon forms.

Apart from the specialist dung-feeders and carrion-feeders, yet other flies are generalized as scavengers. Examples are scavengers in nests, whether of mammals, birds or bees (this last category often involving bee-mimic flies); the seaweed flies (Ephydridae and others), frequenting the shoreline debris; and many larval flies living in mud around the edges of ponds, puddles and in damp ruts, feeding on the algae and detritus. Some of these have cuticles which can resist desiccation when necessary, and await re-wetting in the mud, while others just burrow deeper into their mud-patch in dry weather. Some, especially the larvae of Nematocera (thread-horned flies), are genuinely aquatic (see box) and these are generally opportunistic feeders, preying on small insects or scavenging as appropriate.

It is among scavenging and saprophagous

▶ **Mating pair of robber flies,** *Microstylum* species (Asilidae), in Kenya, the female also feeding on a cotton-stainer bug (*Dysdercus* species). With their acute vision and powers of rapid and maneuverable flight, robber flies are efficient aerial predators of other insects. Like other predacious flies, they have mouthparts modified as sturdy but sharp piercing weapons to penetrate the prey and suck out its juices. An individual robber fly may patrol a regular beat in search of prey.

▼ **Common yellow dung fly,** *Scathophaga stercoraria*, feeds on the body fluids of a hover fly. *Scathophaga* dung flies seek prey at both flowers and dung pats. They always pierce their victims in the neck region (Scathophagidae).

flies (those which feed on dead or decaying organic material) that some of the most interesting examples of dipteran behavior have been recorded. Most notable among these are interactions with mating strategy.

Probably the best-known fly to scientists is the fruit fly *Drosophila melanogaster*, one member of the genus which has long been favored for studies of genetics because its chromosomes are readily visible, its reproductive rate is high, and many mutants occur. But *Drosophila* is also renowned for its courtship displays; these small yellowish flies, with bright red eyes, congregate wherever fruit is stored and where fermentation occurs naturally (fallen fruit, sap from tree wounds, etc). A male approaches a stationary female and taps her with his forelegs, extending his tongue and coming face to face with her. Both then "dance" with a series of side-to-side steps, the male gradually opening and waggling one or both of his wings until the female stands still again, when he circles round and mounts her from behind.

A somewhat similar dance can be observed in long-legged flies which frequent muddy puddles in woodland; the male has a conspicuous white wing spot, which he flashes at the female by vibrating the wings prior to leaping right over her, twisting in mid air to land neatly with his chosen female still in view. Many flies with wing spots and patterning seem to use their wings in sexual signaling of this type. Dolichopodids are also remarkable for their elaborate male genitalia and leg adornments, presumably again important in courtship.

Two other examples do not involve courting dances. The stalk-eyed flies (diopsids, and some other acalyptrates) are remarkable for having immensely broadened heads with the eyes (and sometimes antennae) set out on stalks. These mostly tropical flies feed on decaying plant matter, and will compete for occupancy of a small patch of such material by threats to any intruder. The stalked eyes give a good resolution up to 2ft (60cm) away from the fly and are used in ritualized fights between males in particular: two males will "measure" each other's size by comparing their eye separations, and the fly with closer-set eyes normally retires! Similarly, male flies with particularly long eyestalks seem to be preferred by female diopsids.

Finally, the fascinating story of the dung flies (*Scathophaga* species) should be considered. Male dung flies have developed the strategy of waiting for their hairy yellowish females around new pats of dung, since the female must come there to lay her eggs, so that the larvae can hatch and feed in fresh dung. Males will compete for each arriving female, and she may be mounted by a tussling heap of several males; it pays the males to put a lot of effort into this struggle, since the last mating before egg-laying occurs will secure most (about 80 percent) of the fertilizations. (In *Scathophaga*, as in many other flies, "sperm displacement" occurs, each successive male displacing the sperms of previous copulations with its own sperm mass.) Females, by contrast, seek to lay their eggs as quickly as possible, since the dung rapidly cools and solidifies and is soon unsuitable for ovipositing. Males also recognize this; they begin to leave older dung pats for newer ones, balancing the chances of a few females still coming to older, harder dung, where there may be fewer competitors, against the chances of competing successfully for the last mating at a new and crowded pat.

Plant-feeding flies exploit green plants, yet another habitat where flies can find both liquid food and a moist, sheltered microclimate. Although relatively few adult flies utilize living greenery, as their mouthparts cannot readily penetrate tough cellulose walls, eating green plants (phytophagy) has evolved several times in fly larvae, probably from saprophagous ancestors, and it is a common way of life. Two of the largest plant-feeding families are the gall midges and the leaf miners. For these larvae plants provide an ideal moist, protected habitat, since the larvae burrow and bore within shoots, leaves and roots. Miners in particular, produce conspicuous damage, as the tiny larvae tunnel within the living tissue, leaving their pale "trails" through leaves. Gall midges produce a variety of effects: simple blotches of distorted tissue, or complex rosette galls and cigar galls. Perhaps most destructive of all, though, are the large fruit flies such as tephritids, which lay their eggs in developing orchard fruits (often leaving chemical signals to stop another female trying to use the same fruit); the fruit flies, which can seriously affect cereal crops as the larvae consume the developing seeds; and a variety of root-feeding fly larvae, including carrot flies, cabbage-root flies, and crane flies (leather-jackets).

The larvae of true flies are structurally less diverse than the adult stages, but they vary in appearance more than any other insect order and they live in a vast range of different habitats. Adult females, when ready to lay their eggs, seek out every conceivable niche where food supplies and a moist, pro-

tected atmosphere can be found. They usually insert their mobile and often telescopic egg guide (ovipositor) deep into the chosen substrate, so that the larvae hatch and grow secure from predators or parasites, and with little danger of desiccation or starvation.

Larvae of higher flies tend to be "terrestrial," but nearly always occur in almost liquid habitats, whether in the soil, within plants (as galls, or in leaf mines) or in association with other animals. In the last category come the many parasitic flies, but also the dwellers in dung and many scavengers around bird or bee nests or indeed around human habitation. Generally all these flies have simple maggot larvae, with no legs and very limited sensory organs. The maggots pursue a wriggling worm-like existence in whichever semiliquid site their mother selected for them, feeding voraciously with very simple mouthparts and a strong suction action until they are large enough to pupate. In only a few cases, such as the aphid-feeding hover fly larvae, do genuinely free-living terrestrial larvae occur.

Among the nematoceran flies, especially, truly aquatic larval forms are found. Egg-laying females rest on the surface film, using their ovipositor either to reach down and attach eggs to underwater stones or weeds, or to assemble a floating "egg raft" on the water surface. Most of the resultant aquatic larvae are freshwater forms, preferring still ponds, puddles and lakes: midges and mosquitoes in particular will colonize

▲ **Infested with red parasitic mites,** a Common yellow dung fly (Scathophagidae). The mites feed on body fluids by piercing thin areas of cuticle between the body segments.

▶ **Encased in a gelatinous mass** secreted by the last larval stage, a midge pupa (family Chironomidae) attached to vegetation in a fast-flowing stream. The covering protects the pupa from buffeting and, possibly, from predators.

▼ **Galls on a beech leaf,** the tree's response to the presence of gall midge larvae, *Mikiola fagi* (Cecidomyiidae). Each gall contains a single larva derived from an egg laid in spring. The gall drops from the leaf in late summer, when the midge larva pupates. Next spring an adult midge emerges from the gall's tough coat.

Underwater Survival of Fly Larvae

Many flies have freshwater larvae: the mosquitoes, hanging from water surface films, the mud-burrowing "bloodworms," larval midges and "rat-tailed larvae" of hover flies, and the stream-bed blackflies are classic examples (though many other larvae live in effectively "liquid" habitats). Such insects face two main physiological problems: respiration and osmotic control.

Many fly larvae are not strictly aquatic when it comes to breathing: they use "siphons," tubes extending from their own spiracles to the water surface. Mosquito larvae hang from the surface film by the unwettable hairs on their abdominal siphons, and can breathe directly from the air. The "rat-tailed" larvae of the drone fly have long telescopic siphons and can reach the air even with their bodies buried 2.4in (6cm) deep in the stream bed. Some dipterans even get oxygen by thrusting sharp siphons into pond weed, tapping the plant's air spaces!

Smaller larvae can survive on dissolved oxygen, which diffuses through their thin cuticles. The bloodworms are almost unique amongst insects in containing hemoglobin, which enables them to carry and store extra oxygen. In blackflies oxygen diffusion is assisted by a fine network of tracheae just beneath the cuticle, or sometimes by special "tracheal gills."

In fresh water, salts will leach out of animals and must be replaced. Many dipterans have special salt-uptake tissues, especially on tracheal gills; although this uptake requires energy, it prevents loss of essential ions, or swelling and bursting due to excess water inflow. Such control mechanisms allow flies to survive and breed in highly variable freshwater habitats (even transient puddles), and also to cope with intertidal pools.

Some larvae can survive even when their freshwater pools totally evaporate. African midges of the genus *Polypedilum* survive for years in a shriveled state until the rains return: these dehydrated larvae can withstand temperatures of $-310°F$ ($-190°C$) or $+212°F$ ($100°C$) for brief periods!

rapidly any standing water in summer, including unprotected swimming pools and water butts. The larvae of a few species, notably the blackflies or buffalo gnats, inhabit fast-running streams and rivers, where they hang on to stones by a sucker-like pad, and filter small particles of food from the current with special mouth-brushes. One species of fly (*Heleomyia petrolei*) has larvae which are "aquatic" in pools of petroleum!

Transition from an aquatic larval and pupal stage to a terrestrial flying adult is not easy, and here the flies have again achieved some strange adaptations. Blackfly pupae become inflated with air, and when the pupal case splits the incipient adult fly rises to the surface surrounded by a bubble, and so avoids being wetted. In a few cases, emerging flies are actually catapulted clear of the water surface by the sudden splitting of their pupal cases. Thus a new dry and pristine fly leaves its protected larval environment for its brief and hazardous flying existence in pursuit of a mate.　　PGW

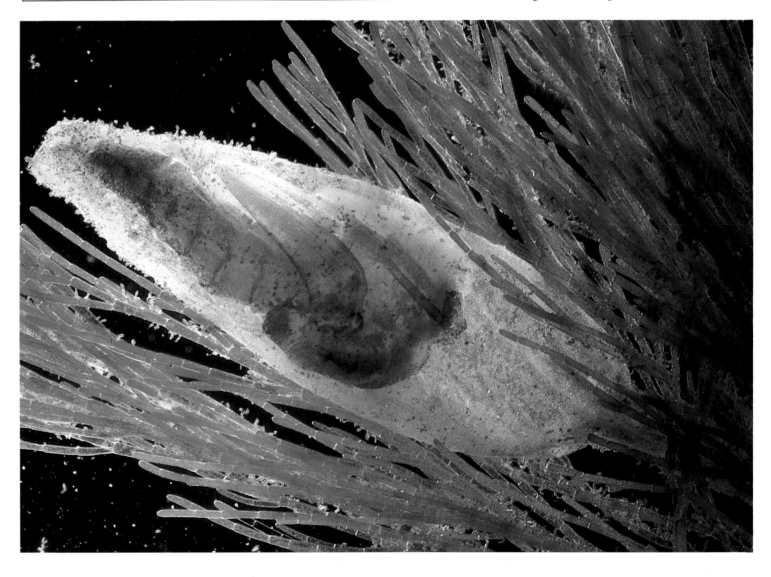

Fly-borne Disease
Scourge of human societies

The two-winged flies are by far the worst insect scourge of mankind. Despite advances in the fields of insecticides and drug treatment, fly-borne diseases continue to mold the organization and distribution of many human societies.

Flies impinge on human health in three major ways. Firstly, they act as simple, mechanical transporters of disease organisms. Houseflies (*Musca* and *Fannia* species) and bluebottles (*Calliphora* species), which feed and breed in feces or rotting organic matter, may contaminate food. A huge range of bacterial, viral and protozoal infections are transmitted in this way. In the third world, it accounts for millions of infant deaths per year due to dehydration associated with severe diarrhoea.

The contaminated mouthparts of blood-sucking flies may result in a "flying pin" type of mechanical transmission. Thus, mosquitoes may transmit the virus of serum hepatitis after feeding on an infected person. Horseflies and mosquitoes may also be transmitters to humans of the bacillus of pseudoplague (tularemia) which is normally transmitted between rodents by ticks. When humans become indirectly involved in this way in an animal disease cycle, the disease is called a zoonosis.

The second type of impact of flies on humans and animals (notably domesticated breeds) is via a condition called myiasis, in which the larvae of certain flies feed on living tissues beneath the skin. Examples are the Human botfly (*Dermatobia hominis*, Oestridae) in the tropical Americas and, in Africa, the Tumbu fly (*Cordylobia anthropophaga*, Sarcophagidae). The wounds caused by the feeding larvae are an entry route for infections.

The third and most important effect of flies on human health occurs with the biological transmission of disease organisms. In biological transmission, the pathogen has a complicated development cycle, part of which is spent in the body of a blood-sucking fly, and part in the human victim. Malaria is the most prevalent and widespread of these diseases and is transmitted by about 30 species of *Anopheles* mosquito, most important being the African species, *A. gambiae*.

The disease organisms of malaria are four species of *Plasmodium*, a genus of unicellular protozoans. *Plasmodium falciparum* is the most dangerous species and has a pantropical distribution. In 1980, 13.5 million cases of malaria were reported, 5.5 million of them in tropical Africa. Given that in the third world millions of cases must go unrecorded, it has been calculated that half the world's population either have the disease or are at risk from it.

The war against a disease like malaria has to be fought on a broad front. Adult mosquitoes and the aquatic larvae can be killed with insecticides, the *Plasmodium* stages in man can be treated with drugs, and people can help themselves by using insect repellents and mosquito nets. But attempts at total eradication have been successful only in the warm, temperate fringes of the malarial zone. Elsewhere, despite the best efforts of international bodies such as the World Health Organization and dozens of control programs, the results look dismal and are worse now than several years ago. In India, cases of malaria were reduced to 50,000 in 1961; by 1977 the numbers had risen by a factor of 60,000, to 30 million.

Although it is easy to name political instability in some regions as the reason, the

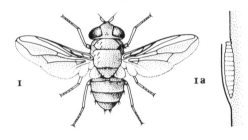

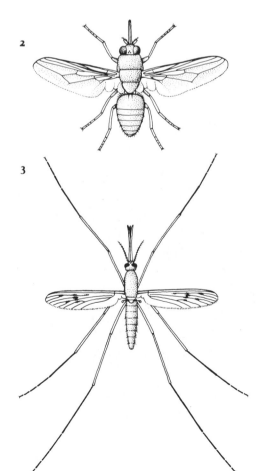

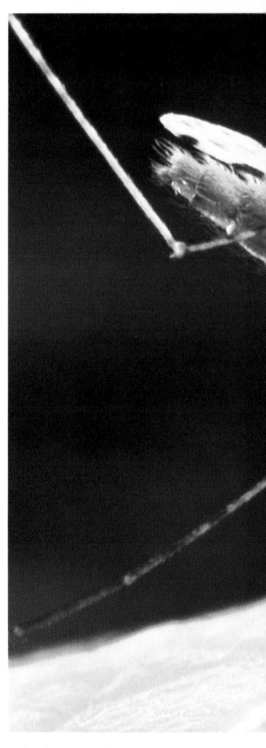

▲ **Her body engorged,** a female malaria mosquito, *Anopheles gambiae* (Culicidae), in the act of taking a blood meal from a human. Only the females can suck, and so transmit to humans the disease organism of malaria, a single-celled protozoan of the genus *Plasmodium*. Once a female is fertilized, she requires a meal before laying eggs.

◄ **Three types of dipteran flies** that cause disease in other animals. (1) The Tumbu fly, whose larvae leave wounds where they enter the skin (1a), exposing domesticated animals in Africa to infections. (2) Tsetse flies, which infect humans with a protozoan that causes sleeping sickness, another disease of Africa. (3) Blood-sucking *Anopheles* mosquitoes, which carry malaria.

► **Head of a disease carrier,** the tsetse fly *Glossina austeni* (Glossinidae).

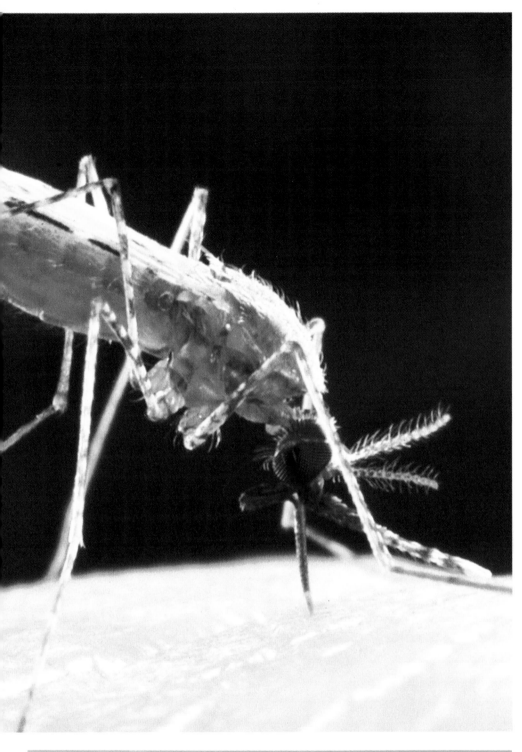

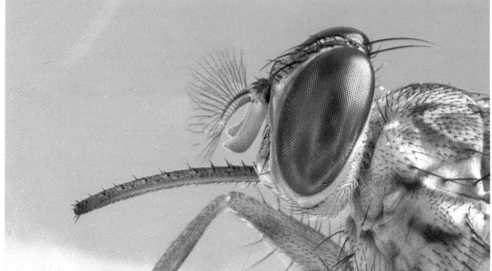

failure is in large part due to the ease with which both *Anopheles* mosquitoes and the malaria parasite developed resistance to the battery of chemical weapons deployed by entomologists and physicians. The ability of the malarial parasite rapidly to change the chemistry of its outer coat has made the development of a vaccine virtually impossible. However, recent developments in the artificial culture of the parasite, in conjunction with new techniques in genetic engineering, offer some hope.

The total eradication of *Anopheles* is now recognized as an impossible dream. Efforts are now centred on integrated control. By the judicious timing of insecticide applications, acting in concert with drug treatment and screening of populations at risk, it is hoped to keep the level of disease down to acceptable levels. An "acceptable level" is one where mortality is reduced substantially and the number of people experiencing the debilitating and economically damaging recurrent fevers is kept as low as possible.

Complete success, if it is ever achieved, will bring its own problems. This is especially true of sleeping sickness, a disease confined to Africa and caused by trypanosome protozoans in the blood (*Trypanosoma gambiense*), transmitted by five species of tsetse flies (*Glossina* species). Sleeping sickness (nagana) is found also in cattle and it is endemic in the large herds of wild grazing animals. The disease has profound effects on human ecology. Cattle ranging is impossible in many parts of Africa because of the transfer of nagana from game to domestic stock. In colonial times, this resulted in whole peoples being forcibly relocated to disease-free areas.

Control of sleeping sickness could be affected by large-scale slaughter of wild game, which acts as a reservoir. Another method, used to a limited extent so far, is the clearing of vegetation belts which provide specific resting places for tsetse flies. Both methods would seriously damage the environment and ultimately, human populations. Further problems would follow if tsetse flies and sleeping sickness were eradicated. Cattle raising would be extended further, resulting in competition with game animals and increased likelihood of desertification through over-grazing. A further consideration is that game animals provide many countries with a valuable income from tourists. The major fly-borne diseases therefore present man with pressing and immediate problems. Their solution will present new problems to challenge us in the future.

AWRM, CO'T

CADDIS FLIES

Order: Trichoptera
Class: Insecta, subclass Pterygota.
Phylum: Uniramia.
About 5,000 species in 18 families.
Distribution: worldwide, always near streams, ponds, small lakes.

Features: the only insects undergoing complete metamorphosis that have primarily aquatic larvae. Adults slender, elongated—0.06–1.4in (1.5–35mm), moth like, with long thread-like antennae and usually 4 membranous wings (absent in females of some species) usually held roof-like at rest over the abdomen: mouthparts reduced, with long maxillary palps at side of head or covering "face." Larvae (caddis worms) caterpillar-like, and often construct a case which they carry about and in which they later pupate. Pupae have movable mandibles and appendages free of body.

Families that make cases include: **large caddis flies** (Phryganeidae), **micro caddis flies** (Hydroptilidae), **northern caddis flies** (Limnephilidae), **primitive caddis flies** (Rhyacophilidae), **snail-case caddis flies** (Helicopsychidae); **net-makers** include: Hydropsychidae, Philopotamidae, Psychomyiidae; **case-makers** include: Leptoceridae.

ALMOST every place where fresh water flows or collects has its caddis fly larvae. The typically drab-colored adults are somewhat moth-like in appearance, but the order is better known for the often elaborate cases constructed and inhabited by the larvae of many species.

The caddis flies are in fact closely related to the butterflies and moths, but they lack their overall covering of wing scales and coiled proboscis, and have long maxillary palps. Caddis flies might be confused with lacewings, but have fewer cross-veins, or with stone flies and mayflies, from which they differ in, among other features, the way they hold their wings at rest.

The forewings of caddis flies are normally hairy—hence the scientific name for the order (Greek *trikhos*—hair, *pteron*–wing); the forewings generally bear a small semitransparent, horny spot (nygma or thyridium) and are usually a little longer than the hindwings. In addition to longitudinal veins, the wings of many groups have some cross-veins and occasionally scales along some of the veins. The head has well-developed compound eyes. The outermost segments of the five-segmented maxillary and three-segmented labial palps are sometimes long and flexible. The three segments of the thorax are well developed, and the upper surface bears warts.

The best fliers have a strong coupling between front and rear wings, narrow forewings, expanded hindwings, and long antennae. The wings are coupled by means of curved hairs (macrotrichia) along the veins and simple overlapping of the margins. The abdomen has quite distinct segments and breathing vents (spiracles) on segments 1 to 7. The legs are relatively long and slender; the lower legs (tarsi) have five segments, and above these the femora and tibiae may be equipped with dense spines or strong bristles and long spines.

Adult caddis flies are chiefly active in the evening and at night; they rest in cool, dark places during the day. Some species swarm

The females of many families, especially those whose larvae do not make cases (see below), enter the water to lay their eggs on submerged objects.

The generally omnivorous larvae are caterpillar-like, with a well-sclerotized head and thorax (ie with hardened cuticle) and a soft abdomen. The larva's head bears small antennae, a patch of simple eyes (ocelli) on each side, and chewing mouthparts. The three pairs of legs arising from the thorax are used for walking or crawling, for capturing prey, and for constructing the larval case. The abdomen has nine segments and a pair of prolegs at the tip which serve to anchor the larva in its case, into which it can withdraw completely when disturbed or at rest. There are no functional spiracles, but most species have external filamentous, tracheal gills attached to the respiratory tubules on the segments of the abdomen and thorax. Some species respire through the cuticle; some have a tuft of anal blood gills.

The larvae are fairly active, and the members of many families construct a portable case made of various small objects fastened together with a glue-like substance or with silk from the tip of the labium. Each species of caddis fly larva is to be found in a particular kind of habitat (slow-running or fast streams, ponds, small lakes) and constructs its own specific type of case. The micro caddis flies make purse-shaped cases, northern caddis flies make cases of various kinds, snail-case caddis flies make snail-shell-shaped cases, and large caddis flies make cases of spirally arranged strips of plant material.

Some larvae do not make cases but construct silken nets between underwater plants, debris and stones. The nets are made to face upstream and catch prey items such as small crustaceans and plankton. Most larvae feed on plant material—algae, moss or decaying vegetation; carnivorous larvae take their prey with their forelegs.

Caddis fly larvae are very important in the food chains of freshwater streams and pools; they are eaten by many species of fish, some predacious insect larvae, and birds and frogs. In consequence, the larvae are used as models for human anglers' lures, as are the adults, and many have attractive names such as black silverhorns, great red sedge, grouse wing and grannom. The larvae and pupae may be parasitized by an ichneumon wasp, *Agriotypus armatus*, whose females submerge and pull themselves down to lay eggs near their prospective hosts. The larvae of some species in the family Leptoceridae are pests of paddy fields. GCM

▲ **Leaving behind the protective case** from which it has wriggled, a northern caddis pupa (Limnephilidae) on its way to climb emergent vegetation for its debut as an adult. The case stays on the surface to which it was attached by the fully grown larva before it pupated inside, having partially sealed the open ends. In primitive species without a larval case, the larva makes a special pupal cell, often from sand grains. The pupa has well-developed mandibles and cuts its way out of the case.

The pupae of caddis flies are capable of a fair degree of movement, unlike most insect pupae. The filaments on the abdomen of this individual are respiratory gills.

◄ **Glued to waterside vegetation** by a gelatinous secretion of the female, these caddis fly eggs are well protected from desiccation. On hatching, they will drop to the water below, where the larvae will build the protective case characteristic of the species. Caddis worm cases vary considerably in shape and materials—they may be slender, oval, straight, curved or helical, with a round or square cross-section, and be made of vegetable matter, sand grains, small pebbles or a hollow stick. As the larva grows, the case may be increased in size, or the larva may leave, to make or adopt a larger case.

in daylight. The mouthparts are adapted for licking fluid, but adults have rarely been observed feeding and it is certain that some species don't feed at all. Some visit flowers.

The adults are to be found near fresh water, though there is an Australian species, *Philanisus plebeius*, which breeds by the sea in rock pools near the low-tide mark. Newly emerged adults can be seen in large numbers dancing, often in vertical swarms. Mating occurs on the wing. Males locate females by using their large eyes and antennae; the flight movement of males in swarms may also serve to attract females.

Caddis flies reproduce once a year. They overwinter as larvae, pupate in the spring, and emerge as adults in early summer. The females lay small, more or less spherical 0.1in (0.3mm), eggs that are usually pale blue-green or whitish. The eggs are usually deposited in masses or strings covered in a sticky secretion that attaches them to stones and other objects in or near the water, or else on vegetation overhanging the water.

MOTHS AND BUTTERFLIES

Order: Lepidoptera
Class: Insecta, subclass Pterygota.
Phylum: Uniramia.
Some 150,000 to 200,000 species.
Distribution: widespread wherever there is vegetation, up to snowline.

Features: adults usually have wings that bear overlapping scales; modified scales (often hairlike) also on rest of body and often legs; adult usually has a long, sucking proboscis or "tongue" for nectar feeding; wingless larvae (caterpillars) usually have chewing mouthparts for plant diet; complete metamorphosis via egg, larva, pupa (chrysalis) and adult (imago); common defenses include vivid warning, or camouflage, markings, spines or irritant hairs, poisons or repugnant taste, or mimicry of poisonous species. Wingspan in adults 0.1–12in (0.3–30cm).

▶ **Day-roosting moths** are often camouflaged to avoid being eaten by birds and lizards. The wing pattern of this moth, *Epipristis nalearia* (Geometridae) resembles the mottled, lichen-covered tree trunk on which the insect rests in Borneo.

▼ **Characteristic overlapping scales** of the order Lepidoptera, here highly magnified on the wing of a tropical moth (family Uraniidae). Wing scales are modified hairs and are responsible for the colored wing patterns of moths and butterflies.

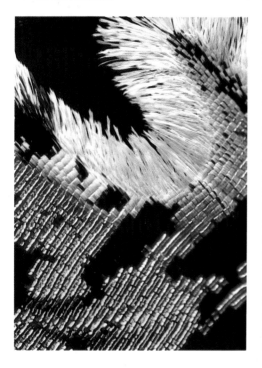

For most of us, the emergence of a large-winged, often brightly colored, butterfly or moth from its chrysalis is the archetypal metamorphosis, a sudden, long-awaited and stunning transformation. The moths and butterflies are one of the largest orders of insects (beetles are the largest). Yet, despite the spectacular variety of size and color in both adults and larvae members of the order Lepidoptera show a high level of structural uniformity. Their closest relatives are the caddis flies.

The presence of overlapping scales on the wings is the order's most notable characteristic (Greek: *lepis*—scale, *pteron*—wing). If a butterfly or a moth is handled, the fine "dust" that gets rubbed off is composed of these tiny scales. Scales also clothe other parts of the body. Those on the head are often hair-like and stand erect to form a tuft. Alternatively they may be scale- or plate-like, and flattened on the head-capsule. The legs often appear to be hairy, but again, these "hairs" are modified scales. The wing scales in most lepidopterans have a cavity (lumen) between the upper and lower surfaces, but in the most primitive moths they are solid.

Underneath the covering of scales the wings are glassy, transparent structures, as in other insects. Wing color either results from pigments in the scales, or from the physical structure of the scales. The "metallic" iridescent blue of the South American morphos (*Morpho* species) is an example of the latter. The exact way in which scale structure relates to color is complex, and at present often beyond our understanding.

The variety of color patterns on the wings of butterflies and moths seems infinite, yet many of them can be derived from the modification of a few basic elements. For example, if each of a series of eyespots on a wing becomes elongated during the development of the insect, a band is formed.

We generally think of butterflies as having brightly colored wings and clubbed antennae, and moths as being drab insects with antennae that are not clubbed. Strictly speaking the division of the order into Heterocera (moths) and Rhopalocera (butterflies) is an artificial one. Firstly, many moths are brightly colored and also have clubbed antennae, such as burnets and foresters (family Zygaenidae), and the Castniidae. Secondly, a detailed study of structure demonstrates that many "moths" (even without those features) are more closely related to butterflies than they are to other moths. (Some moths, too, are day-active, a "butterfly" character.) It is best to regard the division as of colloquial value rather than as a natural primary division of the Lepidoptera.

Broadly speaking, colors either function to camouflage an animal or to advertise it, so there is a strong link between coloration and life-style. Moths, with some notable exceptions, fly at dusk or during the night, and they tend to lie up during the day. Those that rest in exposed places, such as on tree-trunks, are often camouflaged, which protects them from predators. Some of the most cryptic moths are found in the family Geometridae—popularly called the waves, pugs and carpet moths.

Butterflies and moths advertise either to warn of their unpalatability to predators (or deceive predators by mimicking unpalatable models), or to display their attractiveness to potential mates.

It is not only through color that scales play a part in the attraction between the sexes. Special scales, called androconia, are found on males of many species of Lepidoptera. These scales, which help to disseminate scent from glands on the wings, are scattered over the female during courtship. Sometimes modified scales are bunched together to form brushes and "pencils," which function for the same purpose. At the end of the abdomen an "anal tuft" is usually found. This is also thought to function in the dissemination of scent.

Next to the scales the most characteristic feature of adult lepidopterans is the sucking proboscis or "tongue." At rest the proboscis is generally rolled up underneath the head, but when the insect feeds it is extended. A channel runs through the proboscis so that the organ functions like a flexible drinking straw up which liquid (particularly nectar) is sucked. The length of the proboscis varies. In the primitive Micropterigidae it has not been developed. In some families such as the tussock moths (Lymantriidae) the structure has been lost, and the adults do not feed at all. In others the proboscis is present but short, as in the tiny Nepticulidae. The longest tongues are found in the hawk-moths, enabling them to suck nectar from the deep-seated nectaries of tubular flowers. Hummingbird hawkmoths hover while they draw nectar. The genus to which they belong is appropriately called *Macroglossum* ("great tongue").

Also on the heads of lepidopterans are the antennae. In adults these vary in structure and length. In primitive families they are composed of short, simple segments, but in more advanced groups they may bear fine hairs (be ciliated) or have their segments

extended into long filaments to give a comb-like (pectinate) appearance so that the antennae resemble feathers. Pectinate antennae occur in many species of tussock moths.

The adult's thorax bears three pairs of legs and two pairs of wings. Each forewing is coupled with the hindwing on the same side. In this way both forewings and hindwings beat in the same direction at the same time (unlike for example dragonflies).

With few exceptions the larvae (caterpillars) have chewing mouthparts, which is appropriate since they spend most of their time feeding. This is the growing stage in the life cycle. Consumption is related not only to the growth of the larvae but also to the needs of the winged adult. Since many adults do not feed at all, reserves have to be built up by the caterpillar.

Most caterpillars have both true legs and false legs, although in some species some or all of these have been lost. There are three pairs of true legs, which are found on the thorax. False legs (prolegs) are present on the abdomen. Usually there are five pairs of these fleshy structures, one pair on each of segments 3–6, and a terminal (anal) pair on segment 10. Each false leg can grasp stem

The 24 Superfamilies of the Lepidoptera

Unless stated otherwise, all superfamilies are distributed worldwide.

Micropterigoidea

1 family of about 100–150 species. The most primitive group of moths, very small with chewing mouthparts in adults.

Kauri moths

Agathiphagoidea

2 species from SW Pacific in one genus (*Agathiphaga*). Caterpillars feed in seeds of kauri pines (*Agathis* species); adults have not developed "tongues."

Heterobathmioidea

2 named species from temperate S America in 1 genus (*Heterobathmia*). Caterpillars mine leaves of southern beech (*Nothofagus* species); adults lack developed "tongues."

Eriocranioidea

About 20 species from the Holarctic, most in family Eriocraniidae. Very small moths; larvae usually leaf miners.

Ghost moths and Swift moths

Hepialoidea

Small to large moths; larvae often feed in roots or stems. Includes **Venus** or **Silver-spotted ghost** (*Leto venus*, Hepialidae).

Pigmy moths and relatives

Nepticuloidea

Minute moths; larvae generally leaf miners. Includes **pygmy moths** (family Nepticulidae) and Opostegidae.

Incurvarioidea

Small to very small moths frequently "metallic" in coloring; larvae are often leaf miners (eg Heliozelidae); includes also **yucca moths** (*Tegeticula* species, Prodoxidae), **longhorn moths** (Adelidae).

Tischerioidea

Tiny moths; larvae are leaf miners.

Clothes moths, Bagworms and relatives

Tineoidea

Large group of small or very small moths. Includes **clothes moths** (Tineidae), **bagworm moths** (Psychidae), and several families with leaf-mining larvae, including **leaf blotch miners** (Gracillariidae).

Case bearers and relatives

Gelechioidea

Large group of small moths divided into many families, including **case bearers** (Coleophoridae) and species with larvae that mine grasses (Elachistidae).

Copromorphoidea

Small moths, including the metallic-colored and day-flying family Glyphipterigidae.

Web spinners and relatives

Yponomeutoidea

Small moths; larvae of family Yponomeutidae often spin communal nests.

Clearwings and relatives

Sesioidea

Small to medium-sized moths; **clearwings** (Sesiidae) mimic wasps and bees.

Leaf rollers, Bell moths and relatives

Tortricoidea

Small moths; larvae often live in leaves rolled up with silk; also in the Tortricidae, the **Codling moth** (*Cyclia pomonella*) is a serious pest of fruit.

Carpenter moths and relatives

Cossoidea

Small to large moths; larvae bore into trees. Includes the **Goat moth** (*Cossus cossus*) (family Cossidae).

Silk moths, Emperors, Hawkmoths

Bombycoidea

Medium-sized to very large moths; larvae often hairy. Among the families are the **eggars, lappets** and **tent caterpillars** (Lasiocampidae); **silk moths** (Bombycidae) including the domestic **Silkworm moth** (*Bombyx mori*); **emperor moths** and **giant silkworms** (Saturniidae), including the **Atlas moth** (*Attacus atlas*), **Venezuelan emperor moth** (*Lonomia achelous*) and **Mopane moth** (*Gonimbrasia belina*); and the **hawkmoths** (Sphingidae), including the **Elephant hawkmoth** (*Deilephila elpenor*), **Death's-head hawkmoth** (*Acherontia atropos*), and **hummingbird hawkmoths** (*Macroglossum* species).

Skippers

Hesperoidea

Some 3,000–3,500 species in family Hesperiidae. See separate Table.

Butterflies

Papilionoidea

About 14,700 species. See Table.

Castnioidea

Colorful, day-flying, medium-sized moths that often resemble butterflies. In tropical regions.

Burnets, Foresters and relatives

Zygaenoidea

Colorful **burnets** and **foresters** (Zygaenidae), and **"slug" larvae** (Limacodidae).

Geometers, Loopers and relatives

Geometroidea

Includes **carpet, wave** (*Sterrha* species) and **pug** (*Eupithecia, Chloroclystis* species) **moths, geometers, loopworms** and **inchworms** (all Geometridae); **hook-tips** (Drepanidae); Uraniidae includes some colorful species with hindwings extended into tails.

Snout and Plume moths

Pyraloidea

The family Pyralidae has an enormous number of species, including **snout moths** and many pests; adults of *Cryptoses* live in the fur of sloths; the Thyrididae resemble leaves; **plume moths** (Pterophoridae) are delicate, with wings usually cleft to form plumes.

Many-plumed moths

Alucitoidea

In Alucitidae, forewings are divided into 6 and hindwings into 6 or 7 plumes

Noctuoidea

Most numerous are the **armyworms, cutworms, owlet** and **underwing, moths** (Noctuidae), which include the **Alder moth** (*Acronycta alni*); among other families are the **tiger moths, footmen, ermines** and **woolly bears** (Arctiidae); the **prominents** (Notodontidae) including the **Puss moth** (*Cerura vinula*); the **processionary caterpillars** (Thaumetopoeidae); the **handmaidens** (Ctenuchidae); and the **tussock moths** (Lymantriidae), including the **Yellowtail moth** (*Euproctis similis*).

◄ **This "micro" moth's close resemblance** to a crinkled, dead leaf is one of many protective ploys evolved by insects to avoid predation. The accuracy of such mimicry of inedible objects reflects the acute vision of insectivorous birds and lizards, and the intense selection pressures they exert (Micropterigidae).

▼ **Egg-laying emperor moth,** *Gonimbrasia belina* (Saturniidae), in South Africa. The female must first locate a plant which will provide suitable food for the hatched larvae. This she does by sight or smell, and confirms that it is a suitable species by receptors on the feet, antennae or tip of the abdomen. Finally she lays eggs on part of the plant which gives egg and larva the best chances of survival.

or leaf surfaces by means of a ring of hooks (crochets) around its base. In the geometrids two or three of the neighboring pairs are lost and the caterpillars progress by "looping." Some caterpillars spin a mat of silk to provide a foothold on smooth surfaces. Prolegs are absent in slug caterpillars, which have an adhesive "sole" with suckers.

Caterpillars are vulnerable to predation and they protect themselves in various ways. Some are clothed with irritant hairs, others bear clusters of sharp spines, some are distasteful or even poisonous, and some depend on camouflage. (A subsequent section discusses these defenses in greater detail.)

In the pupa (chrysalis) the chewing, wingless larva undergoes its transformation into the winged adult. The most primitive pupae have functional mandibles which help to break open the cocoon before the adult emerges. In the family Eriocraniidae the mandibles are very large.

Lepidopterists are often divided into those who study the small moths ("Microlepidoptera") and those who study the larger species ("Macrolepidoptera"). As with the separation of the moths from the butterflies, this division is largely a useful colloquialism; it does not closely reflect evolutionary relationships. Nevertheless, primitive moths are generally small, and more advanced species generally larger. Also, size reflects lifestyle. Small moths, not surprisingly, develop from small larvae, and small larvae are able to occupy habitats quite different from those occupied by large ones. Small larvae tend to feed inside seeds, galls, fruit, stems, flowers and leaves (as leaf miners). Larger larvae are generally external feeders: they are what we think of as typical caterpillars, and they spend this stage of their life cycle eating leaves. This ecological division is reflected not only in larval (and usually adult) size, but often in structure and habits as well. For example, internal feeders tend to have reduced legs.

The most primitive species of moth alive today are small, and the belief that the first moths also were small received confirmation a few years ago when a small moth was found preserved in Lebanese amber dating from the early Cretaceous, at least 100 million years ago. What makes this find so exciting is that the fossilized specimen belongs to the Micropterigidae, which is considered, on grounds of structure, to be the most primitive family of moths. The adults of this widespread family are remarkable in having chewing mouthparts instead of the typical adult lepidopteran's sucking proboscis. They visit flowerheads and feed on pollen grains, which they grind with their mandibles. Those components of the mouthparts destined to form the proboscis in more advanced members of the Lepidoptera are tiny vestiges in the Micropterigidae. Micropterigid larvae are found in leaf litter and probably feed on detritus or fungal hyphae.

There are two other groups of moths that have not developed a proboscis, the Australian kauri moths (family Agathiphagidae), and the recently discovered South American genus *Heterobathmia* (family Heterobathmiidae). The larvae of both

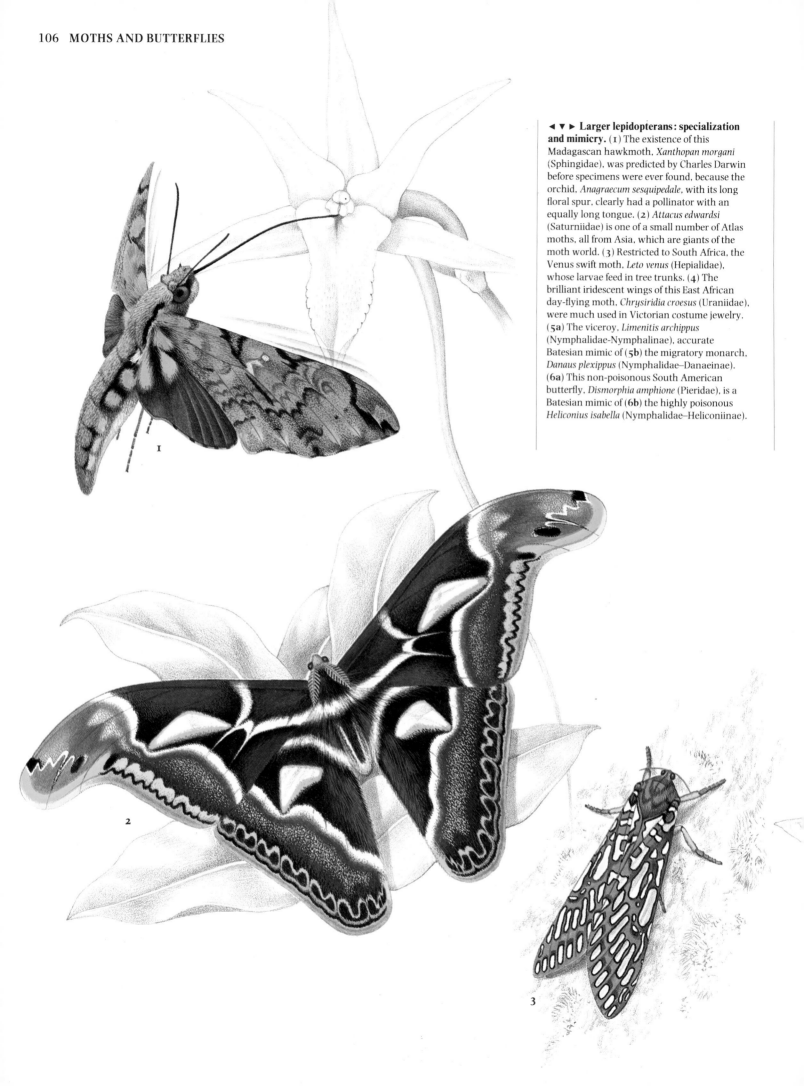

◄ ▼ ► **Larger lepidopterans: specialization and mimicry.** (**1**) The existence of this Madagascan hawkmoth, *Xanthopan morgani* (Sphingidae), was predicted by Charles Darwin before specimens were ever found, because the orchid, *Anagraecum sesquipedale*, with its long floral spur, clearly had a pollinator with an equally long tongue. (**2**) *Attacus edwardsi* (Saturniidae) is one of a small number of Atlas moths, all from Asia, which are giants of the moth world. (**3**) Restricted to South Africa, the Venus swift moth, *Leto venus* (Hepialidae), whose larvae feed in tree trunks. (**4**) The brilliant iridescent wings of this East African day-flying moth, *Chrysiridia croesus* (Uraniidae), were much used in Victorian costume jewelry. (**5a**) The viceroy, *Limenitis archippus* (Nymphalidae-Nymphalinae), accurate Batesian mimic of (**5b**) the migratory monarch, *Danaus plexippus* (Nymphalidae–Danaeinae). (**6a**) This non-poisonous South American butterfly, *Dismorphia amphione* (Pieridae), is a Batesian mimic of (**6b**) the highly poisonous *Heliconius isabella* (Nymphalidae–Heliconiinae).

4

5a

5b

6a

6b

groups feed inside plant tissue, those of the kauri moths in the seeds of the Kauri pine (*Agathis*) and those of *Heterobathmia* within the leaves (as leaf miners) of southern beeches (*Nothofagus*).

Leaf mining is widespread among the lower Lepidoptera. Since leaf miners live between the two outer (epidermal) layers of leaves their appendages are usually reduced or absent. Leaf mining is characteristic of the pygmy moths (family Nepticulidae). Although not frequently encountered, the family occurs all over the world. Close examination of the leaves of such trees as oak and beech will often reveal the signs of leaf-mining larvae at work. As the insect eats the tissue of the plant, a channel or blotch is formed. This becomes visible when the chlorophyll-bearing cell layers, which give the leaf its green color, are eaten.

Many leaf miners restrict their feeding to a particular host plant, so that with a correctly identified leaf bearing the marks of a larva, it is often possible to identify the species of leaf miner from an empty "mine."

The leaf-mining habit has probably evolved more than once in the Lepidoptera. In one family of case bearers (Coleophoridae) the larvae are often leaf miners at first, but in later stages (instars) construct protecting cases and feed externally. Larvae of the Heliozelidae cut oval pieces from the leaf at the end of their mining life, and make them into a case within which pupation takes place.

Related to the Heliozelidae is the family Incurvariidae, which includes the remarkable yucca moths of the genus *Tegeticula*. These moths are found in North America and Mexico and have developed a close association with the yucca plants (*Yucca* species). The female moths lay their eggs in the ovaries of the yucca flowers before applying pollen that they have previously collected. As a result of the pollination the yucca produces seeds, some which germinate and some of which are eaten by the moth larvae. Thus plant and insect depend on each other for surival.

Although some members of the ghost or

swift moths (family Hepialidae) are among the largest lepidopterans, the affinities of the group lie within the small members of the order rather than with the larger ones. Hepialid larvae feed in or among roots or in trunks of trees. The family is well represented in Australia where one species, *Aenetus eximus*, forms tunnels as long as 20in (50cm) in the stems and roots of certain trees. One of the most beautiful hepialids is the Venus or Silver-spotted ghost (*Leto venus*), a species confined to the coastal forests of the southern Cape of South Africa. The larvae tunnel in the trunks of a leguminose tree called *Virgilia oroboides* (the keurboom). Shortly before emergence, the pupa protrudes from the tree trunk. The moth, when freshly emerged, is a rich, deep purple covered with silver patches.

Many of the smaller moths are rather drab. For example, members of the enormous family Tineidae, to which the notorious clothes moths belong, are often yellowish-brown or gray. However, there are some that are exquisitely colored. The delicate little moths that belong to the Gracilariidae (leaf blotch miners) often have their long-fringed wings adorned with eyespots and colored bands. It is difficult to imagine the function of the complex patterns and variety of colors in this group of tiny moths, if indeed there is one.

There is little doubt about the function of pattern in the clearwings (family Sesiidae), which mimic wasps and bees. Their wings are largly devoid of scales, leaving them transparent as in wasps. The bodies of clearwing moths bear wasp- or bee-like stripes, they are usually similar in shape to their models, and may even make a buzzing sound when they fly. Clearwings do not sting, of course, but by mimicking insects that do sting they usually avoid the attentions of predators.

Another colorful group of moths is the Zygaenidae, which includes the burnets or foresters. Like clearwings, they are day-flying; but while clearwings are harmless mimics, zygaenids are colorful to advertise their distastefulness. Some species store toxins of great potency, such as hydrogen cyanide, in their tissues.

One of the most primitive families of larger moths is the Cossidae, the carpenters. The larvae generally bore into trees—hence their colloquial name. *Cossus cossus* is known as the Goat moth because the larvae are said to smell like goats. The species is widespread, being found in Europe (including Britain), North Africa, and central and western Asia. It takes 3–4 years to mature.

► **Denizen of tropical rain forests** in New Guinea and northern Australia, this day-flying moth, *Alcides zodiaca* (Uraniidae), pays frequent visits to flowers in daylight and spends the evenings circling trees at canopy level.

► **Larva of the Death's-head hawkmoth** BELOW RIGHT (Sphingidae) feeding on a plant of the potato family. In so doing, it absorbs toxins from the plant and both caterpillar and adult moth enjoy a measure of chemical protection from predators.

▼ **A Narrow-bordered five-spot burnet moth,** *Zygaena lonicerae*, drinks nectar at a willowherb flower. The warning coloration of burnets (Zygaenidae) indicates that the moth is highly poisonous, containing cyanide compounds sequestrated by the larva from its foodplants, clover and vetches.

Day-flying species of the swallowtail moths (Uraniidae) are startlingly similar to swallowtail butterflies: not only are they brightly colored, but the hindwings bear the typical papilionid "tails."

Nearly all moth larvae are herbivores. Occasionally, however, a truly carnivorous life-style has arisen. Some species feed on scale insects or other homopteran bugs. The only larvae known to ambush prey are certain species of pug moth (*Eupithecia*), a genus belonging to the enormous family Geometridae, to which the Uraniidae are related. Many geometrid larvae are cryptic and resemble twigs. Normally this gives them a measure of protection from predators, but some species of *Eupithecia* take advantage of their camouflage to hunt prey. By gripping the substrate with the claspers at the end of the abdomen and keeping the rest of the body erect, a *Eupithecia* caterpillar remains motionless until suitable prey comes within range: then it strikes. Although the genus is widespread, only the species on the Hawaiian Islands have adopted the predatory habit.

The moths most noted for their powerful flight are the hawkmoths (Sphingidae). Some are known to fly considerable distances, and some species have an intercontinental distribution. One of the most widespread is the Death's-head hawkmoth, so-called because of the skull-like markings on the thorax. The adults of this species are known to raid beehives for honey. Like many hawkmoths, they have a long proboscis. Sphingid larvae (hornworms) have a prominent horn that projects from a position near the end of the abdomen.

Among the most serious of lepidopteran pests are the "cutworms" and the "armyworms," which are larvae of the enormous family Noctuidae. The African armyworm *Spodoptera exempta* attacks the leaves and stems of cereals, sometimes in immense swarms.

Except for some of the colorful Ctenuchidae (handmaidens), all species belonging to the Noctuoidea have "ears" on the thorax. These structures basically comprise a membrane that picks up sound vibrations. Noctuoid moths probably use their "ears" to pick up the high-pitched, ultrasonic sounds of hunting bats. Certain species of the tiger moth family (Arctiidae) actually produce ultrasonics themselves. Many arctiids are distasteful and these auditory signals probably function to warn bats of this fact in much the same way that day-flying insects advertise distastefulness with bright colors.

Among the most dramatic of the moths are the larger emperors (Saturniidae). All bear prominent eyespots on the wings. The enormous Atlas moth is among the largest of all lepidopterans, with a wingspan of up to 12in (30cm). Emperor moths lack a proboscis: each antenna resembles a comb (bipectinate). The larvae bear fleshy protuberances called scoli. The larva of the Mopane moth is eaten in southern Africa by the locals. It is an attractive caterpillar with bright red, yellow and black markings on a white background, and feeds on leaves of the Mopane tree. "Mopane worms" are often sold dried, and they have a rather nutty flavor.

A family closely related to the emperors is the Bombycidae, which includes the well-known Silkworm moth. The copious quantities of silk spun by the larva when it makes its cocoon have been used for 2,000 years in the commercial production of silk.

Some of the large moths look more like butterflies than moths. The Castniidae is a fairly small family found in the tropics and subtropics, excluding Africa. Often the hindwing has a bright "flash" coloration while the forewing is camouflaged. Like butterflies, the Castniidae have clubbed antennae, and the two groups may be closely related.

Although the Noctuoidea include thousands of rather similar-looking moths, two particularly curious habits have arisen—one larval the other adult. Processionary caterpillars (eg *Thaumetopoea processionea*) set off at night in a long line, one following the other, to feed. The remarkable adults of the genus *Calpe* (Noctuidae), instead of using their tongues to suck nectar, pierce fruit, and, in one species, suck blood—usually from cattle.   MJS

Of all insects, the colorful and highly visible **butterflies** have always particularly attracted naturalists and laymen alike. The Victorian mania for cataloguing the natural world was enthusiastically directed toward the butterflies and because of this interest, there are now over 17,700 described species of butterfly (including skippers), and more are added each year. Yet despite this body of knowledge, we still know relatively little of living butterflies and their early stages.

Like moths, butterflies have four main life stages: the egg, caterpillar (larva), chrysalis (pupa) and the adult (butterfly). Female butterflies lay their eggs on or near a suitable food plant for the caterpillars. The female usually distinguishes the correct plant from the rest of the vegetation visually or by detecting a specific odor given off by the plant. She then tests the leaves with receptors on her feet, antennae or the tip of her abdomen. If it is the correct species, she lays her egg(s) on the plant at a site with the correct microclimate (ie balance of humidity, temperature and protection).

Many butterflies are restricted to one species of food plant, though many use a range of related species, the one used depending on season or location. The North American Checkerspot butterfly was originally thought to feed solely on plantain (*Plantago erecta*), but it is now known to eat a whole range of plant species, some of which are totally unrelated to plantains and others only used by one or two populations of the Checkerspot butterfly.

Many subtle factors operate when a female butterfly seeks an egg-laying site. These include temperature, position of the plant relative to its neighbors and the presence or absence of other eggs or insects. Many species select warm microclimates in order to speed up development and thus increase survival chances for the egg and caterpillar by reducing exposure to predators. Cabbage white butterflies prefer to lay their eggs on cabbages around the edges of fields rather than in the center.

The presence of eggs similar to their own will deter females of most butterflies from laying on a plant. This is exploited by certain species of passion flower which produced small, raised yellow blisters on their tendrils and leaves; these mimic eggs and may deter female *Heliconius* butterflies from laying there. (The poisonous *Heliconius* adults are also mimicked by palatable members of the butterfly family Pieridae.) The Mistletoe butterfly of Australia selects food plants which are visited by a certain species of ant. The caterpillars of this butterfly live in mixed age groups and are protected from small

The 6 Families of Butterflies

Hesperiidae

About 3,000–3,500 species worldwide.
Small to medium-sized **skippers**, with stout bodies, narrow, sharp-angled wings and pointed antennae; flight short, darting; some have short "tails," wings often have metallic markings. Subfamilies include the Hesperiinae (2,500 species) and Pyrginae (both worldwide), Megathyminae (C and N America), Pyrrhopyginae (neotropics), Coeliadinae (Africa, India to Australia) and Trapezitinae (Australia).

Papilionidae

About 700 species. Includes the **swallowtails** (eg *Papilio dardanus*, *P. machaon*, and *P. polyxenes* of subfamily Papilioninae, wordwide) and the **apollos** and **festoons**

(*Parnassius* species, subfamily Parnassiinae, Palearctic). Medium to large, conspicuous and powerful fliers, usually with large "tails" and bright markings.

Pieridae

About 1,100 species. Includes the **whites** and **jezebels** (Pierinae, worldwide), including *Pieris* species; the **sulphurs** and **yellows** (Coliadinae, worldwide), including *Colias* species; and the **whites** of the neotropics (Dismorphinae). Medium-sized; wing ground color usually white or yellow, some very colorful; many are migrants.

Nymphalidae

About 5,500–6,000 species. Among the subfamilies are the **nymphalids** (Nymphalinae, worldwide), including the **viceroy** (*Limenitis archippus*) and

checkerspot (*Euphydryas editha*); the **browns** and **satyrs** (Satyrinae, worldwide); the **ithomiids** (Ithomiinae, neotropical); the **tigers** and **danaids** (Danainae, worldwide), including the **monarch** (*Danaus plexippus*), and **Queen butterfly** (*D. gillippus*); the Brassolinae (neotropics), including the **Owl butterfly** (*Caligo belatro*); the Heliconiinae, including *Heliconius* species, mainly neotropical; the **morphos** (Morphinae, neotropical); Charaxinae, including *Charaxes* species, mainly African, also Asian; and the Acraeinae, including *Bematistes* species, African. Predominate in N temperate regions but still well represented in tropics; medium to large, very colorful; life-styles varied but all with forelegs modified with brush-like hairs acting as chemo-receptors.

Riodinidae

About 950 species. Includes the mainly neotropical **metalmarks** and **judies** (Nemeobiinae) and about 10 species of **snout butterflies** (Libytheinae, worldwide). Small to medium-sized adults with colorful markings.

Lycaenidae

About 6,450 species. Includes the **blues** (Polyommatinae, eg **Mistletoe butterfly**, *Ogyris amarillis*), **hairstreaks** (Theclinae) and **coppers** (Lycaeninae), all worldwide in distribution, and the **blues of Africa** (Lipteninae) and **blues of China**, (Poritiinae). Small, predominate in tropics, often in association with forest trees; often metallic blue wing colors; larvae with varied habits.

insect predators by the ants. In return, the caterpillars secrete a sweet liquid which the ants eat.

The specializations that make a caterpillar such an efficient eating machine involve body forms that are very different from those of the sexually mature adult (imago). Caterpillars make the transformation by way of inactive stage, the pupa. During its life the caterpillar molts, usually four times. Most earlier molts are followed by rapid growth before the new cuticle hardens, but the last molt reveals the chrysalis, with the outlines of the adult butterfly-to-be clearly visible. The pupa or chrysalis provides a molded case within which the caterpillar's tissues are broken down and used to feed dormant groups of cells called imaginal buds. These have remained inert inside the caterpillar since it hatched and are now activated to form the adult butterfly within the "mold." The chrysalis can develop as rapidly as in a week in some species but may last for several (up to six or more) months in some temperate region species.

As with caterpillars, the commonest strategy used by the immobile pupa is camouflage and concealment. Most are some shade of brown or green and many mimic leaves, both dead and alive, often to the extent of using gold and silver spots to mimic raindrops. Caterpillars which gain their protection from poisons, however, have relatively brightly colored pupae, often positioned in quite open situations.

The adult butterfly usually lives in association with flowers. Most species spend much

▲ **A mating pair of Coolie butterflies,** *Anartia amathea* (Nymphalidae) in Trinidad. Mating in butterflies usually follows a more or less complicated courtship, which often involves the male drenching the female in an aphrodisiac scent. The scent may be derived from chemicals in the foodplant of the larva or compounds collected by the adult male from dried plants.

◄ **Only a few minutes old** ABOVE, the fresh pupa of a Comma butterfly, *Polygonia c-album* (Nymphalidae), will spend the winter in this state, protected by its resemblance to a dead leaf.

▶ **An Orange emesis butterfly,** *Emesis fatima fatima* (Riodinidae), feeds on a *Bidens* flower in Trinidad. Most members of this brightly colored family mimic the color patterns of other, distasteful species.

▷ **Clustered on dung** OVERLEAF male butterflies, *Actinote alcione salmonea* (Nymphalidae), replace amino acid and salt losses incurred during mating, when a sizeable spermatophore is deposited in the female's reproductive tract.

of their time seeking nectar as a readily available source of energy. However, not all butterflies are flower visitors. Some, such as the charaxes butterflies (family Nymphalidae) of Africa, feed on rotting fruit, tree sap and dung, while many forest-dwelling butterflies feed on the sticky honeydew of aphids and other plant-feeding bugs.

Few of the butterflies obtain much in the way of protein from their food: when developing eggs or repairing body tissues they rely upon food reserves laid down by the caterpillar. Certain species of *Heliconius* butterflies are exceptions to this rule; these denizens of Central and South American tropics eat amino acids and proteins derived from pollen grains, which they rupture by means of their specially modified tongues. They may live up to 130 days, producing eggs for much of that time. By contrast most butterflies, particularly those of temperate regions, have a protein-free diet and rarely live for more than a week or two.

Butterflies all over the world visit patches of mud or damp ground. This "puddling" is particularly common among tropical species and is restricted to males. At first entomologists assumed that the butterfly was seeking water, but could not explain why only males were involved. It has recently been suggested that swallowtails and whites "puddle" in order to absorb sodium. When the adults emerge, both sexes have enough sodium in their bodies for the functioning of their muscles and nerves. On mating, many male whites deposit a sperm package into the female's body. This contains much of the male's free sodium. The female uses the sodium in the package surrounding the sperm to replace sodium she has put into egg production. The males make up for this deficiency by absorbing sodium salts where evaporation of ground water has concentrated this element. In a little-known variation on puddling behavior some male butterflies extract sodium from perfectly dry stones, gravel or even the dried carcasses of animals. Species from a wide range of families use their proboscis to daub dry surfaces with saliva and then drink the dissolved salts.

Each butterfly species has its own unique approach to reproduction. Most females mate several times during their lifetime and develop eggs when necessary fat reserves or food are available. Others, such as the apollos (*Parnassius*) or *Euphydryas* species, mate only once, after which the male deposits a secreted plug in the genital aperture of the female, in this way preventing matings by other males.

The number of eggs produced by a female and the pattern in which they are laid varies greatly from species to species. Most butterflies lay 100–500 eggs during their lifetime. Some place their eggs in batches—the number of eggs ranging from up to 350 in *Euphydryas* to less than 10 in the metalmarks and many others. These species seem to violate the old advice not to "put all your eggs in one basket." However, they usually adopt this strategy because the collective action of many caterpillars may reinforce some protective feature of the individuals, such as spininess or distastefulness and warning coloration. Moreover there is safety in numbers.

The large wing areas of butterflies have uniquely favored the development of pattern and color for use in communication. Almost all of the known species can be identified by pattern alone. There are notable exceptions of course: the skippers often have 20 or more different species almost identical in pattern and size.

In a world full of visually orientated predators such as birds and reptiles, the patterns of butterflies may fulfill two main functions; firstly they can help butterflies to escape detection in their natural habitat, and secondly they can enable members of the same species to recognize each other. These needs are often in conflict, a dilemma that is often resolved by males and females having different patterns, the male to be recognized by the female, and thus facilitate mating, even at the risk of being eaten by a predator, and the female to escape detection by predators through camouflage. It is far more important that the female avoids predators because, unlike the male, once mated she holds the key to further generations through her egg-laying capacity. Many lycaenid butterflies, for example, have brilliant blue males and dull brown females, a typical form of sexual dimorphism among butterflies.

Several wing patterns evolved as a means of deflecting the attack of predators, or even intimidating them. Eyespots are found in a wide range of species and may act in one of two ways. They may deflect the predator's attack away from the more vulnerable parts of the butterfly: virtually all the browns and satyrs (subfamily Satyrinae) have eyespots of this type on the edges of their wings. Large eyespots may be used to startle the potential predator by their sudden display. The so-called Owl butterfly of the South American rain forests is an excellent example of this form of defense.

Other methods of deflecting predator attack include tails which resemble antennae, and the combination of brilliant upperside coloring and very well camouflaged undersides. Such a butterfly may confuse a predator simply by landing and concealing the bright colors which first attracted the predator.

A less well-known use of wing color is in the regulation of body temperature by basking. Dark pigments absorb the radiant heat from the sun more efficiently than pale colors and therefore accelerate the warming up of the butterfly's body before flight. In genera such as the clouded-yellows (*Colias*) and some whites (*Pieris*), the amount of dark pigment in the pattern varies with season, altitude and latitude. The cooler the environment, the darker the pattern, so that the insect's mobility is enhanced. However, in nature things are never what they seem, and at least one tropical butterfly with black wings has been shown to *avoid* overheating by wing-scale pigments which, although black in appearance, do not absorb infrared rays.

The wings of some butterflies incorporate pigments and patterns which are invisible to our eyes, and presumably also to many potential predators. These patterns reflect ultraviolet light, which is invisible to vertebrates but to which the insect eye is sensitive. This enables members of the same species to communicate visually without giving any clues to vertebrate predators. Many apparently plain white or yellow pierids have distinct ultraviolet patterns which enable the two sexes to recognize one another. To the human eye the brilliant metallic blue of *Morpho* butterflies is already

▲ **A Green hairstreak,** *Callophrys rubi* (Lycaenidae), a widespread Eurasian butterfly frequenting open country and heathland, where the caterpillars feed on plants such as heather, gorse, broom, bramble and bilberry.

▲ **Egg batch** TOP of the South American Small lacewing, *Actinote pellenea* (Nymphalidae), on a leaf of *Eupatorium*, in Trinidad. Some butterflies lay relatively few eggs, singly, a strategy which makes it difficult for egg parasites and predators to find them. Another strategy, adopted here, is to lay a very large number of eggs in a dense batch and rely on the safety-in-numbers principle.

▶ **Drinking at damp soil,** a skipper butterfly, *Jemadia* species (Hesperiidae), in rain forest in Peru. Skippers are so-called because of their rapid, darting flight. The larvae of most species feed on grasses and related plants.

spectacular in flight, but if viewed through a video camera viewer sensitive to ultraviolet light, they are seen to flash like a beacon—their wings reflect ultraviolet far more than visible blue light.

Wings are the secret of the success of butterflies, as of most insects. They gave them potential mobility to colonize new habitats and have larger territories and breeding areas. A few species are regular migrants, and travel huge distances across oceans and continents. This ability has been responsible for the spread of the New World monarch throughout most tropical and subtropical regions of the world.

In North America the monarch undertakes regular movements from south to north in spring, a subsequent generation returning again in the fall. Only recently have we appreciated where these butterflies spend their winter. It has long been known that communal wintering roosts existed in selected trees in the southern USA but no one had anticipated the immense congregations of these butterflies, when they were recently discovered roosting in the pine forests of northern Mexico. The migratory behavior of the monarch is especially interesting to biologists because of the species' apparent ability to return to hibernate in the same roost after traveling vast distances. Such abilities are normally only associated with higher organisms, such as birds or mammals. The individual monarchs which have been tagged have traveled 1,180mi (1,900km) in a few days, attaining average speeds of up to 80mi (130km) per day: there have been some suggestions that the mass return to communal roosts in Mexico is a very recent phenomenon and the direct result of large-scale deforestation by man.   KP

Predators Beware!
The defenses of caterpillars

Caterpillars are vulnerable. They are nearly always slow moving, are often exposed, and present an often readily available plump morsel to birds and other predators. It is not surprising, therefore, that they have developed a wide range of defenses.

Many of the small species gain indirect protection by their concealed lives within roots, stems, galls, seeds and other plant tissue. Some large species benefit from similar shelter; for example caterpillars of the ghost and swift moths (family Hepialidae) live in tree trunks or roots, while the larvae of carpenter moths (Cossidae) bore into tree trunks.

The "bagworms" (family Psychidae) construct cases in which larvae (and the usually wingless adult females) live. The bags are made of silk to which the larvae stick grains of sand, twigs or leaves. In some of the larger species, such as those in the African genus *Eumeta*, the bags are extremely tough and difficult to tear apart, and give the vulnerable larvae considerable protection. The larvae of many species of web spinners (Yponomeutidae) live colonially concealed in the large thick silken webs which they spin.

Camouflage is very common among animals and lepidopterans are certainly no exception. Some of the most remarkable examples occur among the "looper" caterpillars of the geometer family, many of which resemble uncannily the twigs of the plants on which they feed. The ability to remain motionless while anchored only by the hind claspers perfects the twig-like effect of the looper.

Other caterpillars resemble bird droppings, such as the early larval stages (instars) of the swallowtail butterfly *Papilio machaon*, which have a white patch in the middle of an otherwise black body. The same disguise is employed by the early instars of the Alder moth.

Some insects protect themselves from predators by looking alarming. The caterpillar of the Elephant hawkmoth bears "eyespots" on its body. When disturbed, it draws in its head, suddenly exposing the eye spots. There is some evidence that this kind of behavior may startle predators into leaving the insect well alone. Certain caterpillars combine this so-called flash coloration with an unpleasant odor. The larva of the European Puss moth not only assumes a threatening posture, but is also capable of ejecting a strong irritant (formic acid) from glands on its thorax. The battery of defenses is completed by a pair of bright red filaments which can be extruded from the "tails" at the end of the abdomen and waved about. These are believed to deter approaches from parasitic hymenopterans.

Those who have unwittingly handled certain hairy caterpillars will know that they can cause unpleasant skin rashes. Sometimes symptoms can be very severe and acute. Indeed, a clinical term—"erucism"—has been coined for the adverse effects of the lepidopteran caterpillars on humans. The hairs that are responsible for such reactions are called urticating hairs. There are two main kinds: those that have a poison gland at their base and discharge venom into an aggressor, and those that are non-poisonous but barbed and extremely irritating. The urticating hairs of the Yellowtail moth are said to number 2,000,000 on a single, last-stage caterpillar. The Yellowtail moth belongs to the family Lymantriidae (tussock moths), a group noted for its hairy caterpillars. The caterpillar of the Venezuelan emperor moth (*Lonomia achelous*) can inject a powerful anticoagulent which may result in serious haemorrhage.

"Slug" caterpillars (family Limacodidae) often bear tufts of sharp, stinging spines sometimes loaded with toxic compounds. The name "slugs" refers to both their squat, broad shape, and their undulating or gliding motion. Contact with the spines may cause acute pain and swelling. Limacodid caterpillars are generally green, but are often bedecked with bright colors, probably as a warning to potential predators.

There is little value in being toxic or distasteful if you do not advertise the fact. If a predator does not learn to associate particular colors with unpleasantness, the prey, albeit toxic or distasteful, may suffer fatal damage while the predator finds out. Hence many larvae have developed warning colors. The caterpillars of the burnet moths are black and yellow—two of nature's most widespread warning colors. Cyanide compounds have been found in the tissues of these larvae.

Among the butterflies, the predominantly black and yellow caterpillars of the Danainae (to which the migratory monarch belongs) store heart-toxins derived from their food plants (eg milkweed—*Asclepias*) and pass them on to the adult.

The caterpillars of the swallowtail butterflies bear a forked process (known as the osmeterium) on the thorax that releases a pungent odor when everted. It is said that this is used to defend the caterpillars particularly from the attention of parasitic insects.

MJS

▲ ► **Variety of defense policies in caterpillars.** Irritant spines TOP containing toxins are the forte of the Emperor gum moth, *Antheraea eucalypti* (Saturniidae), in Australia, while the caterpillar of the Citrus swallowtail butterfly, *Papilio thoas* (Papilionidae) ABOVE resembles a fresh bird dropping on a leaf. If disturbed, the Puss moth caterpillar, *Cerura vinula* (Notodontidae) RIGHT squirts out a jet of formic acid, and threatens by rearing up both front and end of the body, while the head is retracted. The pair of red filaments extruded at the tail end are believed to deter parasitic wasps.

WASPS, ANTS AND BEES

Order: Hymenoptera
Class: Insecta, subclass Pterygota.
Phylum: Uniramia.
Probably at least 280,000 species (120,000 described) in about 105 families.
Distribution: all continents, except Antarctica.
Features: 0.08–2in (0.17–50mm) long, with chewing mouthparts and four membranous wings coupled by a row of hooks called hamuli, forewings larger than hindwings. Males haploid, ie derived from unfertilized eggs. Wings develop internally (endopterygotous), metamorphosis complete. Larvae caterpillar-like in externally feeding Symphyta, legless maggots in Apocrita.

Sawflies, horntails, wood wasps
Suborder Symphyta
Some 10,000 species in 14 families, worldwide except Antarctica.

Most primitive of living hymenopterans; wing venation complex, generalized; abdomen broadly attached to thorax (no "wasp waist"); ovipositor usually saw-like for inserting eggs in plant tissue. Larvae (except wood borers) have segmented legs on thorax and abdomen and segmented labial and maxillary palps.

Parasitic wasps, wasps, ants, bees
Suborder Apocrita
Some 110,000 species described in about 92 families.

First abdominal segment incorporated into rear of thorax to form propodeum; marked "wasp waist" constriction between propodeum and rest of abdomen. Larvae legless.

Division Parasitica (an estimated 200,000 species in 51 families, probably not a monophyletic grouping) comprises mainly **parasitic wasps** or **parasitoids**, in which the ovipositor retains its egg-laying function, and larvae develop as internal or external parasites of insects and other terrestrial arthropods. Includes **ichneumon flies, gall wasps, fairy flies.**

Division Aculeata (41 families) comprises mainly non-parasites, in which the ovipositor is modified as a sting for defense and for immobilizing prey. Larvae of most species feed on maternally provided food. Includes **ants, hunting wasps, paper-making wasps, bees.**

THE ubiquitous Hymenoptera are highly specialized insects second only to the beetles in numbers of species. Many thousands more species probably remain to be discovered, especially among the parasitic wasps.

The tremendous diversity of the Hymenoptera reflects the order's ecological importance. In the temperate forests of North America ants recycle as many soil nutrients as earthworms. In tropical South America the biomass of ants, together with termites, exceeds that of all other animals put together, including capybaras, tapirs and people! The parasitic wasps can exert tremendous pressure on their insect host populations, and many species are used as biological control agents against pests. As pollinators, the Hymenoptera (especially bees) play a vital and economically important role in maintaining much of the earth's vegetation. Worldwide, about 150 crop species depend largely or entirely on bees for pollination. In North America alone, the value of such crops in 1972 was $11,565m. The annual value of the world's honey crop is about $240m.

The oldest known fossil hymenopterans are sawflies of the superfamily Xyeloidea dating from the Triassic period, 225–195 million years ago. The order with which hymenopterans share the most recent common ancestor are the scorpion flies (Mecoptera), dating from the Permian, 280–225 million years ago, by which time the Hymenoptera must have been established.

Sawflies (suborder Symphyta) owe their name to the saw-like blades of the egg-laying tube (ovipositor) with which the females insert eggs into plant tissues. In the wood wasps, whose larvae feed inside dead or dying wood, the ovipositor is a tough drilling tool which protrudes from the apex of the abdomen, and siricids are therefore often called horntails (the ovipositor sometimes being mistaken for a sting).

In most sawfly species, the short-lived adults are active in spring and early summer. Some species appear not to feed, but most visit flowers for nectar and some eat small insects. Females lay eggs in leaves, stems or wood, though some members of the family Pamphilidae glue their eggs onto the surfaces of leaves, which the larvae of some species roll up and live inside.

The larvae of most sawflies resemble the caterpillars of moths and butterflies. They differ in having only one pair of simple eyes (ocelli) and more than five pairs of abdominal prolegs. Those which feed internally, such as the larvae of wood wasps, have only vestiges of thoracic legs and resemble the grub-like larvae of other hymenopterans. Wood-feeding larvae may take several years to complete development, but the external leaf-eating species take about two weeks. The eggs of some species (eg *Pontania*) induce tumorous growths (galls) in the host leaf and the larvae feed inside these.

One sawfly family, the Orussidae, has abandoned plant feeding. Instead, the larvae are internal parasites of wood-boring beetle larvae. It is also thought that some species feed on the fungal-infected larval feces of boring beetles.

Sawflies often achieve pest status in dense single-species stands (monocultures) of forest trees. The European Pine sawfly is a

▲ **Larvae of an Australian sawfly,** *Perga* species (Pergidae), wave their warning-colored heads in a threat display. If disturbed, they exude from their mouths a foul-smelling, distasteful concentrate of oils sequestered from their foodplants, *Eucalyptus* trees.

◀ **With her drill-like ovipositor** penetrating the bark, a female Giant wood wasp, *Urocerus gigas* (Siricidae), lays an egg in a larch tree. The surface of the egg is coated with fungal spores from a sac at the base of the female's ovipositor. The fungus lives in the galleries excavated by the larva and may eventually kill the tree. The wasp provides the fungus with access to its substrate, wood, from which the fungus liberates nutrients for the larva.

major problem in young plantations, where the larvae may strip the trees of needles completely. The wood wasp *Urocerus gigas* is a pest of spruce, the larvae transmitting a fungus which may eventually kill the tree. However, some sawflies are allies rather than enemies of man. *Uncona acaenae*, for instance, has been introduced into New Zealand from Chile to control a pernicious weed of the rose family, *Acaena*, which was itself an accidental introduction.

The body plan of sawflies has persisted for at least 225 million years. However, by the Jurassic (195–135 million years ago) a major new evolutionary trend had appeared. It is from this period that the first fossils of the "wasp-waisted" suborder

Apocrita are known. Instead of the abdomen being broadly attached at its base to the thorax, the first abdominal segment is incorporated into the thorax to form the propodeum and the latter is separated from the *apparent* first abdominal segment by a highly flexible hinged joint. The flexibility allowed by this development of the wasp waist is a vital part of apocritan life-styles; it allows precise movement in egg-laying female parasitic wasps and permits solitary hunting wasps and bees to turn around in the confined spaces of the nest burrow.

The Apocrita show two other structural advances over the sawflies. The mouthparts are retractible into the mouth cavity and the forelegs are armed with a neat device for grooming the antennae. Moreover, in the larvae the mid- and hindgut are not united until the larval stage, thus delaying defecation until just before pupation. By this means they avoid fouling the food, an adaptation of obvious importance for parasitic larvae living in their food and for bee larvae feeding in their natal cells on a mixture of pollen and nectar.

In the Jurassic period and Cretaceous (135–65 million years ago), the wasp-waisted Apocrita diversified into the Parasitica, a vast assemblage of wasps. In some forms (the Aculeata) the egg-laying function of the ovipositor was lost, to be replaced by evolution of the sting with which hunting wasps paralyze their prey by injecting venom. Also in the Cretaceous, flowering plants began to diversify, providing new sources of food. Some hunting wasps gave up insect prey as food for their larvae in favour of pollen and nectar, evolving a range of structures for handling and transporting the new food. So, flowering plants and bees invented each other.   CO'T

Most **parasitic wasps** are neither parasitic nor predatory. Unlike true parasites, the larval stages invariably kill the host on which they feed, and unlike predators they require only one host ("prey") individual for their complete development. Members of the division Parasitica are therefore more accurately referred to as "parasitoids."

The adult female forages for hosts. Using her ovipositor, she deposits eggs either in or on the host, or nearby. Thereafter, she displays no further involvement with either offspring or host. After hatching, larvae begin feeding, but cause little damage. Toward the end of their development however, they feed extensively on host tissues, causing the host to die. Larvae finally pupate, either within or outside the host's remains.

Endoparasitoids develop within the host, whereas ectoparasitoids develop externally, feeding through a lesion produced by the larvae in the host's cuticle. Ectoparasitoids are associated particularly with hosts that live in concealed situations (eg leaf mines, galls). A distinction is also made between those parasitoids that develop singly in hosts (solitary) and those that develop in groups (gregarious).

Some endoparasitoids complete their development in the host stage originally attacked—that is, they utilize a non-growing host such as the egg or pupa, whereas other endoparasitoids complete their development in a later stage—they utilize a growing host (eg egg-larval, egg-pupal, larval-pupal, larval-adult parasitoids). In contrast, most ectoparasitoids complete their development on the stage originally attacked, because the female parasitoid paralyzes the host when she lays her egg, and also because the larvae grow very rapidly.

Parasitoids tend to be host-species specific. For example, among ichneumon flies which attack western Palaearctic aphids, about half the parasitoid species are restricted to one aphid species, while most of the remainder attack closely related species (belonging to a single genus or subfamily). Many other species of ichneumon fly, along with some chalcid wasps, by contrast attack a diverse array of unrelated hosts, in a distinct microhabitat—they are microhabitat- or "niche"-specific.

Female parasitoids forage for hosts in a two-phase search: first for the host's habitat, and then for the host itself. In both phases, she responds to two sorts of stimuli, "attractant" stimuli which cause her to orient to host-containing areas (patches), and "arrestant" stimuli which bring about a reduction in the distance or area searched within a patch.

Some "attractant" stimuli emanate from the host's food medium. Parasitoids such as the ichneumon flies *Diadromus pulchellus*, which parasitizes the Leek moth (*Acrolepia assectella*), and *Diaeretiella rapae*, which attacks the Cabbage aphid (*Brevicoryne brassicae*), are initially attracted to the hosts habitat by odors from the host's food plant (mustard oils in the case of *Diaeretiella*). Feeding by insects, especially on plants, produces chemical or visual stimuli which attract parasitoids. The chalcid wasp *Heydenia unica* (family Pteromalidae), for example, responds to a volatile terpene released from conifers as a result of feeding by its host, the dark beetle *Dendroctonus*

Agents of Biological Control

The accidental introduction of an insect species into a new geographical region, without its natural enemies, may result in its becoming a serious pest. Many parasitoid wasps are used in biological control programs involving the importation and release of these natural enemies of pest insects in an attempt to reduce pest numbers and crop damage.

Such a program begins with a search for suitable parasitoid species in the pest's native country. The parasitoids are imported and then investigated under quarantine conditions, with particular attention paid to their life cycles, reproductive and searching behavior, so that their mortality effects upon host populations can be predicted. If the introduction of more than one species is contemplated, competitive interactions between them are also studied. Great care is taken not to introduce hyperparasitoids, as they will drastically reduce the effectiveness of the primary parasitoids. Finally, one or several species are chosen and released. They may become established, increase in abundance, and reduce pest numbers.

Biocontrol is used not only to reduce pest numbers, but also keep them at the new reduced level. An example of such an interaction is the control in Barbados of the Sugarcane stem borer (*Diatraea saccharalis*), a moth larva, by two introduced parasitoid species, the braconid wasp *Apanteles flavipes* and the tachinid fly *Lixophaga diatraeae*. Following introduction in 1966–67, the three populations (host and the parasitoid species) fluctuated very little and the percentage of cane plants damaged remaining at around one-third of previous levels.

To date, over 180 species mainly of parasitoid wasp, but also fly and beetle parasitoids, have been successfully established against insect pests.   MAJ

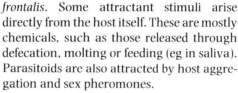

◄ **"Oak apple" galls** induced by the presence of larvae of a gall wasp, *Biorrhiza pallida* (Cynipidae), which feed inside. Males and females emerge from the galls in summer and mate. The females migrate to the roots of the tree and lay eggs. These induce other galls which give rise to wingless females the following spring. The females reproduce asexually and lay eggs in young twigs. Another growth of "oak apples" is produced, and the cycle of alternating generations continues.

▼ **Having fed inside** this moth caterpillar, at least 50 parasitic wasp larvae (Braconidae) have burst out to spin cocoons and pupate.

frontalis. Some attractant stimuli arise directly from the host itself. These are mostly chemicals, such as those released through defecation, molting or feeding (eg in saliva). Parasitoids are also attracted by host aggregation and sex pheromones.

"Arrestant" stimuli are visual, tactile or chemical in nature. Walking parasitoids commonly concentrate their search in response to chemicals deposited by hosts. These "contact chemicals," being of low volatility, cause parasitoids to respond only upon contact. For example, when a female ichneumon fly *Venturia canescens* encounters a deposit of mandibular gland secretion from larvae of the meal moth *Plodia interpunctella*, she stops and begins tapping the tips of her antennae rapidly on the substrate (usually milled and stored grain products). She then moves over the patch at a reduced walking speed, occasionally stopping to probe with her ovipositor. When she contacts the edge of the patch, she turns back sharply into the secretion-contaminated area.

Once a host has been located, the female parasitoid examines it in order to identify it (species and stage of development), performing a series of "tests" usually with her antennae and ovipositor, which bear sense organs of various kinds. *Telenomus heliothidis* (family Scelionidae), for example, recognizes eggs of its host, the moth *Heliothis virescens*, by means of a chemical substance present on their surfaces. The substance is derived from the accessory gland of the female moth's reproductive organs. Host eggs that lack this substance are not attacked by *Telenomus*, whereas glass beads resembling the eggs and coated with accessory gland material stimulate the female parasitoid to drill with her ovipositor.

The final stimuli for the release of eggs are received when the female probes the host with her ovipositor. At this point, egg-laying may depend on whether or not the host is already parasitized. If a solitary parasitoid lays more than one egg, the excess progeny will die as a result of competition. Larvae of many species eliminate rivals with their mandibles. In gregarious species, if more eggs are deposited than the host will support, some or all of the brood will perish, or the larvae will develop into undersized adults. Not surprisingly, superparasitism— egg-laying into an already parasitized host—is usually avoided.

The number of eggs produced per parasitoid female may vary considerably from species to species, even within the same family. Such differences can be viewed as adaptations to the abundance and distribution of hosts. Parasitoids that attack the advanced larval or pupal stages of the host tend to carry fewer eggs than those that attack its early stages. Parasitoids of concealed hosts (eg those found in mines, tunnels, silk webbing) likewise tend to be less fecund than those attacking exposed hosts.

Parasitic wasps belonging to the families Eucharitidae, Perilampidae and Trigonalidae deposit their eggs on foliage, often some distance from the host. In the former two families, the first stage larvae ("planidia") remain near the site where the eggs were laid, and await the arrival of a potential host. Eucharitid planidia attach themselves to foraging worker ants, and are then carried to the ants' nest, where they transfer to the ants' offspring. In the Trigonalidae, the eggs have to be eaten by a caterpillar host before they hatch. In these parasitoids, the chances of first-stage larvae becoming established in hosts are very low. Females therefore tend to lay very large numbers of eggs during their lifetime. Total egg production in the Eucharitidae for example, ranges from 1,000 per female in some species to 15,000 in others. One female was observed to lay 10,000 eggs in six hours!

Some female parasitic wasps emerge from the pupa with their full complement of eggs, while other species are able to produce new eggs during their adult life, provided that they can obtain suitable food such as host body fluids or even honeydew and nectar. Some parasitoids of hosts concealed in, for example, plant tissues, cocoons or puparia, unable to reach the host directly with their mouthparts, construct a special feeding tube. *Pteromalus semotus* (family Pteromalidae) stings its host, the larva of the grain moth *Sitotroga cerealella*, then withdraws its ovipositor until only the tip protrudes within the cavity surrounding the larva in the grain. A clear, viscous fluid oozes from the ovipositor and is molded, before hardening, into a tube by movements of the ovipositor. When the tube linking the puncture in the cuticle to the exterior is complete, the ovipositor is reinserted into the original puncture and then carefully withdrawn. The female then applies her mouthparts and imbibes the fluids, which pass up the tube by capillary action. Many parasitoids, in the absence of hosts and suitable food, are able to resorb eggs. Energy and materials contained in the eggs can then be used for adult maintenance.

Parasitic wasps usually inject glandular secretions (venoms) into their hosts during or before oviposition. Often, these venoms, particularly those produced by ectoparasitoids, paralyze the host, enabling the female to lay eggs and feed unhindered. The venoms of many endoparasitoids by contrast, do not cause paralysis, but they may nevertheless have major effects on host physiology. Endoparasitoids of growing hosts commonly cause alterations in their host's condition—in food consumption rate, growth rate, development, reproduction (parasitic castration for example), morphology, behavior, respiration and other physiological processes. Symbiotic virus-like particles are present in the calyx and calyx fluid of various parasitoids (the calyx is the region between the ovary and oviduct). When injected, along with an egg, they invade certain host tissues, and then apparently suppress the host's immune response to parasitoid eggs and larvae, diverting energy and materials. Parasitoid wasps therefore resemble platyhelminth and other true parasites, in manipulating their hosts.

Each host species can support a number of parasitoid species that together form a structured community. The parasitic wasps are often organized into groups of species that utilize the host in similar ways, eg egg parasitoids, larval parasitoids, pupal parasitoids. The community can also include several trophic levels: parasitoids that attack the non-parasitoid host (primary parasitoids) and secondary and tertiary parasitoids (or hyperparasitoids) which are parasitoids of parasitoids. Many hyperparasitoids, including nearly all tertiary species, are able to develop either hyperparasitically or in the primary role. These facultative hyperparasitoids are largely responsible for the extremely complex structure of food webs found within many galls and leaf mines.

The division Parasitica contains many non-parasitoid species, the vast majority of which have secondarily reverted to a plant diet. Many Gasteruptiidae, together with a few ichneumon flies (eg *Grotea, Macrogrotea* species) kleptoparasitize solitary bees. The first-stage larva devours the host egg or young larva, and then develops on the food store in the host's nest cell. Larvae may also move to either one or a succession of cells within the nest, consuming the contents.

Large numbers of plant feeders occur within the families Eurytomidae and Torymidae. Some develop in seeds, while others produce galls. Some members of the Pteromalidae and most, if not all, Tanaostigmatidae produce galls. The best known gall causers however, are members of the family Cynipidae. In Britain, at least 31 species of cynipid gall causer are associated with oaks alone. Most of them have an alternation of sexual and parthenogenetic generations during a year, and the galls produced by the two generations of each species differ markedly both in structure and in their position on the oak tree. Associated with these species are about half as many species of "inquiline" Cynipidae, which do not form their own galls, but develop in the galls of other species, eventually taking them over (most of them destroy the gall maker). Another group of plant-feeding Parasitica is the family Agaonidae, members of which are involved in symbiotic relationships with fig plants, which they pollinate. Larval agaonids develop within the ovules of the fig fruit, inducing gall formation.   MAJ

Wasps, ants and bees are all members of the wasp-waisted suborder Apocrita. They comprise the division Aculeata, in which the ovipositor is modified as a sting, having lost its egg-laying function. They range from obscure parasitoids to the more familiar nest-building solitary and social groups of which most are hunters. The bees are vegetarians and are the indispensable pollinators of flowers.

▲ **A female ichneumon wasp,** *Rhysella approximator*, lays an egg on the concealed larva of an Alder wood wasp, *Xiphydria camelus* (Siricide), flanked by two waiting females of *Pseudorhyssa alpestris* (Ichneumonidae). One will lay an egg via the hole drilled by the *Rhysella*; her larva will eat those of the *Rhysella* and the wood wasp.

◄ **Midgets of the insect world,** these female parasitic wasps, *Trichogramma semblidis*, are no more than 0.02in (0.5mm) long. They are laying eggs inside the eggs of an alderfly; each wasp larva will complete its development inside the host's egg. Males which develop in alderfly eggs are wingless, with the last four antennal segments distinct; males parasitic in moth eggs are fully winged and the last four antennal segments are fused. *Trichogramma semblidis* may cause up to 90 percent mortality among moth eggs, and as early as 1912, this wasp was used as a biological control agent against Codling moth, a pest of apples. Some adults of the family Trichogrammatidae are just 0.007in (0.17mm) long; fairy flies of the Mymaridae, though slightly longer, are more slender, so probably the smallest of all insects.

The **ants** (Formicidae) are just one of over 40 families in the division Aculeata. All ants are social, forming perennial societies which parallel those of the honeybees, but have workers that are wingless.

Ant queens shed their wings after a single mating flight. Males also fly and mating takes place on the wing or on special surfaces such as bare soil patches where members of the same species gather. The mated queens may then attempt to rear workers and hence start a new nest, or adopt another strategy (see below).

Ants commonly indicate the position of food sources by scent trails, laid by satiated ants using visual orientation to return to the nest. Scent trails are readily observed in species such as the Jet black ant of temperate Eurasia. *Leptothorax* species and others avoid attracting more aggressive ants by not emitting odors. An ant returning to a large food source is followed closely by a second nest mate. Further doubling can be surprisingly rapid.

The food is regurgitated and passed to other ants or fed to larvae back in the nest. Mutual antennal tapping precedes food transfer (trophallaxis) between two adults. The begging ant may also stroke the cheeks of the donor ant in Wood ants and other *Formica* species. Rather more violent antennal strokes may be used to alert others to potential danger, but the main alerting signal in most species is a chemical secretion which may contain several components of different volatility to provide progressively stronger stimulus nearer to the site of disturbance, as in the Old World tropical weaver ants (*Oecophylla* species). Larger quantities of chemicals may be sprayed out as a defense against predation. The formic acid produced by Wood ants can easily be seen and smelt by humans—or felt painfully in the eyes.

The chemical messengers (pheromones) usually differ between species, although in closely related species the difference is often only in the proportions of constituents. An ant will therefore generally recognize a member of a different ant species; furthermore an ant of the same species from a separate nest is usually recognized as a stranger and attacked. However, some ant societies have "slaves" from other species, for example the Slave-maker ant of Europe normally has *F. fusca* workers as auxiliaries. These slaves hatch from pupae robbed from their parent nest and they behave and are treated as normal members of their adopted nest.

Ant societies have been looked upon as "superorganisms." Component parts (ie individuals, as opposed to a head or limb of an individual) may be lost without disabling the superorganism. The apparent altruism of ant and other hymenopteran workers has attracted much attention (see below). Many activities can take place simultaneously in societies, while ordinary individuals cannot usually do two things at once if they involve elaborate behavior. Some ant species have one or more special subcastes, for example, workers with very large heads for seed crushing (eg *Pheidole* species) and special soldiers or nest-entrance blockers (eg *Colobopsis* species) have been evolved in others.

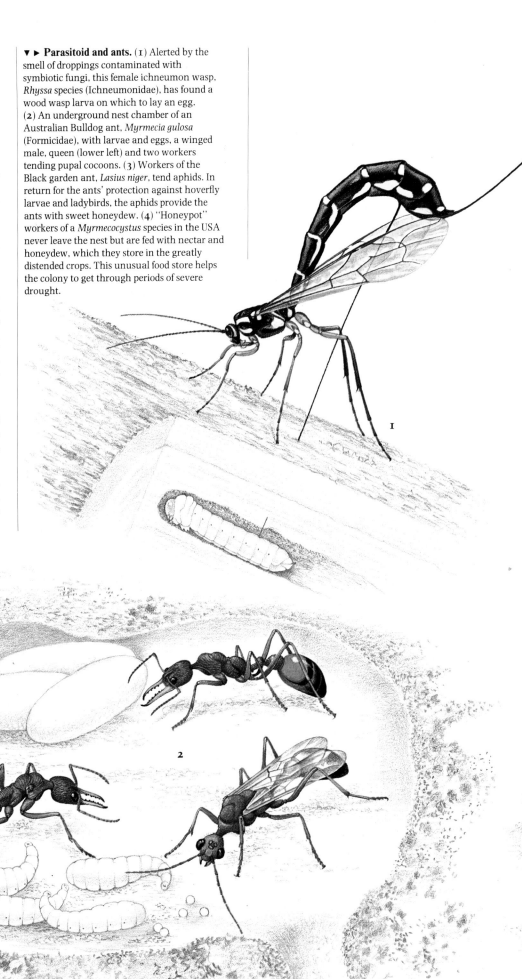

▼ ▶ **Parasitoid and ants.** (1) Alerted by the smell of droppings contaminated with symbiotic fungi, this female ichneumon wasp, *Rhyssa* species (Ichneumonidae), has found a wood wasp larva on which to lay an egg. (2) An underground nest chamber of an Australian Bulldog ant, *Myrmecia gulosa* (Formicidae), with larvae and eggs, a winged male, queen (lower left) and two workers tending pupal cocoons. (3) Workers of the Black garden ant, *Lasius niger*, tend aphids. In return for the ants' protection against hoverfly larvae and ladybirds, the aphids provide the ants with sweet honeydew. (4) "Honeypot" workers of a *Myrmecocystus* species in the USA never leave the nest but are fed with nectar and honeydew, which they store in the greatly distended crops. This unusual food store helps the colony to get through periods of severe drought.

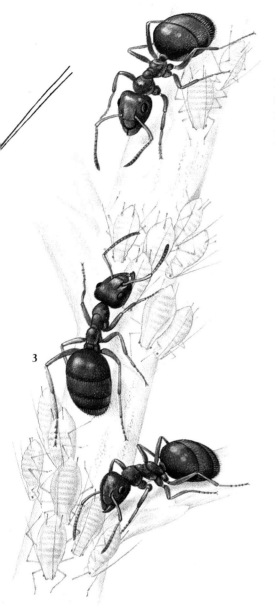

3

However, most species retain the more flexible system whereby workers can transfer from one task to another according to demand. Weaver ants are unique in that their silk-emitting mature larvae are employed by workers as "shuttles," enabling them to weave leaves together in making nests in trees.

Ant societies are very successful, if success is measured by ecological dominance. The tropical driver or army ants made famous by writers of fiction are certainly spectacular examples (eg *Eciton* in South America, *Anomma* in Africa). With up to several million per society, driver ants need to move on to new areas as they use up the prey in a locality in a few days. Most animals (notably other ants) must either move out of their way or be eaten. Ants which reach high numbers but remain in static nests must adopt more advanced ecological strategies. Continuous food supplies which are not so easily overexploited by the ants include the sweet feces (honeydew) of sap-sucking insects such as aphids. The tropical American parasol or leafcutter ants and their relatives carry into their nests pieces of leaf on which they cultivate a fungus (the species is different for different ant species) which is the ants' main food, and found only in nests of the ant genus *Atta*. Seed eating enables some harvester ants to survive semi-desert conditions by storing dormant seeds in their nests for use during long periods of drought. The "honeypot" ants use the abdomen of immobile workers as storage vessels for liquid honeydew or nectar.

Ants' saturation of tropical and temperate habitats has resulted in many interactions between different species of ants, and in highly evolved associations with other organisms. One example of ant interaction is temporary social parasitism as an alternative strategy of nest founding. Pioneer species (eg *Lasius flavus, L. niger*) invading disturbed land have normal queen-founded nests, but saturation of an area by these species makes further entry of queens impracticable because they are eaten. Species such as *L. umbratus* and *L. mixtus* which follow the pioneers therefore produce larger numbers of smaller queens which do not found colonies alone, but seek adoption in nests of the pioneer species. A third stage in this sequence is provided by the Jet black ant, a woodland species that is in turn adopted by *L. umbratus*. Most of the invading queens are killed, but some are successful, perhaps in queenless host nests, and nests with a mixture of workers result. Slave makers maintain this mixture by raiding, but *Lasius* nests soon consist purely of the take-over species.

In ant/plant interactions the plants may gain either protection from defoliators (eg moth larvae in the case of *Cecropia* species in tropical America) or nutrients from the ants' rubbish dump (some epiphytes) and the ants may be positively catered for by the plants. For example *Cecropia* trees produce special Müllerian bodies which are eaten by ants (*Azteca* species) for their glycogen, protein and lipid content and have no other apparent function. The evolutionary arms race has been taken a stage further by some lepidopteran larvae which have evolved defenses against the ants. Plants exploit ants in other ways, notably for seed dispersal. Many non-seed-eating ants carry certain plant seeds (eg *Viola* species) which have edible outgrowths (elaiosomes), but very hard smooth coats; the seeds are discarded eventually on the ants' rubbish dumps, which may provide a fertile growing medium. AJP

4

Most **true wasps** or **aculeate wasps** are solitary hunters, but some are social and some (the bees) vegetarian, while the parasitoid aculeates have a life-style similar to that of the division Parasitica.

None of the aculeate parasitoid wasps builds a nest. Instead, the female lays one or more eggs in or on the host. Although,

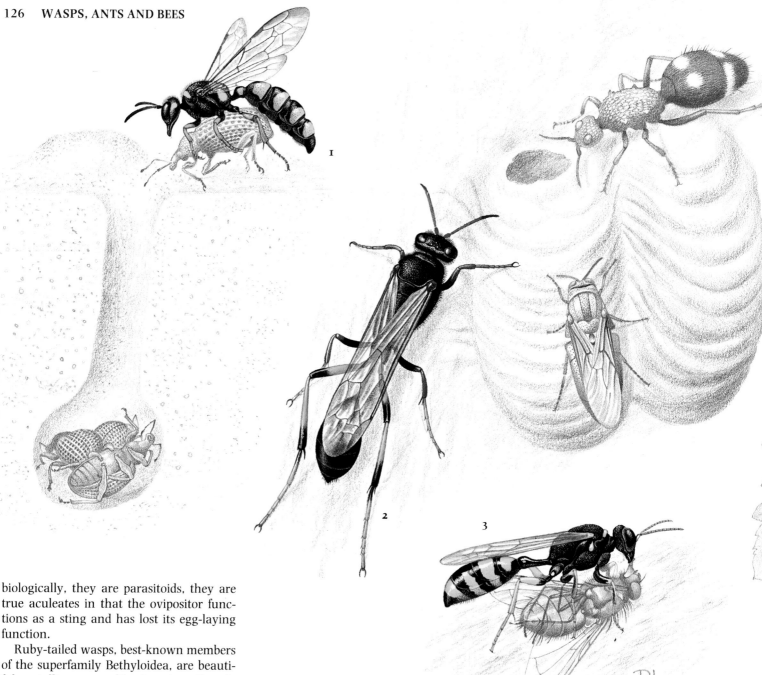

biologically, they are parasitoids, they are true aculeates in that the ovipositor functions as a sting and has lost its egg-laying function.

Ruby-tailed wasps, best-known members of the superfamily Bethyloidea, are beautiful, metallic green or blue insects, with only three visible abdominal segments. Females have neither sting nor ovipositor; they lay eggs via a retractable tube formed by the fused segments of the tip of the abdomen. Ruby-tailed wasps parasitize other wasps and bees. Some are true parasitoids and their larvae feed on the fully grown host larva; others are cuckoos (kleptoparasites) and eat the host egg or larva and then feed on the stored food.

The principal parasitoid families in the superfamily Vespoidea are the Scoliidae, Tiphiidae and Mutillidae. All scoliids and most tiphiids develop as external parasitoids of subterranean larvae of chafer beetles (family Scarabaeidae). The tiphiid genus *Methocha* parasitizes the larvae of tiger beetles (*Cicindela* species) in their burrows; females are wingless and resemble ants. Wingless females are characteristic of an entire tiphiid subfamily, the Thynninae, found in Australia and South America. The

Australian *Diamma bicolor* parasitizes mole crickets, but most thynnines are assumed to attack scarabaeid larvae. Courtship and mating in thynnines involves the females being carried in flight by the males, attached by the genitalia (phoretic copulation). The male feeds the female ritually with nectar.

The females of the so-called velvet ants (Mutillidae) are also wingless. They run about on the ground, in leaf litter or on tree trunks, with an agitated, ant-like gait. Mutillids always parasitize the prepupae or pupae of other insects. Most attack other wasps and bees and are fairly host-specific. Two African species, *Chrestomutilla glossinae* and *Smicromyrme benefactrix*, parasitize the puparia of tsetse flies. They are currently under investigation as potential control agents against these vectors of sleeping sickness. Female velvet ants have an extremely

▲ **Hunting wasps and a solitary bee.**
(1) A weevil-hunting wasp, *Cerceris arenaria* (Philanthidae), at her nest. (2) This female African mud-dauber, *Sceliphron spirifex* (Sphecidae), left, is watched at her nest by two enemies, the wingless female of a "velvet ant," *Dolichomutilla guineensis* (Mutillidae), above, and a female ruby-tailed wasp, *Stilbum cyanurum* (Chrysididae), below. (3) A fly-hunting wasp, *Mellinus arvensis* (Mellinidae). (4) American thread-waisted wasp, *Ammophila alberti* (Sphecidae) returning with prey to her nest. (5) Another digger wasp, *Astata boops* (Astatidae), stings her prey, a shieldbug nymph. (6) A solitary mining bee, *Colletes succinctus* (Colletidae), and her cluster of cells, each with an egg attached to the cell wall. On hatching, the larvae will drop into the liquid mixture of honey and pollen below.

▶ **A queen paper wasp,** *Polistes dorsalis* OVERLEAF, at her newly built nest, Mexico. The short stalk bearing a single horizontal comb has a shiny black ant-repellant coating (Vespidae).

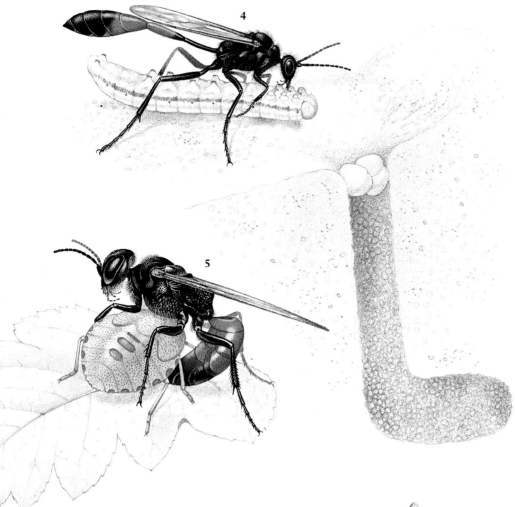

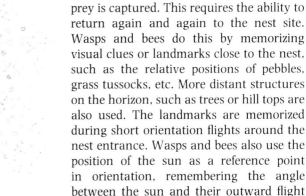

into which she drags her paralyzed victim before laying an egg on it. This is the situation in many spider-hunting wasps and in the primitive sphecoid family Ampulicidae.

In the more advanced spider-hunting wasps, solitary vespoids and remaining sphecoid families, the nest is built before any prey is captured. This requires the ability to return again and again to the nest site. Wasps and bees do this by memorizing visual clues or landmarks close to the nest, such as the relative positions of pebbles, grass tussocks, etc. More distant structures on the horizon, such as trees or hill tops are also used. The landmarks are memorized during short orientation flights around the nest entrance. Wasps and bees also use the position of the sun as a reference point in orientation, remembering the angle between the sun and their outward flight path. An internal clock enables them to adjust for the ever-changing position of the sun.

According to species, the nest may be excavated in the ground or dead wood, or the wasp may use existing cavities such as hollow stems or beetle borings in dead wood. Mason and other wasps collect mud and build exposed nests on rocks of the underside of leaves. Whatever the architectural details, the nest comprises one or more cells and a single larva develops in each. The female provides each cell with several prey insects (mass provisioning), sufficient for the complete development of the larvae. She usually dies before her offspring emerge.

The best known hunting wasps are the nine families in the superfamily Sphecoidea. They comprise just over 7,600 species and hunt a wide variety of insect prey. A few isolated species collect spiders. Some advanced species of *Bembix* (family Nyssonidae), such as *B. texana* in North America, practice progressive feeding of their developing larvae. They provide the fly prey as and when the growing larva needs it, rather than through mass provisioning. Females of the American caterpillar-hunting wasp *Ammophila azteca* not only practice progressive feeding, but also maintain several nests simultaneously, in varying degrees of development.

The families of sphecoid wasps were probably established by the early Cretaceous period (ie soon after 135 million years ago). Other groups of insects diversified at this time and provided new sources of prey. The prey of modern sphecoids reflects this: primitive wasps tend to hunt primitive prey, while the more advanced hunting sphecoids hunt more highly evolved insects.

painful sting and, not surprisingly, are warningly colored. Males are fully winged and usually larger than the female. Some species indulge in phoretic copulation like the thynnines. In others, the males carry females in flight clasped in their mandibles, braced against a modified area of the head. Wingless females have evolved many times independently in the order Hymenoptera (eg worker ants) and are presumed to be adapted for host or prey searching underground or in confined spaces, where wings would be a hindrance.

The evolution of nest-building behavior was a major evolutionary advance in the aculeate wasps. In the superfamily Vespoidea, it is found in varying degrees in the spider-hunting wasps and reached its most complex developments in the social species of the family Vespidae. Nest building is also well developed in the superfamily Sphecoidea.

In its simplest form, a nest is a space prepared by the female wasp or bee in which she stores food for her offspring and which provides physical protection for the developing larva. Primitively, the female wasp finds and stings a single insect prey and only then excavates a simple nest in the ground

The complexity of social wasp society ranges from loose associations of egg-laying females which cooperate only in nest contruction, to the highly social paper wasps or yellow jackets with their well-defined worker caste of sterile females.

Most species of social wasps are in the family Vespidae but the superfamily Sphecoidea includes (as well as the bees) hunting wasps which have a simple social organization. In the Central American species *Trigonopsis cameronii* (Sphecidae), up to four females cooperate in constructing the mud nest, but each provisions its own cells with cockroach prey. This is known as a communal level of social organization. There is very little aggression between nest mates and prey stealing is rare. The nest mates are likely to be closely related. Two obvious advantages of such communal societies are that the labor of nest building is shared and nest defense is improved, because the nest is rarely left unattended.

A more complex form of social behavior is found in another Central American sphecoid wasp, *Microstigmus comes* (family Pemphredonidae). Up to 11 females share a single, thimble-sized nest. They cooperate in building the nest and in provisioning the cells with springtails. Only one cell is mass-provisioned at a time. Although the females are morphologically identical there is a reproductive division of labor: only one female has developed ovaries and lays eggs; the others function as worker caste. Moreover, it is believed that more than one generation is present in the nest. The society of *M. comes*, while small in numbers, is an example of the most developed level of sociality in hymenopterans, eusociality, which is typical for example of paper wasps and honey bees.

Many vespid wasps (and also bees) are of an intermediate level of social development. Three of the six currently recognized subfamilies of the Vespidae (Stenogastrinae, Polistinae and Vespinae) consist entirely of social species. All provision their nests with chewed insect prey rather than whole insects. As in all vespids, the egg is laid in the cell before any food is provided. The Stenogastrinae are communal, except for one unnamed species of *Parischnogaster* which appears to be semisocial. The nests of polistine and vespine wasps are made of tough paper comprising wood fibers mixed with saliva.

Polistine colonies may be founded by either one female (haplometrosis) or several females (pleometrosis). Although there is no morphological distinction between females,

one always emerges at the apex of a dominance hierarchy. She is the sole or major egg layer, or queen, and seldom leaves the nest. The ovaries of subordinate females more or less atrophy and these insects function as workers, foraging for food and feeding the queen and larvae. In species of the African genus *Belonogaster*, in some *Ropalidia* and many *Polistes*, the female which manages to eat most eggs laid by nest mates eventually assumes dominance. In other species of *Polistes*, dominance is asserted by outright aggression.

The exchange of food between adults and larvae is characteristic of polistine and vespine wasps. Larvae solicit food from workers by exuding from the mouthparts a droplet of liquid which contains carbohydrates and possibly enzymes the adults cannot make themselves. Workers and queens consume this liquid; it seems that the latter require it for continued egg production.

Species of the South American polistine genus *Polybia* have the beginnings of a morphological caste distinction. There may be one to many queens in a colony and colonies may have up to 10,000 workers. As well as having developed ovaries, *Polybia* queens are usually larger than the workers, although this distinction is not always clear cut. With such large colonies, it is obvious that the queen(s) cannot assert dominance by mere aggression or differential egg eating. Instead, they and vespine wasps secrete a "queen pheromone," a scent which inhibits development of the ovaries of the workers.

Polybia is also more advanced than *Polistes* in its nest architecture. A mature nest comprises several horizontal combs, connected by vertical pillars and enclosed in a durable paper envelope. The colony is perrenial, and may persist for up to 25 years. A colony is formed through swarming: one or more queens and several hundred workers leave the old nest and establish a new one.

The subfamily Vespinae is characterized by a clear-cut size distinction between the larger queen and smaller workers. Colonies are always established by a single queen, which behaves as a solitary and then as a subsocial wasp, until the first generation of workers emerges. Nests are either suspended under branches or made in cavities in the ground. Although vespines are often a nuisance and frequently are pests of bee hives, on balance they are beneficial insects, as they kill a wide range of pest species for their larval food.   CO'T

Bees are sphecoid hunting wasps which have become vegetarians; they collect pol- and nectar from flowers. This change in diet probably took place in the middle of the Cretaceous period (135–65 million years ago), soon after flowering plants appeared. The earliest known fossil bees, from late in the Eocene epoch (54–38 million years ago), already include members of specialized, long-tongued families such as the honeybees and stingless bees. Today, many bees specialize in one plant species, or a group of related species, as a source of pol- len. Examples are *Macropis* species which visit only *Lysimachia* flowers and the economically important *Peponapis* which pollinate melons. These bees, termed oli- golectic, are most abundant in dry warm regions, where they may account for over 60 percent of bee species. In such areas, where the climate induces the simultaneous flowering of many flower species, oligolecty

reduces competition between bees and prob- ably results in more successful pollination.

The vast majority of bees have a solitary life-style. They are most abundant and diverse in regions such as deserts of south- western North America and in the Medi- terranean basin. From their sphecoid ancestors, bees inherited the nesting habit, including the ability to find their way back to the nest. Superimposed on this inheritance are structures such as longer tongues, branched body hairs and scopae ("brushes") adapted to deal with the collec- tion and transport of nectar and pollen; some specialists (eg *Macropis* species and some *Centris*) are adapted for collecting plant oils.

There are two main types of nest-building behavior in bees. The females of short- tongued mining bees line their underground brood cells with the secretions of the abdominal Dufour's gland. The resultant waterproof, fungus-resistant lining is important in maintaining the right level of humidity inside the cell and prevents the cell and its contents from being inundated if the soil becomes waterlogged. In only a few spe- cies with cell linings of this type does the larva spin a cocoon before pupation.

The second type of nesting behavior is found mainly in one family, the Megachilidae, whose members use collected materials rather than glandular secretions in nest construction. Moreover, most species use existing cavities—old insect borings in dead wood, hollow twigs, snail shells and often the crumbling mortar of old walls— rather than dig nests in the soil. Some species also build exposed nests on rocks or shrubby plants. According to species, the building materials include mud, resin, a mastic of chewed leaves, petals, pieces of leaf and plant and animal hairs, or a combina- tion of these substances. Those which use soft, malleable substances are often called mason bees. Megachilid larvae spin a tough, silken cocoon.

Because megachilids nest in almost any suitable cavity, especially in wood and stems, many species have been accidentally dispersed from their normal range by human commerce. Thus, a mason bee, *Chalicodoma lanata*, common in the southeastern United States and islands of the Caribbean, originated in Africa and is thought to have been brought to the New World by the slave trade. The leafcutter bee *Megachile rotundata* is another accidental introduction. A native of Eurasia, it first appeared in the United States in the 1930s and is now managed by American farmers

▶ **A female cuckoo bumblebee,** *Psithyrus vestalis* (Apidae), on wild thyme. Female cuckoo bees have no pollen-collecting apparatus and there is no worker caste. As the name implies, cuckoos lay eggs in the nests of bumblebees, and their offspring are reared by the host's workers).

▶ **Worker stingless bees** BELOW, *Trigona* species (Apidae) gather honeydew secreted by plant bugs in a forest in Peru.

The Language of Dance

Worker honeybees communicate information about food sources to their nest mates by "dancing." The dance is performed within the darkness of the hive, on the vertical surfaces of the wax honeycomb. The dancer is always attended by several "followers," which inspect her closely with their antennae.

Foragers returning from a food source within 80ft (25m) of the hive perform a "round dance" (1) of circular runs with more or less frequent changes in direction. The greater the frequency of direction changes, the greater the calorific value of the nectar at the food source being indicated.

To indicate a food source distance of between 80 and 380ft (25–100m), a bee performs a figure intermediate between the round dance and the "waggle dance." The latter, used for longer distances, is a contracted figure-of-eight (2) in which the bee waggles her abdomen from side to side during the straight run between the two semicircles at the ends of the figure. Distance is indicated by the duration of the straight run and the frequency of waggles which accompany it. Direction is indicated by the angle from the vertical of the straight run, which corresponds to the angle between the direction of the food source and the sun, as viewed from the hive entrance. Waggling, and the high-frequency buzzes which accompany it at about 250 cycles per second, may together impart information on food quality.

The bees recruited by a dance perceive all this information by touching the dancer with their antennae and by their sensitivity to air- borne vibrations (sound). The specific scents of flowers on the body of the dancer may also be important. Thus, the dance language is a "multi-channel" system of communication.

CO'T

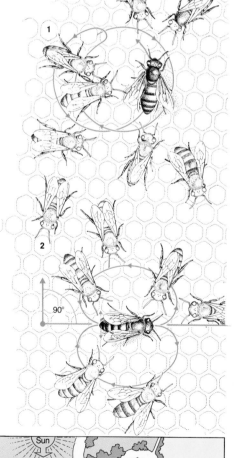

as the major pollinator of alfalfa or lucerne.

Like the vespine wasps, bees show all the grades of sociality. The Halictidae are of particular interest because a single genus, *Lasioglossum*, contains communal, subsocial, primitively eusocial and eusocial species, as well as many which are solitary.

Bumblebees (*Bombus* species) are the most familiar social bees in temperate regions. There are a little over 200 species only a few of which have penetrated the tropics. Each colony is founded in spring by a lone queen which was mated the previous season and which spent the winter in hibernation. Bumblebees are at the primitively eusocial level of organization. There is no clear-cut morphological difference between queen and worker. Indeed, in some species there is little or no difference in size, and the queen apparently asserts her dominance by aggression.

The advanced eusocial bees in the family Apidae comprise the pantropical stingless bees, *Melipona* and *Trigona*, and the four species of honeybees. They differ from the bumblebees in that their large colonies are perennial, there are clear-cut morphological differences between castes, and workers can communicate the direction of food and other resources and recruit additional bees from the hive to exploit them.

Stingless bees usually nest in hollow trees or in cavities in the ground. A few species nest in termite mounds. A large colony of *Trigona* may contain 180,000 bees, including one to several queens. Brood cells and food storage pots are kept separate and are made of wax, secreted by the bees, mixed with resin and/or animal feces. Stingless bees practice mass provisioning of brood cells. Foragers communicate the source of food by laying a scent trail between it and the nest. Although they do not sting, meliponines are not helpless. They attack vertebrate nest intruders by biting the skin and some species also secrete a corrosive fluid via the mandibular glands. In all the stingless bee genera except *Melipona*, queens are derived from larvae reared in larger than usual cells, provisioned with extra food. By contrast, in *Melipona* species "queenness" is determined by genetic factors.

In the honeybees (*Apis* species), larvae destined to be queens are reared entirely on royal jelly (or "bee milk"). This is a mixture of sugars, proteins, vitamins, RNA and DNA and the fatty acid *trans*-10-hydroxy-decenoic acid and is secreted by the mandibular and hypopharyngeal glands of young workers. Larvae destined to be workers are deprived of royal jelly after about three days, then feed on pollen and honey.

Worker honeybees use secreted wax to build double-sided vertical combs of hexagonal cells. Pollen and honey are stored in cells the same size as those used to rear worker larvae. Males (drones) are reared in larger cells and queens develop in large cells suspended from the comb. Honeybees also use resin, but unlike stingless bees do not mix it with wax. Instead, they use the resin only to stop up gaps or to reduce the size of the nest or hive entrance. Like the stingless bees, however, the honeybees collect resin from plant sources and transport it back to the nest in the pollen basket (corbiculum) on the tibia of the rear leg.

A healthy colony of the Western honeybee will contain some 40,000–80,000 workers, 200 drones and one queen. The queen may lay up to 1,500 eggs a day and exerts physiological dominance over the workers by means of a pheromone called queen substance (as do vespine and some polistine wasps). This is *trans*-9-keto-2-decenoic acid; it is produced in the mandibular glands, and not only does it inhibit the development of the workers' ovaries but it also suppresses the building of special queen cells for potential rivals. The queen may live from one to five years. Either when her powers wane or when the number of workers is very large, there is proportionally less queen substance to go round and the workers begin to build queen cells. A swarm may then ensue and the old queen leaves the colony to be taken over by the first of the young queens to emerge. The latter usually kills any subsequent queens which emerge.

The activities of worker honeybees are age-related. Their first three days are spent as cleaners. Then, from days 3 to 10, a worker is a nurse; her mandibular and hypopharyngeal glands become active and she feeds the larvae. At about day 10, these glands atrophy and the abdominal wax glands become active: now she is a builder. From about day 16 to day 20, she receives pollen and nectar loads from returning foragers and places them in the comb. At about day 20, she acts as a guard at the nest entrance and thereafter, for the rest of her six weeks or so of life, she is a field bee, foraging at flowers.

The allocation of duties is not inflexible, however. If the age structure of a colony is disrupted, whether experimentally or by a large predator, duties are reallocated among the survivors according to the colony's needs.

Colony defense is the hallmark of eusociality and in *Apis* is triggered by an alarm pheromone, secreted from glands at the base of the sting apparatus. This recruits additional workers to a point of danger. The barbed sting and the venom gland are left behind as the bee struggles to free itself. The bee soon dies, in apparently "altruistic" self sacrifice, but the venom sac continues to pulsate and inject venom.

Concerted defense strategies of this kind evolve where a bee (or ant or wasp) colony has valuable resources to protect. In the case of honeybee species, the large numbers of larvae and the stored pollen and nectar attract predators. It is the honey, an energy-rich mixture of plant sugars (nectar) modified by the bees, that attracts man. Honeybees, the Western honeybee particularly, have been managed in hives for at least 3,000 years.   CO'T

▼ **Swarm cluster of the honeybee,** *Apis mellifera* (Apidae). Swarming is the method of colony multiplication in honeybees and stingless bees. In honeybees, the old queen leaves the colony with a large number of workers. The swarm settles in a cluster around the queen while scout bees seek out a new nest site. When one is found, the scouts communicate the direction and distance of the new site by "dancing" on the swarm cluster. In stingless bees, swarming is not so abrupt. Workers from the parent colony find a new nest site and construct the nest entrance characteristic of the species. They then build the rest of the nest, except for brood cells. The food pots may even be provisioned with pollen and honey. Only then do one to several young queens leave the parent colony. These together with the workers, form the swarm proper and take up residence in the new nest.

"Altruism"—A Paradox Resolved?

The existence of social insects was felt by Charles Darwin seriously to challenge his theory of natural selection. How could selection have favored "altruistic" traits in a worker caste (such as caring for the young of others) if the workers did not reproduce and pass on these traits? Darwin covered this dilemma with an "escape clause": social insects were a special case, selection acting on the colony as a whole rather than on individuals.

Highly social behavior has evolved independently at least 11 times in the Hymenoptera but only once in all the rest of the insects (in the termites). The "selfless" behavior of worker hymenopterans is not really altruism but has a lot to do with an unusual method of sex determination. In most insects and other animals, males and females are derived from fertilized eggs. They have two sets of genes, one from each parent; they are said to be diploid. Sons and daughters share, on average, one half of their genes with each other and with either parent. In the Hymenoptera, however, while all females are diploid, the males arise from *un*fertilized eggs and have only *one* set of genes; they are haploid. (Males therefore have a single, maternal, grandfather, but no father.)

Because a male hymenopteran is haploid, all his sperm are genetically identical. Assuming that a female mates only once (not always the case in highly social species), then all her female offspring will receive an identical set of genes from their haploid father. However, since their mother is diploid her daughters have in common only one half of the maternal genes. Adding up the genes received from father and mother, it is clear that hymenopteran sisters share, on average, 75 percent of their genes by common descent (50 percent from the father and 25 percent from the mother). They share only 50 percent of their genes with their mother or, if they have any, daughters.

In terms of the numbers of genes identical with her own which pass into the next generation, it pays a female hymenopteran not to have daughters, but to help her mother rear sisters, some of which will become queens and reproduce. The pay-off is the extra 25 percent of genes identical with her own which are pepetuated in this way. This "kin selection" theory offers the most elegant explanation to date for the evolution of insect sociality; it also solves Darwin's dilemma.

CO'T

The Key Families of the Order Hymenoptera

Sawflies
Suborder Symphyta
Sawflies, wood wasps, horntails. About 10,000 species in 14 families, including: Pamphilidae, **web-spinning sawflies** with larval stage solitary or gregarious in silk web or rolled up in leaf held by silk; Pergidae, S America and (mainly, with at least 136 species) Australia, some eucalyptus feeders (eg *Perga, Pergagrapta* species) which may be serious defoliators; Argidae, cosmopolitan, over 800 species; Tenthredinidae, most commonly seen **sawflies** of N temperate regions, over 5,000 species, some (eg *Pontania*) induce galls; Siricidae, about 85 species of **wood wasps** or **horntails**, worldwide except S America, larvae wood borers in conifers, eg *Urocerus gigas* in spruce; Diprionidae, eg **European pine sawfly** (*Neodiprion sertifer*); Orussidae, 66 species of **parasitic sawflies**, cosmopolitan, larvae parasitic on larvae of wood-boring beetles and wood wasps; Cephidae, 100 species of **stem sawflies** whose larvae bore into grass stems, eg *Cephus pygmaeus* in wheat.

Parasitic wasps
Suborder Apocrita, division Parasitica
Parasitic wasps, parasitoids.
An estimated 200,000 species (many still to be described) in 51 families, including:

Trigonalyoidea
Family Trigonalidae, parasitic on caterpillars.

Ichneumonoidea
Includes **bracon flies** (Braconidae, probably 40,000 species); Aphidiidae, parasitic on aphids; **ichneumon flies** (Ichneumonidae, probably 60,000 species).

Evanioidea
Includes Gasteruptiidae, with many species kleptoparasites of solitary bee eggs and larvae.

Chalcidoidea
Possibly 80,000–100,000 species, including **fig wasps** (Agaonidae), gall makers in figs; Pteromalidae; Eurytomidae, larvae of many species seed eaters; Eulophidae; Encyrtidae; **fairy flies** (Mymaridae), and Trichogrammatidae, both parasites of insect eggs; Eucharitidae, parasitic on ant larvae; Perilampidae, some hyperparasites of caterpillars; Torymidae, many plant feeders; Tanaostigmatidae, mostly gall makers.

Cynipoidea
Parasitic and gall wasps, including Ibaliidae, larvae parasitize those of wood wasps; Anacharitidae, larvae parasitic on lacewing pupae; Eucoilidae, larvae parasitic on pupae of dipteran flies; **gall wasps** (Cynipidae), including many species in galls made by other cynipids, eg **Oak marble wasp** (*Andricus kollari*).

Proctotrupoidea
Includes Proctotrupidae, larvae internal parasites of beetle larvae; Diapriidae, parasites of flies; Scelionidae, parasites of insect and spider eggs; Platygasteridae, parasites of flies and mealybugs.

Wasps, ants and bees
Suborder Apocrita, division Aculeata
Some 70–85,000 species, 41 families.

Bethyloidea
At least 3,500 species in 9 families, including Bethylidae, larvae gregarious ectoparasites of beetle and moth larvae; Cleptidae, parasites of mature sawfly larvae; **ruby-tailed wasps** (Chrysididae), larvae cuckoos in nests of other wasps and bees; Dryinidae, parasites of leaf hoppers.

Vespoidea
Some 40–50,000 species, 12 families, including Scoliidae and Tiphiidae, larvae parasitic on those of scarabaeid beetles; **velvet ants** (Mutillidae, 4,000 species), parasitize larvae, pupae of bees and wasps, pupae of tsetse flies, hyperparasitize scarab beetles; **spider-hunting wasps** (Pompilidae); solitary **hunting wasps** and social **paper-making wasps** (Vespidae), eg **hornets** (*Vespa* species), **yellow jackets** or **common wasps** (*Vespula, Dolichovespula* species), *Polistes, Polybia* species; **ants** (Formicidae, about 14,000 species), including **army** or **driver ants** (eg *Eciton, Anomma* species), **honeypot ants** (*Myrmecocystus* species), **Jet black ant** (*Lasius fuliginosus*), **leafcutter** or **parasol ants** (*Atta* species), **Slave-maker ant** (*Formica sanguinea*), **weaver ants** (*Oecophylla* species), **Wood ant** (*Formica rufa*).

Sphecoidea
Some 29,600 species in 20 families, 9 of **hunting wasps** (7,600 species) and 11 of **bees** (about 22,000 species): **Cockroach-hunting wasps**

(Ampulicidae); **thread-waisted wasps** (Sphecidae), preying on spiders, cockroaches, crickets, caterpillars (eg *Ammophila, Sphex*); Pemphredonidae, preying on springtails, thrips and aphids; Larridae, preying on orthopterans, some on bugs; Mellinidae, preying on flies; Crabronidae, preying on flies, some on beetles; **sand wasps** (Nyssonidae), including *Gorytes* species preying on plant hoppers and their cuckoos *Nysson*, and *Bembix*, fast-flying hunters of flies; Philanthidae, eg *Philanthus triangulum*, the European **bee wolf** pest of honeybees, and the weevil- and bee-hunting genus *Cerceris*.

Mining bees in the families Colletidae (eg *Colletes* and *Hylaeus*), Halictidae (eg *Halictus, Lasioglossum*, include some social species), Oxaeidae (eg *Oxaea*), Melittidae (eg *Melitta, Dasypoda*), Andrenidae (eg *Andrena, Panurginus, Perdita*), all with short to medium-length tongues; Anthophoridae (eg *Anthophora, Centris, Melissodes, Eucera, Ceratina, Xylocopa*), long-tongued, fast-flying, mainly ground nesters, some primitively social, and some cuckoo genera (eg *Epeolus, Nomada, Melecta*); Fideliidae, with pollen scopa on underside of abdomen, not hindlegs; Megachilidae, long-tongued bees with abdominal scopa, including **mason bees** (eg *Osmia, Hoplitis, Chalicodoma*) and **leafcutter bees** (*Megachile* species); Apidae, including **orchid bees** (*Euglossa, Eulaema*), **bumblebees** (*Bombus* species) and their cuckoo *Psithyrus* species, **stingless bees** (eg *Melipona, Trigona* species), and 4 species of **honeybee** (eg **Western** or **"Domestic" honeybee** (*Apis mellifera*).

ARACHNIDS

CLASS: ARACHNIDA

Phylum: Chelicerata.

About 70,000 known species in 11 subclasses.
Distribution and habitat: worldwide, some
subclasses more restricted. Primarily terrestrial
but 45 families of mites (and 1 spider species)
aquatic. Practically all habitats, including
forests, woodland, grassland, desert, seashore,
caves, mountains. Most species are predators.
Some mites and all ticks parasitic, harvestmen
and some mites plant eaters.

Features: body (0.003–7in/0.08mm–18cm
long) divided into two regions—the
cephalothorax (or prosoma) with 6 segments
and the abdomen (opisthosoma) with 12
segments. Externally segmentation often not
visible. The cephalothorax bears 6 pairs of
appendages: piercing, pincer or fang-like
chelicerae, leg- or pincer-like pedipalps, and 4
pairs of walking legs. Apart from pectines
(scorpions) and spinnerets (spiders) the
abdomen has no appendages. Arachnids lack
the antennae, mandibles and wings of insects.
Excretory system includes coxal glands; book
lungs present in many groups. Fertilization
usually indirect; newly hatched nymph
resembles small adult.

Subclasses:

Scorpions
Scorpiones

Pseudoscorpions
Pseudoscorpiones

Sun spiders
Solifugae

Micro-whip scorpions
Palpigradi

Schizomida

Whip scorpions
Uropygi

Whip spiders
Amblypygi

Ricinulei

Harvestmen
Opiliones

Ticks and mites
Acari

Spiders
Araneae

THE Arachnida boasts some of the best
known, but least loved animals, including the spiders, scorpions, mites and ticks.
Apart from a few families of mites which
have returned to an aquatic way of life,
arachnids are primarily land dwellers. They
have been so successful that members can
be found in just about every land, freshwater and marine habitat. For the most part,
arachnids are free-living predators, mainly
of other arthropods. Harvestmen, however,
will also eat such things as fungi and decaying plants and insects, while mites are
unique as they include plant and detritus
feeders as well as parasites of vertebrates
and invertebrates. The ticks are exclusively
blood-sucking parasites of vertebrates.

The Arachnida is an economically
important group. Certain scorpions and
spiders have venom which is highly toxic to
humans, while the mites and ticks include
species which transmit human diseases or
are pests of domestic livestock; a number of
species of mites cause damage to horticultural and agricultural plants. However,
many other species are beneficial as they
feed on harmful arthropods, while the large
numbers of detritus-feeding mites in the soil
play an essential part in the breakdown of
organic material and the consequent recycling of nutrients.

The class Arachnida is an ancient group.
The earliest fossil arachnid, a scorpion, dates
back to the Silurian period, some 400 million years ago. Fossil evidence suggests that
the ancestral arachnids were scorpion-like,
primarily marine animals, the Eurypterida,
belonging to the class Merostomata, whose
only living members are five species of
horseshoe or king crabs. Arachnids are
grouped with horseshoe crabs and sea
spiders (class Pycnogonida) in the phylum
Chelicerata, distinguished from other
arthropods by differences in the appendages
at the front of the body. In chelicerates, the
first are a pair of feeding organs, the chelicerae, the second is a pair of leg-like
pedipalps. (The other arthropods have one
or two pairs of antennae in front of a pair
of "chewing" mandibles.)

Arachnids are often wrongly referred to
as insects, but they have many differing
characters. For example, arachnids lack
antennae, mandibles, wings and compound
eyes, while, perhaps most obviously, they
have four pairs of legs, not three as in
insects. Also, instead of the three body divi-
sions of insects (head, thorax, abdomen),
arachnids have only two regions—the
anterior cephalothorax, or prosoma, and
the posterior abdomen, or opisthosoma. The
two parts are joined along their whole width
in scorpions, pseudoscorpions, ticks, mites
and harvestmen, whereas whip spiders,
spiders and ricinuleids have a connecting
narrow waist (pedicel) between them. In
spiders, the pedicel is particularly narrow,
while in ricinuleids it is hidden below an
extension of the abdominal exoskeleton. The
remaining subclasses are broadly waisted.

External signs of segmentation are often
hidden by chitinous plates. In most subclasses, the back of the cephalothorax is entirely
covered by a shield (carapace). Schizomids,
micro-whip scorpions and sun spiders, however, have a divided carapace. Abdominal

segmentation is evident in all groups apart from spiders, ricinuleids, ticks, the vast majority of mites and some harvestmen. In ticks and mites fusion is so extreme that there is no distinguishing boundary between the cephalothorax and abdomen. Scorpions also differ as the abdomen narrows in its posterior half to form the "tail" which ends in the familiar sting. At the end of the abdomen of whip scorpions, micro-whip scorpions and schizomids, there is a slender, articulated extension, the flagellum. In the first two subclasses, it is about as long as the body and consists of some 15 articulations, but in schizomids the flagellum is short and comprised of only three.

In spiders and whip spiders the chelicerae are fang-like for piercing, while in plant-parasitic mites they are long and needle-like for penetrating plant cells. Apart from feeding, chelicerae are sometimes used to burrow, as defensive weapons and to transfer sperm to females during mating. Spiders and pseudoscorpions respectively have a poison and a silk gland opening into the tips of their chelicerae.

The second pair of appendages, the pedipalps, flank the mouth and are also variously modified. They can be leg-like, sometimes flexed for grasping or, as in scorpions and pseudoscorpions, end in a large pincer. A poison gland opens into the pedipalps of pseudoscorpions, those of certain plant mites have silk glands, while the end segment of the pedipalps of male spiders is adapted to store sperm and impregnate the female. The pedipalps are sometimes also used to keep the chelicerae clean. The only arachnids not to have four pairs of legs occur in young ricinuleids, larval ticks and mites and the mite family Podapolipodidae, which all possess three pairs of legs, while the gall mites (family Eriophyidae) have only two pairs. Arachnid legs end in a maximum of three toothed or smooth claws and, particularly on the end segments, are equipped with sensory hairs. The first pair of legs often acts as feelers; in whip scorpions and

whip spiders this specialization is carried to extremes as the front legs are exceptionally long and slender and used solely for sensory purposes, the animals walking on just six legs. Other functions of legs include drawing silk threads, manipulating prey and, in aquatic mites, swimming.

There are no abdominal appendages in most arachnids, the exceptions being the silk-producing spinnerets of spiders and the comb-like organs, the pectines, peculiar to scorpions. Most of the internal organ systems and a number of glands open into the abdomen.

The cephalothorax has large bundles of muscles connected to the chelicerae, pedipalps and legs, anchored to special internal projections of the exoskeleton, while the abdomen possesses only narrow muscle strips, needed for the opening and closing of the various orifices and for movements of the gut. Each segment of the appendages has separate extensor and retractor muscles.

Apart from some species of mites which can ingest solid particles such as fungal spores, arachnids take their food in liquid, partially digested form. Once the body of the prey has been pierced (or the epidermis of the plant in phytophagous mites), salivary juices containing enzymes pour into the tissues and digestion begins. The resulting "soup" is sucked through a shallow tube, the prebuccal cavity, at the bottom of which is the mouth. In some groups, the wall of the prebuccal cavity has cuticular spines to filter out solid particles. Alternate contraction and relaxation of muscles attaching the pharynx to the exoskeleton sucks food into the pharynx and then pumps it out through the oesophagus (the gullet) into the midgut. Blind sacs (diverticula) branching off the midgut fill with the partly digested food, sometimes expanding to fill the whole of the abdomen. The walls of the midgut contain secretory cells which produce the enzymes, and absorptive cells which, when digestion is complete, take up the nutrients and pass them to surrounding storage cells. The waste products are expelled to the outside via the hindgut and the anus which is usually under the tip of the abdomen.

Other waste products are secreted in the form of guanine by paired coxal glands by the base of the first leg segments and Malpighian tubules emptying into the hindgut —some subclasses have one or other type but most have both. Each coxal gland consists of a thin-walled, round sac immersed in blood with a long, often partly coiled, tube leading to the outside; number and position of openings vary between subclasses.

In some mites, larval ticks and microwhip scorpions, respiration is achieved by the simple diffusion of gases through the exoskeleton. More usually, specialized structures are employed in the form of book-lungs or tracheae. A respiratory system consisting of tracheae only is found in pseudoscorpions, in sun spiders, harvestmen, ricinuleids, most mites and ticks and a few spiders. Whip scorpions, whip spiders, schizomids and a small number of spiders have book-lungs only, while scorpions and most spiders have both systems.

Book-lungs occur in pairs at the front of the abdomen, each opening onto the underside via a slit-like pore, the spiracle. The maximum number of four pairs is seen in scorpions; but one or two pairs is more usual.

Sieve tracheae are found in ricinuleids, pseudoscorpions and some spiders. The spiracle opens into an air chamber from which bundles of tracheae arise. The tube tracheae of harvestmen, sun spiders, mites and most spiders, are single-branched or unbranched tubes. The spiracle either opens into a chamber or directly into a trachea.

Arachnids have an "open" circulatory system, with usually a tubular, pumping heart. The blood of arachnids is a colorless liquid and, in some spiders and scorpions, is itself poisonous to predators.

The nervous system is generally greatly reduced, comprising a ring-like "brain" through which runs the oesophagus, giving rise to nerves which innervate the appendages, the various internal organ systems and the cuticular sense organs.

The sexes are always separate. In both male and female the genital orifice occurs on the underside of the abdomen. In the male, sperm passes from the one or two testes, along the vas deferens to the genital orifice. Similarly, the female has one or two ovaries, each with an associated oviduct leading to the outside. Most female spiders have separate orifices for the entrance of sperm and the exit of the fertilized egg.

Sense Organs of Arachnids

The legs of most arachnids bear conspicuous, usually black, erect bristles, the spines. The base of each spine communicates with a nerve ending. Setae, finer than spines (short ones give arachnids their hairy appearance), also are in communication with a nerve cell. Setae are very variable in shape; they can, for example, be serrated, feathered or branched. Most are sensitive to touch, but others detect temperature, humidity levels and chemicals, (eg pheromones). Thread-like trichobothria are considered to perceive air vibrations.

Schizomids, ricinuleids, and certain ticks, mites and pseudoscorpions are eyeless. Where eyes occur, they are simple and found on the upper surface of the carapace. Harvestmen and sun spiders have just one pair of eyes, while most other arachnids with eyes have four pairs. Some scorpions have six pairs.

Slit, or lyriform, organs on the body and appendages of most arachnids help with orientation of its body. The underside of a membrane covering a fluid-filled, slit-like depression in the cuticle touches a hair-like projection originating from a nerve cell. Any change in tension of the exoskeleton (as during movement) is communicated to the nerve via the membrane.

Sperm may be passed in a liquid medium or in stalked packets called spermatophores. The shape of the spermatophore is characteristic, even of individual species. The female either takes up the sperm herself or else it is helped into her orifice by one or more appendages of the male. The males of harvestmen and some mites have a "penis" to transfer sperm directly to the female. There is often an elaborate courtship preceding copulation, enabling the female to recognize the male as a potential mate rather than a potential meal. Stridulatory organs, generally consisting of ridged or toothed areas on the sides of the body and the appendages, have been identified in scorpions, spiders and whip spiders. In some species, only males have these organs.

The first active stage (nymph) is immediately recognizable as an arachnid. In most groups it only differs from the adult in size, the absence of secondary sexual characters and reproductive organs and the smaller number of bristles (setae). The number of nymphal stages varies between the groups. The first active stage of mites and ticks is the highly characteristic six-legged larva, which is then followed by a variable number of eight-legged nymphs. Life span ranges from a few weeks in certain mites, up to 30 years in females of the largest spiders reared in captivity. However, the expectation in nature is not really known.   ABa

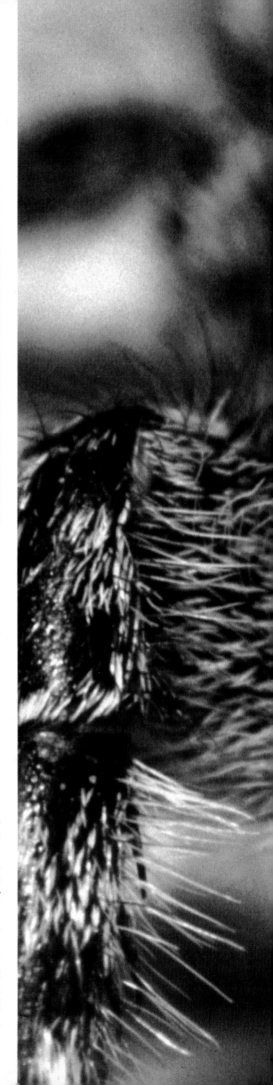

SCORPIONS

Class: Arachnida (part)
Phylum: Chelicerata.
About 8,930 species in 9 subclasses.

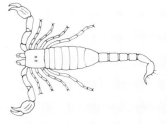

Scorpions (subclass Scorpiones)
1,200 species. 0.4–7in (10–180mm) long.
Worldwide in tropical and warm temperate
regions. From deserts to rain forests; under
stones, in crevices and burrows, a few cave
dwellers. Food: other arthropods.

Pseudoscorpions (subclass Pseudoscorpiones)
Pseudoscorpions or false scorpions.
2,000 species. 0.1–0.3in (2.5–8mm) long.
Worldwide except for Arctic and Antarctic. In
leaf litter, under bark, in birds' nests, moss,
compost heaps. Food: small arthropods.

Sun spiders (subclass Solifugae)
Sun spiders, wind scorpions, sun scorpions,
camel spiders, gerrymanders.
900 species. 0.4–2in (10–50mm). S Asia,
Africa, W Indies, Mediterranean zone, C and
S USA, Mexico. In deserts and other arid places;
at rest may burrow, or sit under stones. Food:
arthropods, small vertebrates, eg lizards.

Micro-whip scorpions (subclass Palpigradi)
60 species. 0.02–0.1in (0.5–2.8mm) long (less
"tail"). S Europe, Madagascar, Africa, SE Asia,
Texas, California to S America. Litter dwellers,
under stones, in soil, some in caves. Food:
possibly small soil arthropods.

Subclass Schizomida (Schizopeltida)
80 species. 0.08–0.6in (2–15mm) long. Asia,
Africa, Americas. In leaf litter, under stones,
will tunnel in soil. Food: other arthropods.

Whip scorpions (subclass Uropygi)
Whip scorpions or vinegaroons.
85 species. 0.6–3in (15–75mm) long (minus
"tail"). Most species in SE Asia, also in India,
Japan, New Guinea, Philippines, S USA to
S America, introduced locally in Africa. In
litter, under stones and logs, will tunnel in soil.
Food: other arthropods.

Whip spiders (subclass Amblypygi)
Whip spiders or tailless whip scorpions.
70 species. 0.2–1.8in (5–45mm) long. Islands
of Aegean Sea to sub-Saharan Africa, W Indies,
Asia, S USA to S America. In forests, in
crevices, litter, under stones and loose bark,
some in caves. Food: other arthropods.

Subclass Ricinulei
35 species. 0.4–0.6in (10–15mm) long.
W Africa, Texas to Brazil. Tropical forest litter,
caves. Food: possibly termites.

Harvestmen (subclass Opiliones)
Harvestmen and harvest spiders.
4,500 species. 0.04–0.6in (1–15mm) long.
Worldwide. Grassland, woodland, forests, on
vegetation, under loose bark. Food: small
arthropods, decaying vegetation, fungi.

THE oldest known fossil arachnid is a
scorpion, *Palaeophonus nuncius*, dating
back some 400 million years. **True scorpions**
(subclass Scorpiones) can be recognized by
their large, menacing, pincer-like pedipalps
and by the narrow "tail" arched over the
body, bearing at its tip a poison gland opening into a sting. They also have a pair of
unique comb-like sensory organs on the
underside of the abdomen. These pectines
probably detect ground vibrations. A
scorpion uses its sting primarily for self-
defense. The potency of the venom varies,
from being innocuous to humans in, for
example, *Heterometrus cyaneus* from Java, to
being lethal as in the Durango scorpion
(*Centruoides suffusus*) from Mexico. All dangerous species occur in the family Buthidae.
Populations of *Buthus occitanus* in southwestern Europe cause a painful sting with
fairly mild toxic effects, but in North African
and Middle Eastern populations, the same
species' venom can cause death. After
indirect fertilization, one to 95 eggs are laid,
depending on the species. The newly
hatched scorpions climb onto their mother's
back, often along the pincers which she
helpfully turns sideways and rests on the
ground to form a ramp. After one molt the
young become independent and disperse.

With their large pincered pedipalps held
at the ready, **pseudoscorpions** resemble tiny
tailless scorpions. These agile creatures dart
backward if threatened from the front.
Pseudoscorpions often cling to flies, beetles
and harvestmen, but they are not parasitizing them, just hitching a lift for dispersal.
Silk from glands in the chelicerae is used to
construct refuges for overwintering, molting and egg laying. Courtship is quite

▲ **Lying in wait** for prey at night, a scorpion by its lair on a tree in South African rain forest. Before mating, scorpions perform a "courtship dance" in which the male holds the female by the claw-like pedipalps or by the chelicerae and leads her back and forth. He eventually deposits a sperm packet (spermatophore) and positions the female over it until she takes it up with the aid of the valves of her genital opening.

◄ **A notoriously aggressive predator,** the swift-running sun or wind spider, *Solpuga* species (Solifugae) will use its long chelicerae to crush prey to death, as it lacks poison glands. Just six legs are used for walking—the markedly slender first pair are used as "feelers." Unique sensory mallet-shaped "racket" organs occur on the underside of the fourth pair of legs, apparently for detecting ground vibrations.

elaborate. The male waves his pedipalps, taps his legs and quivers his abdomen. If the female responds, they "dance" scorpion-like and the female takes up a spermatophore. Two to 40 eggs are laid in a silken sac attached to the female's abdomen. After hatching, the young feed on "milk" from the mother's ovaries, but they become independent after the first molt.

In **sun spiders**, there are few niceties before mating; the male literally jumps onto the female, stopping her in her tracks. She allows her partner to topple her on her side and sperm is transferred to her genital opening by the male's chelicerae. This accomplished, he retires hastily before the female returns to the normal aggressive state. After fertilization, the female digs a burrow to lay 100–250 eggs, sometimes staying to guard them.

The rare **micro-whip scorpions** are agile and delicate. The abdomen ends in a flagellum, which is about the same length as the body and equipped with long, sensory bristles (setae). It is carried vertically and gathers information about environmental conditions.

Schizomids are small subtropical and tropical arachnids with a short flagellum. Prior to mating, the female hooks onto ridges on the male's flagellum and is then dragged over a spermatophore he has deposited. Six to 30 eggs are laid and adhere to the female's genital orifice before hatching.

Whip scorpions have massive, pinching chelicerae and a long, whip-like flagellum. They walk with just six legs as the first pair are slender feelers. "Scent" from glands at the flagellum base containing acetic (hence the common name, vinegaroon) or formic acid or chlorine is sprayed at potential enemies. The female is fertilized by the male pushing a spermatophore into her genital orifice with a projection of the pedipalps.

Whip spiders have a cephalothorax noticeably wider than long and narrowly joined to the abdomen. While all the legs are long and slender, the first pair is particularly so and used just for sensory purposes. Whip spiders characteristically scurry sideways. During mating, the male guides the female over a spermatophore which she takes into her genital orifice. Twenty to 40 eggs are laid in a sac attached to the female's abdomen. The young are initially carried on their mother's abdomen.

Ricinuleids are heavily armored, robust arachnids. They possess a unique hinged flap (the cucullus) at the front of the cephalothorax, overhanging the mouthparts. Before mating, the male climbs onto the female. With a modified copulatory organ on the third pair of legs, he transfers sperm to the female. One or two eggs are laid and are carried between her bent pedipalps and the cucullus.

The round-bodied **harvestmen** lack a narrow waist, characteristic of spiders. Short-legged species exist but the most familiar are the forms with long, stilt-like limbs. A pair of defensive scent glands opens into the edge of the cephalothorax. When threatened, a spray of malodorous liquid is directed at the would-be attacker. Alternatively, a droplet of the scent is spread over the body to give the desired deterrent effect.

Fertilization is direct. Ten to 100 eggs are laid through a long tube, the ovipositor, in damp soil, under stones or similar sites.

ABa

TICKS AND MITES

Subclass Acari

Class: Arachnida.
Phylum: Chelicerata.
About 30,000 species (850 ticks) in 7 orders.
Distribution: worldwide, in practically every terrestrial, freshwater and marine environment.

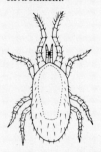

Features: in size from mites 0.003–0.6in (0.08–16mm) to ticks 1.2in (30mm) long, usually black or brown but reds, greens, yellows also common. No division between 2 parts of body, the cephalothorax (prosoma) and abdomen (or opisthosoma), but a furrow may be present between 2nd and 3rd pairs of legs. Chelicerae variously modified round basic pincer-like form, for example, for biting, sucking and piercing; small leg-like pedipalps; usually 4 pairs of walking legs. Abdomen without appendages. Development to adult via egg, 6-legged larva and usually 1–3 (though up to 8 in soft ticks) 8-legged nymphal stages. Ticks are ectoparasites of land mammals, birds, reptiles; there are free-living, and plant- and animal-parasitic mites.

Order Metastigmata
Hard ticks (family Ixodidae) include **Brown dog tick** (*Rhipicephalus sanguineus*), **Wood tick** (*Dermacentor andersoni*); **soft ticks** (family Argasidae) include **Fowl tick** (*Argas persicus*), *Ornithodoros* species.

Orders Cryptostygmata (beetle mites); Notostigmata; Tetrastigmata.

Order Mesostigmata
Includes **Red mite of poultry** (*Dermanyssus gallinae*, family Dermanyssidae).

Order Prostigmata
Includes **gall mites** (family Eriophyidae); **spider mites** (Tetranychidae); superfamily Trombidioidea; **water mites** (45 families, the Hydrachnida, including **chiggers** or **red bugs**, family Trombiculidae); **Follicle mite** (*Demodex folliculorum*, family Demodicidae); **quill mites** (family Syringophilidae); family Podapolipodidae.

Order Astigmata
Includes **Flour mite** (*Acarus siro*) and **Furniture mite** (*Glycyphagus domesticus*) (family Acaridae); **fur mites** (family Listrophoridae); **feather mites** (family Analgesidae); **Scabies** or **Itch mite** (*Sarcoptes scabei*, family Sarcoptidae); family Pyroglyphidae.

IN both structure and habits, the ticks and mites are the most diverse groups of arachnids. They are also the most significant in veterinary, medical and agricultural terms. The ticks are the largest of the subclass Acari and are exclusively blood-sucking ectoparasites of land vertebrates. Some species are pests of domestic livestock, while a number transmit human disease (see box).

To survive, a tick must find a suitable host on which to feed and, having done this, remain attached until it is replete. Ticks possess special sense organs which can detect an approaching host. Among these, bristle-like setae sensitive to humidity and "smell" are concentrated in special depressions in the cuticle; the characteristic "Haller's organs" are located on the end segment of both front legs. When a possible host is detected, a tick climbs to the top of vegetation to "quest," waving its front legs in the air, trying to "home into" the direction of the stimuli and readying itself to climb onto the animal if it brushes past.

Before feeding begins, the skin of the host is punctured by the serrated pincers of the chelicerae. A conspicuous toothed, snout-like projection, the hypostome, lies between the pedipalps and is worked into the wound, the teeth providing anchorage. Blood is sucked up along a groove on the upper surface of the hypostome; anticoagulants in the tick's saliva prevent clotting. After feeding, most ticks drop to the ground, where they molt or lay eggs.

Ticks are classified into three families, all but one species belonging to the Ixodidae (hard ticks) or to the Argasidae (soft ticks). Hard ticks get their name from the thickened shield (scutum) on top of the front of the body. They possess prominent, well-developed mouthparts, needed to secure themselves to their roving hosts during feeding, which can take several days. A common hard tick is the cosmopolitan Brown dog tick. Soft ticks lack a scutum and have relatively weak mouthparts, positioned inconspicuously on the underside. Soft ticks are "habitat" ticks: they remain in the host's retreat, such as a nest or burrow, only feeding when it returns. Soft ticks are able to complete a meal in as little as two minutes. Their mouthparts do not need to be exceptionally well-armed as the host is generally at rest while feeding proceeds, so reducing the risk of the tick being dislodged. The Fowl tick is a soft tick pest of poultry in warm, dry parts of the world.

The Notostigmata and Tetrastigmata are predators of other arthropods, and confined to warmer parts of the world. All other orders are cosmopolitan. The beetle mites (Cryptostigmata) are the most abundant mites in soil and leaf litter. They feed mainly on decaying plants, playing an essential role in the recycling of nutrients. Their robust, rounded dark-colored bodies resemble tiny beetles.

Mesostigmatid mites are mostly large, rapidly-moving predatory species, equipped with strong chelicerae. They feed on nematode worms, arthropods (including other mites) and their eggs.

The Prostigmata include sap-sucking plant parasites, the most important of which are the gall mites and spider mites which cause damage to a variety of agricultural and horticultural plants around the world.

Mites that are pests of stored foods belong to the Astigmata. Probably the most common and important is the cosmopolitan Flour mite. Some species feed on the food itself, while others prefer the molds that tend to grow in these situations.

Certain members of the orders Mesostigmata, Astigmata and Prostigmata are found in association with both vertebrates and invertebrates. Parasitic forms generally attack the external parts of their host. Those considered to be endoparasitic invade via the respiratory openings.

A number of species, such as the Red mite of poultry, live in the retreat of their host and only board it to feed. Mites of the superfamily Trombidioidea and most of the freshwater forms are only parasitic as larvae, subsequent stages being free-living predators. The majority of parasitic mites, though, complete their life cycle on the host.

Other relationships are mutually beneficial to both parties. For example, the "follicle mite" *Demodex folliculorum*, which lives in the hair follicles and sebaceous glands of humans, helps keep the skin clean by feeding on sebum. Fur, feather and quill mites perform similar scavenging duties.

Mites often cling to other arthropods, often to beetles and flies. They are not parasitizing their "host," merely hitching a lift to escape from adverse conditions. Certain Astigmata have a special highly modified immature form, the hypopus, as the dispersal stage. This lacks a mouth, is flattened to fit closely to the host's body, and can project attaching suckers through a perforated plate at the hind end of the under side. A fascinating example of "hitch-hiking" occurs when mites living in the flowers of plants pollinated by humming-birds run up the beaks and into the nostrils of feeding birds, later to disembark at another flower.   ABa

▲ **Giant desert mite** or "red velvet mite" (Trombididae), a free-living mite, in Kenya. Other mites are much smaller, and many are parasites of plants or animals. Uniquely among arachnids, some are aquatic.

▶ **Stuck into a blood meal,** hard ticks (Ixodidae) on a European hedgehog. Such hard ticks have well-developed mouthparts for hanging on to the moving host while feeding, which may take several days.

Medical Importance of Ticks and Mites

All but two of the seven orders of ticks and mites (the Notostigmata and Cryptostigmata) include species of medical importance. In itself, the blood-sucking habit of ticks causes irritation and malaise in the host, but it is as carriers and transmitters of human disease organisms that ticks are medically most important. The organisms, chiefly viruses, rickettsiae and spirochaete bacteria, are transmitted in the tick's saliva during feeding, and any one organism can be carried by a range of tick species. The viruses cause hemorrhagic fevers or encephalitis; the different types are usually named after the place where they were first identified, for example Omsk hemorrhagic fever, and Russian spring-summer encephalitis. They occur in Canada, the United States of America, Malaysia, India, and eastern, northern and central Europe. The main human rickettsial infections are the spotted fevers, tick-bite fevers and tick-typhus fevers, one of the most famous examples being Rocky Mountain spotted fever, which, in the western USA, is carried by the Wood tick. Spirochaetes, causing human relapsing fevers, are transmitted by species of the genus *Ornithodoros*. These occur in Africa and the Americas.

Larval mites of the family Trombiculidae, commonly called chiggers or red bugs, are mostly lymph-feeding ectoparasites of vertebrates. About 20 species cause either a dermatitis (scrub-itch), resulting from an allergic reaction to the chigger's saliva, or transmit human disease organisms. Among the latter is the most important of mite-borne diseases, scrub-typhus or tsutsugamushi disease, which occurs in many parts of eastern and southeastern Asia.

Perhaps the most famous of mites infesting humans is the scabies or itch mite. Favored sites for infection are the hands and wrists; severe itching and a rash result.

House-dust mites are primarily beneficial to humans–they clean up by feeding on dead skin cells and other detritus. But in some people they induce allergic reactions in the form of asthma and rhinitis.

Several species of stored food mites cause a dermatitis in people handling infested food. They include Grocer's itch, caused by the Furniture mite and Baker's itch, associated with the presence of the Flour mite.

SPIDERS

Subclass: Araneae
Class: Arachnida.
Phylum: Chelicerata.
About 30,000 known species (perhaps twice this number in reality), in 84 families.
Distribution: worldwide, excluding Antarctica, in forest, heath, grassland, deserts, mountains, caves, mines, houses, marshes; 1 species (*Argyroneta aquatica*) under water.

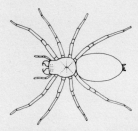

Distinguishing features: distinct from other arachnids in having a copulatory organ on the male pedipalps (2nd pair of appendages), unsegmented abdomen joined by a narrow pedicel to the cephalothorax, and in the widespread use of silk. Length is 0.3–3.5in (0.7mm–9cm) and leg span up to 10.2in (26cm), females in orb web spiders up to 7 times longer than males. Most have both tracheae and book lungs.

SPIDERS are the major example in the animal kingdom of evolution in the production of silk. The silk is put to many uses but, most importantly, builds a prey-catching system which works continuously. Not all spider species construct webs— approximately half are independent hunters which chase or ambush their prey—but all use silk in one way or another.

Some other arachnids also produce silk, but spiders demonstrate further adaptations which help to explain their relative dominance. Such features as poison glands leading to the jaws, hydraulic extension of the legs permitting fast movements and jumps, improved eyesight (chiefly in hunting spiders), and direct sperm transfer, have all contributed to the spiders' success and diversification.

Spiders are found virtually everywhere. They have colonized all the major environments of the terrestrial world. While the greatest diversity occurs in tropical rain forest, they are also well represented in most types of woodland, heathland and grassland. They thrive wherever there is rich vegetation and plenty of insects, but also many species can survive in desert, on mountain tops and down mines.

Spiders are frequently among the leading colonists following the emergence of new islands by volcanic eruptions, such as Krakatoa, and Surtsey near Iceland. Their most spectacular method of migration is known as "ballooning." With the aid of long strands of silk drawn out by the breeze, small and young spiders become airborne and may be transported considerable distances. Spiders are often recorded in samples of aerial plankton from heights of up to 16,500ft (5,000m). At the mercy of the winds, many individuals are dropped in unsuitable places such as the sea, but some will have more luck. When large numbers attempt to take off together, their strands may coalesce and form sheets of gossamer.

In favorable situations, such as unspoilt meadows and woodland glades, spiders can be abundant. The arachnologist W. S. Bristowe calculated that in an undisturbed field in southeast England at certain seasons there were more than 2 million spiders to the acre (5 million per hectare). He further estimated that for the country as a whole, the weight of insects consumed annually by spiders exceeded the weight of its human inhabitants—a conservative estimate in the early 20th century, according to Bristowe but, because of changes in land use, probably no longer true.

When a woodland or grassland habitat is divided into its various layers, or zones, it is found that a different community of spiders occurs in each. Many species are rather difficult to see as they prefer the darkness and humidity of the ground layer (up to about 6in/15cm above the soil surface). Here, assorted hunting and web-spinning

The 3 Suborders and Key Families of Spiders

Liphistiomorphae
Liphistiomorphae or Mesothelae
Trap-door spiders (Liphistiidae). Primitive, with abdominal segmentation; restricted to SE Asia.

Mygalomorphae
Mygalomorphae or Orthognatha
Trap-door spiders (Ctenizidae). Have line of teeth on chelicerae for digging burrows that are usually closed with a hinged door; in most warm parts of the world.

Theraphosidae. Very large, hairy hunting spiders; eyes small, in compact group; tropical and subtropical. Includes **Mexican red-kneed tarantula** (*Brachypelma smithi*).
Funnel-web spiders (Dipluridae). Tropical and subtropical. Includes poisonous species such as the **Sydney funnel-web** (*Atrax robustus*).

Araneomorphae
Araneomorphae or Labidognatha
Tube-web spiders (Segestriidae). Elongated species with tubular retreat and radiating trigger threads; worldwide.

Spitting spiders (Scytodidae). Only 6 eyes; carapace domed; squirt sticky silk at prey; cosmopolitan except cold regions.

Comb-footed or scaffolding-web spiders (Theridiidae). Spin scaffolding-webs; usually small with globose abdomen; worldwide. Include poisonous species such as the **Black widow** or **redback** (*Latrodectus mactans*).

Money spiders (Linyphiidae). Mostly tiny; webs often sheet-like; worldwide.

Orb-web weavers (Araneidae). With sticky silk; usually broad-bodied; worldwide. Include the **Australian bolas spider** (*Celaenia distincta*), **Giant**

wood spider (*Nephila maculata*) and other **golden orb spiders** (*Nephila* species).

Horizontal orb-web weavers (Tetragnathidae). Web has open hub; usually slim bodied with large chelicerae; worldwide.

Cobweb weavers (Agelenidae). Many house spiders; worldwide. Include **Common house spider** (*Tegenaria gigantea*).

Wolf spiders (Lycosidae). Hunters with 4 large and 4 small eyes; worldwide.

Nursery web spiders (Pisauridae). Like wolf spiders, but eyes smaller; many are semiaquatic (**fishing spiders**); worldwide.

Gnaphosidae. Nocturnal hunters; dark colored and often with silvery oval eyes; worldwide.

Sac-spiders (Clubionidae). Similar to gnaphosids but usually paler in color; sit over young in egg sac; worldwide.

Wandering spiders (Ctenidae). Fast-moving hunters, often aggressive (eg *Phoneutria fera*); tropical and subtropical.

Huntsman spiders (Heteropodidae). Fast-moving and crab-like; tropical and subtropical. Include the **Banana spider** (*Heteropoda venatoria*) which often travels in banana shipments.

Crab spiders (Thomisidae). Mostly sedentary ambush-hunters which walk forward, backward and sideways; worldwide.

Jumping spiders (Salticidae). Attractive, alert hunting spiders with large front eyes; worldwide.

Cribellate spiders—main families include Eresidae, Dictynidae, Amaurobiidae, Filistatidae, Dinopidae (**ogre-eyed** or **net-casting spiders**) and Uloboridae—produce dry hackled silk.

▲ **An Australian wolf spider,** *Lycosa godeffroyi*, lurks at the entrance to its silk-lined tunnel. Wolf spiders are active predators, fleet of foot and with acute vision. They hunt insects on the ground and are found all over the world, in habitats ranging from deserts and coastal dunes, to grassland and leaf litter on forest floors. The family Lycosidae also includes the "true tarantulas" of southern Europe, reputedly dangerous to man but in reality harmless; they are infrequently seen because of their retiring habits.

spiders lead a sheltered existence at the base of plant stems, under debris, in decomposing vegetable matter and even in fissures in the soil. Further up, about 6–39in (15cm to 1m) above the ground, lies the field layer, where some species are adapted to life on plant stems and accordingly are elongated in shape. On top of the field layer, among flowers and where light levels are generally high, the more visually acute hunters such as wolf spiders and jumping spiders tend to be dominant. The shrub layer occurs at approximately 3–16ft (1–5m). It is a zone much favored by web builders, which occupy the spaces within and between shrubs. Above 16ft (5m) is the woody layer. This is the most exposed zone and tends to be the domain of nocturnal hunting spiders which shelter during the day in crevices and under bark.

In Japan a study of three species of the orb-web weaver genus *Tetragnatha* (family Tetragnathidae) has revealed the sort of division of habitat, to reduce competition, that is typical of closely related, coexisting spiders. *Tetragnatha praedonia, T. japonica*

and *T. pinicola* all build their horizontal orb webs across small streams where prey density is high. *Tetragnatha praedonia* suspends its web from shrubs about 3–6.5ft (1–2m) above the surface, *T. japonica* uses grasses below 3ft (1m) and *T. pinicola* also uses grasses, but its web, below 8in (20cm), lies very close to the water surface.

Among European species which occur only in strictly defined habitats are a wolf spider (*Pardosa traillii*) on mountain scree slopes, a jumping spider (*Sitticus rupicola*) on coastal shingle, and a money spider (*Glyphesis cottonae*) in sphagnum moss. *Tetrilus macropthalmus* (Agelenidae) and *Lepthyphantes midas* (Linyphiidae), known only from rotten cavities in trees in one or two ancient woodlands, avoid extinction only as long as this habitat survives.

At the other end of the scale, cosmopolitan species demonstrate broad habitat tolerance as well as the ability to disperse widely. For example, the orb-web spider *Argiope trifasciata* is familiar in diverse habitats throughout the warm parts of the world. Often abundant, it is an aggressive colonizer. In Europe the improbable habitat of sewage filter beds has allowed three species of money spiders to expand their range. A food chain based on bacteria feeding on sewage is headed by these species, which sometimes attain high densities. Previously, *Erigone arctica* occurred only in coastal foreshores and saltmarshes; *Leptorhoptrum robustum* is usually an inhabitant of marshes and wet meadows (in woodland in Sweden); and *Lessertia dentichelis* is found otherwise in cellars, mines and caves. This last species is scarce in the upper parts of the filter bed clinker and most numerous in the dark, wet regions at 3.3–6.6ft (1–2m), where temperature, light and humidity are relatively constant, as in a natural cave.

The two parts of a spider's body are joined by a narrow tube, the pedicel. The combined head and thorax (cephalothorax) covered by a hardened shield (carapace) contains the brain, poison glands and stomach. Six pairs of appendages are attached: eight legs, two palps (the male's bearing a copulatory organ), and a pair of jaws (chelicerae). There are no antennae.

The abdomen is usually sac-like and contains the heart, midgut, silk glands, respiratory and reproductive systems. On the underside is the epigastric furrow separating the front third from the rear (apical) regions. On this furrow, either side of the genital opening, are patches revealing the presence of the book lungs (see below). At the end of the abdomen is the anal tubercle and below that the spinnerets. These appendages, usually six in number, issue strands of silk through tiny spigots.

The eyes are generally at the front of the cephalothorax. Most spiders have eight simple eyes (ocelli) as opposed to the compound eyes of insects and crustaceans. Normally sight is poor, as most spiders "listen" to the world around them through vibrations borne on the air, the ground, their webs, or even the surface of water.

Two families, the jumping spiders and the ogre-eyed or net-casting spiders, have

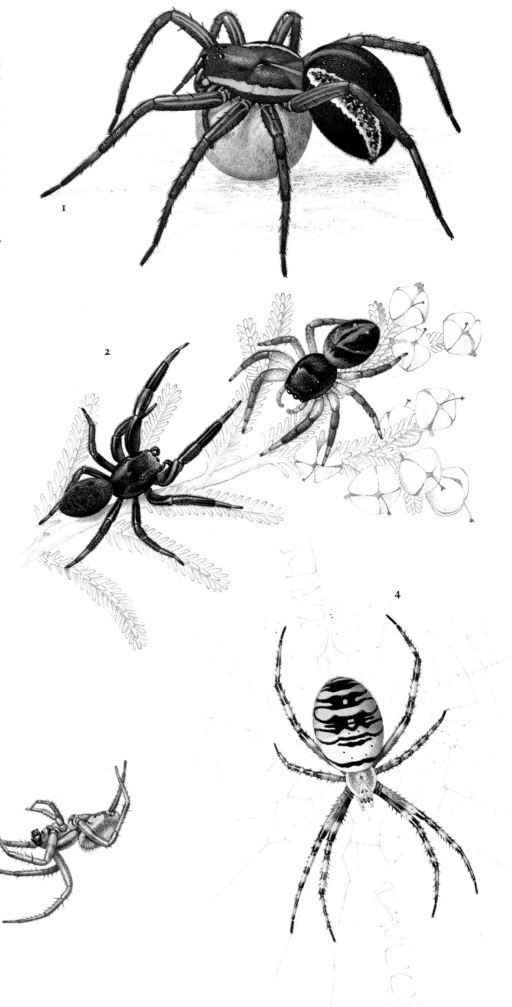

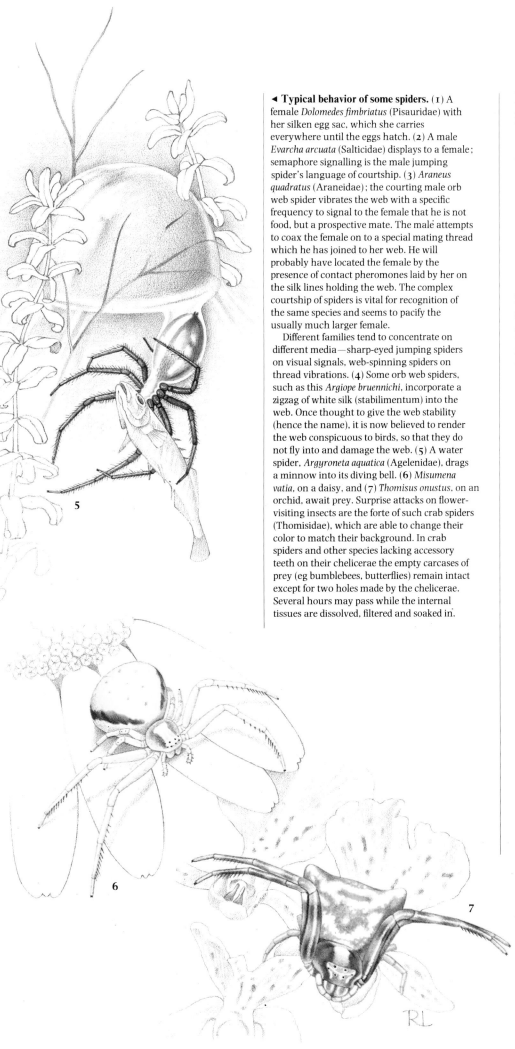

◄ **Typical behavior of some spiders.** (1) A female *Dolomedes fimbriatus* (Pisauridae) with her silken egg sac, which she carries everywhere until the eggs hatch. (2) A male *Evarcha arcuata* (Salticidae) displays to a female; semaphore signalling is the male jumping spider's language of courtship. (3) *Araneus quadratus* (Araneidae); the courting male orb web spider vibrates the web with a specific frequency to signal to the female that he is not food, but a prospective mate. The male attempts to coax the female on to a special mating thread which he has joined to her web. He will probably have located the female by the presence of contact pheromones laid by her on the silk lines holding the web. The complex courtship of spiders is vital for recognition of the same species and seems to pacify the usually much larger female.

Different families tend to concentrate on different media—sharp-eyed jumping spiders on visual signals, web-spinning spiders on thread vibrations. (4) Some orb web spiders, such as this *Argiope bruennichi*, incorporate a zigzag of white silk (stabilimentum) into the web. Once thought to give the web stability (hence the name), it is now believed to render the web conspicuous to birds, so that they do not fly into and damage the web. (5) A water spider, *Argyroneta aquatica* (Agelenidae), drags a minnow into its diving bell. (6) *Misumena vatia*, on a daisy, and (7) *Thomisus onustus*, on an orchid, await prey. Surprise attacks on flower-visiting insects are the forte of such crab spiders (Thomisidae), which are able to change their color to match their background. In crab spiders and other species lacking accessory teeth on their chelicerae the empty carcases of prey (eg bumblebees, butterflies) remain intact except for two holes made by the chelicerae. Several hours may pass while the internal tissues are dissolved, filtered and soaked in.

highly developed eyesight, in some cases more acute than in any other land invertebrate.

Below the eyes lie the chelicerae. They are the offensive weapons of the spider, delivering the poison that most use to paralyze or kill their prey. Each chelicera consists of two segments, a strong basal segment and an articulating fang which is the part that is thrust into the victim. Two of the three suborders of spiders are separated according to the way their fangs move. In the Mygalomorphae (or Orthognatha), which includes the tarantulas and most trap-door spiders, the chelicerae project and strike downward like parallel pickaxes (paraxial). By contrast, in the Araneomorphae (or Labidognatha), the chelicerae project much less and the fangs move horizontally, closing on each other. In the third suborder, the rare Liphistiomorphae (or Mesothelae), the chelicerae are paraxial but these spiders are further distinguished by certain other primitive characters; the suborder is confined to Southeast Asia.

Chelicerae are used not only for attack and defense, but also for manipulation in many other tasks—they are the spider's "hands." Trap-door spiders of the family Ctenizidae use their chelicerae to dig burrows; the basal segment (the rake) is furnished with extra teeth. Fishing spiders (family Pisauridae) use them to carry their large egg cocoons as they run on the surface of the water. Spiders in some families interlock their chelicerae during mating. Often those of the male are larger, to assist in restraining the female.

Apart from the family Uloboridae, all spiders possess venom glands. It does not follow that most are poisonous to man; this would apply to only about 30 species in the world. Unfortunately it can be difficult to distinguish between harmless and dangerous spiders. The Black widow or redback is quite timid. It does not attack without provocation but, of course, this can be unintended. A spider may be forced to defend itself when, for instance it is squeezed against a body by clothing. The Black widow may crawl carefully across one's hand but suddenly bite.

The two venom glands are sac-like in form. In araneomorphs they lie in the head region and connect by a narrow duct to the fang, opening at a pore near the tip, while in mygalomorphs the glands are relatively small and lie within the chelicerae. Venom is ejected voluntarily by contraction of the gland's musculature. The gland is very large in crab spiders and spitting spiders. In the latter, the glands also produce glue and are accommodated in a highly domed carapace. The unique method of prey capture in spitting spiders relies on squirting the mixture of venom and glue through the chelicerae to paralyze the prey, transfixing it to the substrate.

One of the most dangerous spiders is the Sydney funnel-web of eastern Australia. Its venom has been studied in some detail but the production of an antivenene has proved very difficult. The venom is very acidic and this is thought to be the immediate cause of pain in humans. A constituent substance known as hyaluronidase breaks down tissue and assists penetration of the venom. The symptoms are variable, but broadly there is nausea, vomiting, salivation and crying, uncoordinated muscle activity intensifies, with severe abdominal pain and bizarre heart beats; there follows paralysis of the respiratory muscles and a massive accumulation of fluid in the lungs with a severe drop in blood pressure. If delirium and coma occur, death may also follow.

Other poisonous spiders include the aggressive *Phoneutria fera*, a wandering spider of South America, and the rather delicate recluse spiders (*Loxosceles* species, family Loxoscelidae) of South and North America. Other harmful genera in South America include *Lycosa* (wolf spiders), *Trechona* (hunting spiders), the orb-web spider genus *Mastophora*, and *Latrodectus*. The latter is found throughout the warm regions of the world. In America it is called the Black widow, in Europe (France) the malmignette, in South Africa the Button spider, in Australia the redback and in New Zealand the katipo. Its venom causes respiratory paralysis with the risk of death. However, for *Latrodectus* an antivenene is available.

Essentially, spiders take only living prey. Their food is mainly insects and other spiders. Some take crustaceans and worms; many refuse ants, wasps, beetles and distasteful bugs. Diets vary from catholic to highly specific as in, for example, the Bolas spider of Australia, which feeds on males of a single species of moth.

The predatory nature of spiders severely limits social behavior, which is rare, but most common in cribellate families. Large numbers of *Mallos gregalis* (Dictynidae) live together without territoriality, aggression or cannibalism, feeding simultaneously on prey caught in the large communal webs.

The other appendages of the cephalothorax are the single pair of pedipalps and the four pairs of walking legs.

The palps are leg-like but consist of only six, instead of seven, segments. They are not used for locomotion but assist in many tasks such as prey capture. In adult male spiders the tip of the palp is modified into a copulatory organ. The ends of both palps and legs bear taste receptors.

Spiders' legs have seven segments: from the base, coxa, trochanter, femur, patella, tibia, metatarsus and tarsus. On the end of the tarsus are two or three claws. Among araneomorphs, two-clawed spiders (Dionycha) are usually hunters while three-clawed spiders (Trionycha) are usually web builders. The extra claw is used for holding the silk threads. Many two-clawed spiders have a dense brush of hairs called "claw tufts" which facilitate walking upside-down on smooth surfaces—the undersides of leaves are an extremely important microhabitat. Under the microscope these hairs can be seen to split into thousands of fine cuticular extensions ("end feet").

Through the narrow pedicel, from the cephalothorax to the abdomen, pass the ventral nerve cord, the aorta, the digestive tract and sometimes, in the other direction,

▶ **A spider in ant's clothing,** this male jumping spider, *Cosmophasis* species (Salticidae), eats a worker ant in Kenya. The spider's resemblance to the ant involves gait as well as appearance. It confers a double-edged advantage: most birds avoid ants as prey and the spider is mistaken by the ants as one of their own kind.

▶ **Bird-eating baboon spider** BELOW of southern Africa (Theraphosidae).

▼ **Lynx spiders** (family Oxyopidae) are mainly found in warm climates, where they specialize in hunting insects among vegetation. Here, an African species of *Peucetia* eats a winged termite (*Macrotermes* species) in Kenya. Many lynx spiders are partly or wholly green and spend much of their time sitting motionless on leaves. They respond rapidly to the presence of prey and can leap nimbly from leaf to leaf.

Bird-eating Spiders

Bird-eating spiders—tarantulas in North America, mygales in French-speaking countries, baboon spiders in Africa and "arañas peludas" (hairy spiders) in Spanish America—are very large members of the family Theraphosidae. They rival in size the biggest land invertebrates. The largest species, *Theraphosa leblondi* of northern South America, has a leg span in the male of up to 10.2in (26cm), although its weight would be no more than 3oz (85g).

Despite their formidable appearance, many species of bird-eating spider are placid and will attack a human only under extreme provocation. Other species, however, can be irritable and aggressive, quite capable of giving a painful bite, though it is rarely fatal to humans. To attack, these spiders raise the front half of the body, front legs held high in the air, and strike powerfully downward, driving in the large parallel fangs as the victim is grasped by the front legs. With such power, potent venom is relatively unnecessary.

Bird-eating spiders are found in the tropics and subtropics; in all approximately 300 species are known. Essentially they are forest-hunting spiders, though in the southwestern USA and Mexico, for example, there are many desert-adapted forms. Commonly they are black or brown, but some have vivid coloration, for example, the Mexican red-kneed tarantula, with its partly red legs, and *Pamphobetus antinous* from Bolivia, with its purple iridescence. All have a thick covering of hairs, making them highly sensitive to

vibrations. As they are active at night, their tiny eyes are used only to judge light levels. Tree-dwelling forms have adhesive brushes of hairs on the end segments of the legs (tarsi) to allow progress over the smoothest leaves.

Occasionally they may catch nesting or roosting birds. More frequently, the food of "bird-eating spiders" consists of small reptiles and amphibians, beetles, moths, grasshoppers and other spiders. Bird-eating spiders have many enemies; mammals dig them from their burrows and the young are preyed on by birds, reptiles and amphibians. They suffer from the attentions of the tarantula hawk wasps (*Pepsis* species) which sting and paralyze the spider, then drag it to a burrow which is sealed after an egg is laid on the spider. On hatching, the larvae feed on the still-living spider.

fine respiratory tubules. The abdomen is most commonly oval and rather soft but it may be globose, worm-like, capped by plates (scuta) or covered with spines. No other arachnid order exhibits anything like the ornamentation and coloration which occurs among spiders. Camouflage patterns are extremely common. Spiders can also be convincing mimics of ants, distasteful bugs and even bird droppings. Ordinarily, the abdomen shows no trace of the primitive segmentation of arthropods. Only the primitive suborder Liphistiomorphae has visible segmentation, in the form of a series of transverse plates (tergites). Closely resembling fossils from the Carboniferous period (345–200 million years ago), the two surviving genera are *Liphistius*, found today in Burma, Thailand, Malaysia and Sumatra; and *Heptathele*, which occurs in China and Japan.

Spiders breathe air through book lungs and tracheae. The book lung is a lung chamber appearing externally as a pale or dark, hairless patch of cuticle on the underside of the abdomen toward its base. Araneomorphs have one pair, except in the anomalous family Hypochilidae which has two pairs, as do the mygalomorphs and liphistiomorphs. The organ's interior comprises a number of overlapping invaginations, folds or leaves (hence the name). Deoxygenated blood is moved by pulsations of the heart through the stacks of leaves which alternate with air-filled spaces.

Book lungs present a large surface through which water may be lost. To assist water conservation and for greater efficiency, the second pair has, in the majority of spiders, been transformed into tracheae. Like those of insects, the tracheae of spiders carry oxygen directly to the tissues. In most spiders the two spiracle openings of the tracheae have fused into one and moved back towards the spinnerets. The tracheal tubes may be elaborately branched, or unbranched. In some small spiders with high metabolic rates and a tendency to desiccation, all the book lungs have been replaced by tracheae. However, it may be an advantage to have two independent systems, as in the case of wolf spiders, which are among the most active of spiders.

Males can usually be distinguished from females by their smaller size, slimmer body and relatively longer legs. However, to be certain one must look for the copulatory organs carried on the palps of the adult male which are absent in the female. In the mygalomorphs and more primitive groups within araneomorphs, the organs of both sexes are in their simplest form. On the palpal tarsus of the male a bulb arises within which a tapered duct is coiled. The bulb functions like a pipette to take up and expel a drop of sperm which the male has extruded onto a specially spun "sperm web." During copulation the organ is inserted into the female's genitalia, via a single opening that serves also for egg laying. In the more advanced araneomorphs, the structure of the palpal organ is more complex, combining expandable soft tissue with various hardened (sclerotized) appendages. When the palp is inflated by hydraulic pressure these appendages project and interlock with features on the adult female's genital plate (epigyne). The female has three separate genital openings: two introductory ducts, which receive the tip of the male palp (embolus), and a gonopore, through which the eggs are laid.

Soon after completion of the final molt of the exoskeleton (in most spiders there are 4–12 molts), and before approaching a prospective mate, the male charges his palps with sperm, usually from the tiny triangular sperm web, which is then drawn into the palps.

During mating the male introduces his palps alternately, or, in the more primitive spiders, both together. Copulation lasts from a few seconds to many hours; among the orb-web weavers courtship is protracted but the mating is very short. The coupling of two predatory and often short-sighted creatures can be a hazardous affair, particularly for the almost invariably smaller male. Among orb-web weavers males may be one-quarter or even less the size of females. In pantropical golden orb spiders such as the Giant wood spider of Southeast Asia, the female may have a leg span of 6in (15cm), while the male, with a span of less than 0.4in (1cm) is able to walk over her abdomen, virtually immune to attack.

Most spiders live about one year. Eggs laid in the fall or dry season usually hatch in the following spring or wet season. Some spiders live for 2–5 years, and theraphosids in captivity may live up to 25 years.

Spiders are an ancient group and were probably in existence during the Devonian period, almost 400 million years ago. By the Carboniferous period (over 300 million years ago), when insects were in their infancy, many highly developed spiders already existed. Some 20 fossil species have been described from the period, among them 12 from the Liphistiomorphae, which are remarkably like the modern "living fossils" *Liphistius* and *Heptathele* (see p147). It is not until the Oligocene epoch (28 million years ago) that fossil spiders reappear. In Baltic amber and other sources in North America and Europe, many well-preserved fossils have been found.

The discovery of the peculiar family Archaeidae is a very similar story to that of the much more famous coelacanth fish and *Metasequoia* conifer, but it happened much earlier. First described in 1854 as fossils in Baltic amber, they were found alive in Madagascar a quarter of a century later. These bizarre spiders have an enormously elevated head region and grossly developed chelicerae used, apparently, to spear other spiders! Though very rare they are today known from South Africa and Australasia as well as Madagascar, with relatives in South America. Such a distribution, reflecting the ancient continent of Gondwanaland, is also seen in bolas spiders: *Mastophora* in South America, *Dichrosticus* and *Celaenia* in Australia and *Cladomelea* in South Africa.

The enemies of spiders include mammals, birds, reptiles, amphibians and other spiders. Ants, assassin bugs and preying mantises prey on spiders. Insect parasites include minute wasps (Ichneumonidae) which parasitize spider eggs, flies (both endo- and exoparasites) and wasps, including the spider-hunting wasps (Pompilidae, Sphecidae). Many species of fungus also develop on and within spiders.   PDH

▲ **Suspended by a silken thread** from her web, a female orb web spider, *Araneus quadratus* (Araneidae), completes her final molt. A spider's sex only becomes apparent after the final molt.

▶ **Silken nursery tent,** spun by the female when her eggs are about to hatch, gives the nursery web spiders their name. Here, a female guards her spiderlings in their nursery. Previously, she will have carried her eggs around in a silk purse (Pisauridae).

▼ **A mating pair of crab spiders,** *Xysticus cristatus* (Thomisidae). The male is very much smaller than the female and has tethered her to the leaf with strands of silk. However, she will have no difficulty in freeing herself afterward. Rather, the bondage is "symbolic" and part of courtship.

Maternal Care

The hazards of life for spiders are so great that most females must produce tens, hundreds or even thousands of eggs to ensure survival of the species. Cave spiders of the genus *Telema* (family Telemidae) lay a single egg, but *Araneus* and *Cupiennius* (family Ctenidae), for example, lay 2,500 in every egg sac. Some spiders guard and defend their egg sac, but those that produce numbers of egg sacs (up to 20 or more, often from one mating) tend to abandon them, relying on camouflage for their protection. Many spiders never see their offspring, but some actively care for the newly hatched spiderlings, protecting and/or feeding them.

In the abundant widespread wolf spiders (*Pardosa* species) the egg sac, which is carried attached to the spinnerets at the tip of the abdomen, is conspicuous and may be as big as the mother herself, but she will fight and defend it with her life. After 2-3 weeks she bites open the egg sac, whereupon the brood of up to 100 spiderlings climbs onto her abdomen, several layers deep. Living on their reserves of yolk, they hold on for about a week while she continues to hunt and defend herself if necessary.

Experiments with wolf spiderlings have shown that there is no mutual recognition. They accept spiderlings from another female and they will climb onto the backs of other spiders, even male spiders of other species which often simply eat them.

Nursery-web spiders carefully carry their egg sac in their mouthparts (chelicerae) but it is further secured by silk lines to the spinnerets. It is often so large that the mother has to run on tip toes. Close to the time for hatching, the egg sac is fixed to a stem or leaf and surrounded by a network of silk to form a protective tent while the spiderlings undergo their first molts. In North America, Europe and Japan, the mother on guard outside the tent is a common sight during the summer months.

Active feeding of the brood is found in only a tiny minority of spiders. There are two levels of care: passive provision of prey, and feeding by regurgitation as found in two unrelated families, Theridiidae and Eresidae. In the cosmopolitan genus *Theridion* the spiderlings imbibe a fluid mixture of predigested food and the mother's own intestinal cells. Regurgitation may be stimulated by the spiderlings stroking her legs and then clustering round her mouth. After their first molt they begin to share her victims, which she liberally punctures with her fangs. In North America and Europe, spiders of the genus *Coelotes* (Agelenidae) carry maternal feeding to the extreme—when the mother dies, her tissues break down and the spiderlings feed on her.

Silken Webs

Variety of silks is key to spiders' success

Web-spinning spiders spend virtually their whole life in contact with silk threads of their own manufacture. All spiders, even those that do not build webs, use silk for a variety of purposes, including the construction of retreats, egg sacs and nursery tents, the wrapping of prey, making floating threads for "ballooning," and the laying of draglines. Draglines are anchored to the web or to points on the substrate by attachment disks. An orb-web spider, disturbed at its hub, will often drop like a stone on a dragline, then wait, and climb up it again later when the danger has passed. For the jumping spider, which may be hunting on a vertical rock face or wall, it is essential to fix this safety line before any leap is made.

Spider's silk is a fibrous protein (fibroin) which is insoluble in water. Its strength is almost as good as high-tensile nylon but its elasticity is much greater, stretching as much as one-third its length before breaking. The dragline silk of a golden orb spider (*Nephila* species) is the strongest natural fiber known. Silk is not squeezed out of the body but drawn out. Liquid silk, within a gland inside the abdomen, is solidified and transformed from a soluble to an insoluble form (polymerized), not by contact with the air but simply by mechanical stretching. Most silk strands have a diameter of only a few micrometers. As much as 2,300ft

(700m) in length may be drawn continuously from a living golden orb spider.

Different glands secrete silk of a particular chemical composition with physical properties fitted to a specific purpose. Up to seven different types of glands occur in spiders of the orb-weaver family Araneidae, but in hunting spiders (Heteropodidae) with fewer different requirements, there are usually only four. The main silk glands are: ampullate (bellied) glands, producing silk for the dragline and for the dry threads of webs; aggregate (branched), producing the sticky globules of orb-webs (Araneidae and Tetragnathidae) and the scaffolding-webs (Theridiidae); piriform (pear-shaped), for the attachment disks of draglines; aciniform (berry-shaped), swathing bands for wrapping prey and the sperm web; and cylindrical (absent in the adult male), providing silk for the egg cocoon.

Early spiders (400–300 million years ago) probably dwelt in holes or retreats. Around the entrances, accumulated threads would have helped signal the presence of prey through vibrations and possibly assisted in its trapping. Simple webs of this type are found in the tube-web family Segestridae. Their web comprises a tubular retreat with several straight "fishing lines" radiating from the entrance which communicate vibrations from potential prey and indicate the direction of chase. In the cribellate families Filistatidae and Amaurobiidae, the similar but more untidy webs convey vibrations and also entangle victims in the mesh.

Greater, three-dimensional complexity is seen in the scaffolding-webs of Theridiidae (eg the cosmopolitan genus *Steatoda*). Filling spaces such as the corners of disused rooms, *Steatoda's* web is studded with gluey droplets. Tight, criss-crossing threads stretch above and below a central tangle under which hangs the rotund spider. Insects which break the contact of a thread with the substrate, adhere to the gum and are lifted into the web as the thread contracts. Struggling only causes further entanglement in neighboring threads and, after throwing more gummy silk over the hapless victim, *Steatoda* delivers a *coup de grâce* with a bite to the nearest leg.

An advance toward the orb web may be seen in the hammock webs or dome webs of Linyphiidae (money spiders) where the central tangle has become a distinct sheet. With the final transformation from horizontal sheet to vertical orb, the most economical and effective trap for aerial prey has evolved. Remarkably designed structure though it is, the orb web appears to have

▲ **An orb web spider,** *Araneus angulatus*, sits at the center of its web. Orb webs are built in gaps between vegetation or rocks, which are likely to be in the flight paths of insects. The web's sticky threads help to retain insects which have blundered into it (Araneidae).

▶ **Silk is drawn out** by the spider's legs, through tiny spigots on the spinnerets, short or finger-like appendages at the tip of the abdomen. There are usually three pairs, as in cobweb spiders (Agelenidae) (1). But in the several families of cribellate spiders (2), the first pair of spinnerets has developed into a sieve-like field, the cribellum, bearing up to 40,000 tiny spigots. The ultra-fine woolly "hackled" silk is as little as 0.02μm in diameter and has great snagging power, requiring no sticky droplets to catch insects' legs, unlike silk of other spiders.

◀ **Scaffolding web** of a species of *Theridion* in Malaya. The web is an interlocking network of silk strands, with droplets of a sticky glue distributed regularly throughout (Theridiidae).

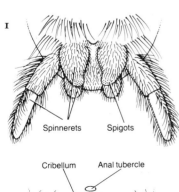

1

Spinnerets   Spigots

Cribellum   Anal tubercle

2

Spinnerets   Spigots

developed twice. The webs of cribellate Uloboridae and ecribellate Araneidae are superficially similar but with dry, woolly cribellate silk on the one hand and glue-coated threads on the other, it may be that here is an excellent example of evolutionary convergence, though this theory is now disputed; many believe that cribellate webs are ancestral to ecribellate.

Webs must to some extent provide a balance between the time and energy used in their construction and their trapping efficiency. For example, cribellate silk is economical, it weathers well and does not require frequent renewal. Gluey silk, on the other hand, catches more but loses effectiveness when subjected to water and dust. The majority of araneid orb-web weavers renew their webs once a day (or, rather, night). However, as they roll up the old web and eat it, conserving the protein, this is not such an extravagant use of nutrients as it might seem. It also helps to combat the problem of kleptoparasites, small uninvited spiders that feed in another's web.

The web spun by members of the araneid orb-web genus *Cyrtophora* illustrates a number of features. It is a horizontal, finely radiating sheet with scaffolding above and below which, unusually for araneids, lacks stickiness. It is a robust, semi-permanent construction which very often is host to numbers of kleptoparasites. The web holds prey less effectively than sticky orbs of the same area, it is more conspicuous and more easily avoided by insects, but it requires less maintenance. Its chief virtue may be that it is still in place after heavy tropical downpours, to catch the moths and other insects which fly immediately after rain.   PDH

BIBLIOGRAPHY

The following list of titles indicates key reference works used in the preparation of this volume and those recommended for further reading. The list is divided into various categories.

General

Alcock, J. (1975) *Animal Behavior: An Evolutionary Approach*, Sinauer Associates, Sunderland, Massachusetts.

Alexander, R. McNeil (1979) *The Invertebrates*, Cambridge University Press, Cambridge, England.

Askew, R.R. (1971) *Parasitic Insects*, Heinemann Educational Books, London.

Barash, D. (1979) *Sociobiology: the Whisperings Within*, Harper and Row, New York.

Barnes, R.D. (1980) *Invertebrate Zoology* (4th edn), Saunders College/Holt, Philadelphia.

Barrington, E.J.W. (1979) *Invertebrate Structure and Function* (2nd edn), Van Nostrand Rheinhold, Wokingham, UK.

Bell, W.J. and Cardé, R.T. (eds) (1983) *The Chemical Ecology of Insects*, Chapman and Hall, London and New York.

Birch, M.C. (ed) (1974) *Pheromones*, Frontiers of Biology no. 32, North Holland, Amsterdam.

Birch, M.C. and Haynes, K.F. (1982) *Insect Pheromones*, Studies in Biology no. 147, Edward Arnold, London.

Blum, M.S. and Blum, N.A. (eds) (1979) *Sexual Selection and Reproductive Competition in Insects*, Academic Press, New York and London.

Boror, D.J., de Long, D.M. and Triplehorn, C.A. (1981) *Introduction to the Study of Insects* (5th edn), Saunders College Publishing, New York.

Boudreaux, H.B. (1979) *Arthropod Phylogeny*, John Wiley and Sons, New York and Chichester.

Breed, M.D., Michener, C.D. and Evans, H.E. (eds) (1982) *The Biology of Social Insects*, Proceedings of the 9th Congress of the International Union for the Study of Social Insects, Westview Press, Boulder, Colorado.

Brian, M.V. (1983) *Social Insects, Ecology and Behavioral Biology* Chapman and Hall, London and New York.

Chapman, R.F. (1982) *The Insects: Structure and Function* (3rd edn), English University Press, London.

Cheng, I., (ed) (1976) *Marine Insects*. North Holland Publishing, Amsterdam and Oxford.

Clausen, C.P. (1940) *Entomophagous Insects*. McGraw-Hill, New York.

Clutton-Brock, T.H. and Harvey, P.H. (eds) (1978) *Readings in Sociobiology*, W.H. Freeman, Reading, UK.

Cott, H.B. (1940) *Adaptive Coloration in Animals*, Methuen and Co, London.

Daly, H.V., Dayen, J.T. and Erlich, P.R. (1978) *Introduction to Insect Biology and Diversity*, McGraw-Hill, New York.

Dawkins, R. (1976) *The Selfish Gene*, Oxford University Press, Oxford.

Dawkins, R. (1982) *The Extended Phenotype: the Gene as the Unit of Selection*, W.H. Freeman, Oxford.

Edmunds, M. (1974) *Defence in Animals*, Longmans, London.

Eisner, T. and Wilson, E.O. (eds) (1977) *The Insects: Readings from Scientific American*, W.H. Freeman, San Francisco.

Emden, H.F. van (ed) (1973) *Insect–Plant Relationships*, 6th Symposium of the Royal Entomological Society, Blackwell Scientific, Oxford.

Evans, H.E. (1984) *Life on a Little-known Planet*, University of Chicago Press, Chicago and London.

Free, J. B. (1970) *Insect Pollination of Crops*, Academic Press, London and New York.

Futuyma, D.J. and Slatkin (1983) *Coevolution*, Sinauer Associates, Sunderland, Massachusetts.

Gilbert, L. E. and Raven, P. H. (eds) (1975) *Coevolution of Animals and Plants*, University of Texas Press, Austin.

Gilbert, P. and Hamilton, C.J. (1983) *Entomology—A Guide to Information Sources*, Mansell Publishing, London.

Gillott, C. (1980) *Entomology*, Plenum, New York and London

Hennig, W. (1981) *Insect Phylogeny*, (transl and ed A. Pont, revisionary notes Dieter Schlee), John Wiley and Sons, New York and Chichester.

Hermann, H.R. (ed) (1979-82) *Social Insects* (4 vols), Academic Press, New York and London.

Johnson, C.G. (1969) *Migration and Dispersal of Insects by Flight*, Methuen, London.

Kaestner, A. (1968) *Invertebrate Zoology*, vol II, *Arthropod Relatives, Chelicerata, Myriapoda* (transl H.W. and L.R Levi), John Wiley Interscience, New York and London.

Kettlewell, H.B.D. (1973) *The Evolution of Melanism: the Study of a Recurring Necessity*, Clarendon Press, Oxford.

Krebs, J. R. and Davis, N. B. (1978) *Behavioral Ecology, an Evolutionary Approach*, Blackwell Scientific, Oxford.

Krishna, K. and Weesner, F.M. (1969-70) *Biology of Termites* (2 vols), Academic Press, New York and London.

Linsenmaier, W. (1972) *Insects of the World* (transl L.E. Chadwick), McGraw-Hill, New York and London.

Manton, S.M. (1977) *The Arthropoda, Habits, Functional Morphology and Evolution*, Clarendon Press, Oxford.

Mound, L.M. and Waloff, N. (eds) (1978) *Diversity of Insect Faunas*, 9th Symposium of the Royal Entomological Society, Blackwell Scientific, Oxford.

Oster, G.F. and Wilson, E.O. (1978) *Caste and Ecology in the Social Insects*, Monographs in Population Biology 12, Princeton University Press, New Jersey.

O'Toole, C. and Preston-Mafham, K. (1985) *Insects in Camera: A Photographic Essay on Behaviour*, Oxford University Press, Oxford.

Owen, D.F. (1980) *Camouflage and Mimicry*, Oxford University Press, Oxford.

Rainey, R.C. (ed) (1975) *Insect Flight*, 7th Symposium of the Royal Entomological Society, Blackwell Scientific, Oxford.

Richards, O.W. and Davies, R.G. (1977) *Imm's General Textbook of Entomology* (10th edn, 2 vols), Chapman and Hall, London.

Rockstein, M. (ed) (1973-74) *The Physiology of Insects* (6 vols), Academic Press, New York and London.

Romoser, W.S. (1981) *The Science of Entomology*, Macmillan, London and New York.

Ross, H.H., Ross, C.A. and Ross, J.R.P. (1982) *A Textbook of Entomology* (4th edn), Wiley, New York.

Sharov, A.G. (1966) *Basic Arthropodan Stock, with Special Reference to Insects*, Pergamon Press, Oxford.

Smith, K.G.V. (ed) (1973) *Insects and Other Arthropods of Medical Importance*, British Museum (Natural History), London.

Snodgrass, R.E. (1935) *Principles of Insect Morphology*, McGraw-Hill, New York.

Southwood, T.R.E. (ed) (1968) *Insect Abundance*, 4th Symposium of the Royal Entomological Society, Blackwell Scientific, Oxford.

Thornhill, R. and Alcock, J. (1983) *The Evolution of Insect Mating Systems*, Harvard University Press, Cambridge, Massachusetts.

Varley, G.C., Gradwell, G.R. and Hassell, M.P. (1973) *Insect Population Ecology: an Analytical Approach*, Blackwell Scientific, Oxford.

Wickler, W. (1968) *Mimicry in Animals and Plants* (trans R.D. Martin), Weidenfeld and Nicolson, London.

Wigglesworth, V.B. (1964) *The Life of Insects*, Weidenfeld and Nicolson, London.

Wigglesworth, V. B. (1972) *The Principles of Insect Physiology* (7th edn), Chapman and Hall, London.

Wilson, E.O. (1971) *The Insect Societies*, Belknap Press of Harvard University Press, Cambridge, Massachusetts.

Wilson, E.O. (1975) *Sociobiology, the New Synthesis*, Belknap Press of Harvard University Press, Cambridge, Massachusetts and London.

Regional

Arnett, R.H. (1985) *American Insects: A Handbook of the Insects of America North of Mexico*, Van Nostrand Reinhold, New York.

Chinery, M. (1976) *A Field Guide to the Insects of Britain and Northern Europe*, Collins, London.

Gertsch, W.J. (1979) *American Spiders*, Van Nostrand Reinhold, New York.

Holm, E. and Scholtz, C. (eds) (1985) *Insects of Southern Africa*, Butterworth, Durban.

Jones, R. (1985) *The Country Life Guide to Spiders of Britain and Northern Europe*, Country Life Books, Feltham.

Main, B.Y. (1976) *Australian Spiders*, Collins, Sydney.

Mani, M.S. (1962) *Introduction to High Altitude Entomology. Life above the Timber-line in the North-West Himalaya*, Methuen, London.

Skaife, S.H. (1979) *African Insect Life* (2nd edn), Country Life Books, London.

Waterhouse, D.F. (ed) (1970) *The Insects of Australia, a Textbook for Students and Research Workers*, Melbourne University Press, Melbourne.

Major Groups

Ackery, P.R. and Vane-Wright, R.I. (1984), *Milkweed Butterflies, their Cladistics and Biology*, British Museum (Natural History), London.

Bristowe, W.S. (1958) *The World of Spiders* (revised edn, 1971), New Naturalist Series, Collins, London.

Butler, C.G. (1954) *The World of the Honeybee*, New Naturalist Series, Collins, London.

Corbet, P.S. (1962) *A Biology of Dragonflies*, Willoughby, London.

Corbet, P.S., Longfield, C. and Moore, N.W. (1960) *Dragonflies*, New Naturalist Series, Collins, London.

Growson, R.A. (1981) *The Biology of the Coleoptera*, Academic Press, London.

Evans, G. (1975) *The Life of Beetles*, George Allen & Unwin, London.

Evans, H.E. (1966) *The Comparative Ethology and Evolution of the Sand Wasps*. Harvard University Press, Cambridge, Massachusetts.

Evans, H.E. and West-Eberhard, M.J. (1973) *The Wasps*, David and Charles, Newton Abbot, Devon.

Foelix, R.F. (1982) *Biology of Spiders*, Harvard University Press, Cambridge, Massachusetts.

Ford, E.B. (1957) *Butterflies* (3rd edn), New Naturalist Series, Collins, London.

Ford, E.B. (1972) *Moths*, (3rd edn), New Naturalist Series, Collins, London.

Free, J.B. and Butler, C.G. (1957) *Bumblebees*, New Naturalist Series, Collins, London.

Frisch, K. von (1967) *The Dance Language and Orientation of Bees* (transl L.E. Chadwick), Belknap Press of Harvard University Press, Cambridge, Massachusetts.

Heinrich, B. (1979) *Bumblebee Economics*, Harvard University Press, Cambridge, Massachusetts and London.

Iwata, K. (1971) *Evolution of Instinct: Comparative Ethology of Hymenoptera*, Amerind Publishing Co, New Delhi, for Smithsonian Institution, Washington, DC and Natural Science Foundation.

Michener, C.D. (1974) *The Social Behavior of the Bees, a Comparative Study*, Belknap Press of Harvard University Press, Cambridge, Massachusetts.

Oldroyd, H. (1964) *The Natural History of Flies*, Weidenfeld and Nicolson, London.

Owen, D.F. (1971) *Tropical Butterflies*, Oxford University Press, Oxford.

Preston-Mafham, R. and Preston-Mafham, K. (1984) *Spiders of the World*, Blandford Press, Poole.

Rothschild, M. and Clay, T. (1952) *Fleas, Flukes and Cuckoos, A Study of Bird Parasites*, New Naturalist Series, London.

Savory, T. (1977) *Arachnida* (2nd edn), Academic Press, London and New York.

Spradberry, J.P. (1973) *Wasps, An Account of the Biology and Natural History of Solitary and Social Wasps*, Sidgwick and Jackson, London.

Stephen, W.P., Bohart, G.E. and Torchio, P.F. (1969) *The Biology and External Morphology of Bees, with a Synopsis of the Genera of Northwestern America*, Oregon University Press, Corvallis, Oregon.

Vane-Wright, R.I. and Ackery, P.R. (1984) *The Biology of Butterflies*, 11th Symposium of the Royal Entomological Society of London, Academic Press (Harcourt, Brace, Jovanovich), London.

Witt, P.N. and Rovner, J.S. (eds) (1982) *Spider Communication Mechanisms and Ecological Significance*, Princeton University Press, Princeton, New Jersey.

GLOSSARY

Abdomen   region of the body of an arthropod behind the THORAX, in insects comprising up to 10 SEGMENTS.

Adaptive radiation   see RADIATION, ADAPTIVE.

Air sac   thin-walled expansion of the TRACHEAL system of an arthropod, which boosts the inspiration and exhalation of air. Air sacs also give buoyancy to aquatic insects and in dragonflies provide insulation around the thoracic wing muscles.

Alimentary canal   the gut or digestive system.

Ametabolous   of insects having no METAMORPHOSIS, ie the Apterygota, in which larvae hatch from the egg in a form essentially identical to the adult except for the size and undeveloped genitalia. The gonads develop and size increases at each molt.

Amino acid   one of about 20 compounds comprising both a basic amino (NH$_2$) group and an acidic carboxyl (COOH) group, which combine in their hundreds to form proteins.

Anaerobic   of physiological processes which take place in the absence of oxygen.

Annelid   a member of the phylum Annelida which comprises the segmented worms, including the familiar earthworms and leeches.

Aorta   the main blood vessel leading anteriorly from the dorsal "heart" of insects.

Apodeme   an ingrowth of EXOSKELETON to which muscles are attached.

Arachnid   member of the class Arachnida (spiders, scorpions, ticks and mites) of the phylum Chelicerata.

Arthropod   "jointed-limbed" invertebrate with a hardened CUTICLE (EXOSKELETON), a condition believed to have evolved independently on several occasions – hence the separate phyla of "arthropods."

Autotomy   the process by which a limb can be voluntarily shed if grabbed by a predator. Found in spiders and grasshoppers, where the leg is shed by the sharp contraction of muscles acting on a special fracture point of weakness.

Axon   long process of a nerve cell; normally conducts impulses away from the nerve cell body.

Bee milk   see ROYAL JELLY.

Biological control   the use of natural predators, parasites or disease organisms to reduce the number of pest insects or weed plants.

Book gill   breathing apparatus in some arachnids, resembling a BOOK LUNG but on exterior of body.

Book lung   a paired chamber invaginated into the ventral abdominal wall of arachnids where the gaseous exchanges of respiration take place across folded, leaf-like LAMELLAE, which have a rich blood supply.

Brood cell   a specially-prepared space or structure in the nests of bees and wasps in which food is stored, an egg is laid and the larva completes its development.

Calamistrum   a row of hairs on the back legs of certain spiders, which are used to comb out silk produced by the CRIBELLUM.

Caste   in colonies of SOCIAL insects, any group of individuals that are structurally and/or behaviorally distinct and perform specialized tasks: eg the "SOLDIERS" of termites and ants and the "WORKERS" of, say, hornets and honeybees.

Catalepsy   death-feigning.

Cell   the basic structural unit of all plant and animal tissues, each comprising a central nucleus surrounded by CYTOPLASM.

Cellulase   an enzyme which digests cellulose.

Cephalothorax   or prosoma, the 6-segmented head-and-thorax of an arachnid.

Cerci   paired, articulated appendages at the end of the abdomen in many arthropods and probably sensory in function.

Chelicerate, chelicerae   member of the arthropod phylum Chelicerata (arachnids, horseshoe crabs and sea spiders) possessing a pair of pincer-like mouthparts (chelicerae) in front of the mouth opening.

Chemoreceptor   a sense organ of taste or smell reacting to the presence of chemicals, as opposed to other receptors which perceive sound waves, vibrations or touch.

Chitin   (adj. chitinous) complex nitrogen-containing polysaccharide which forms a material of considerable mechanical strength and resistance to chemicals : forms the CUTICLE of arthropods.

Chromosome   thread-like structure in the nuclei of cells, which carries the genetic information.

Chrysalis   the PUPA (pupal stage) in moths and butterflies, often enclosed in a silk cocoon.

Cilia   minute hairs which beat with a regular rhythm and are found in many EPITHELIAL tissues which line internal ducts. Cilia also cover the outside of many protozoans and are their means of locomotion.

Claspers   a pair of pincer-like appendages of the male genitalia of insects which clasp the female during copulation.

Click mechanism   a spring-loaded articulation between THORAX and ABDOMEN of beetles of the family Elateridae which enables the beetle to right itself if it falls on its back. This is accompanied by an audible click, which may surprise predators.

Clypeus   the frontal plate or SCLERITE between the COMPOUND EYES and anterior to the antennal insertion.

Cocoon   the silk envelope spun by the mature larva (pre-pupa) of many insects immediately prior to pupation.

Comb   horizontal or vertical ranks of brood cells in SOCIAL paper-making wasps and the highly social stingless bees and honeybees.

Communal   (level of social organization) refers to the situation in insects where members of the same generation share a nest and its construction, but not care of the brood; each female rears her own brood.

Complete metamorphosis   where development from the egg goes through a distinct larval and pupal stage before the adult stage is achieved. Typically, the larva differs from the adult, not only in structure, but also in diet.

Compound eye   type of arthropod eye composed of many long, cylindrical units (ommatidia) each of which is capable of light reception.

Conspecific   of the same species.

Convergent evolution   the evolution of two or more organisms with some increasingly similar characteristics but different ancestry.

Corbiculum   the pollen basket of female bees of the family Apidae, comprising a slightly concave area of the outer face of the hind TIBIA, fringed with stiff bristles.

Corpus allatum   see JUVENILE HORMONE.

Cosmopolitan   found everywhere.

Courtship dance   dance-like actions which precede mating in many arthropods and which enable prospective mates to recognize each other as being CONSPECIFIC and to assess each other's quality.

Coxa   basal section of an arthropod APPENDAGE, joining the limb to the body.

Cribellate (noun cribellum)   of spiders which have a cribellum, a plate through which a special kind of silk is produced, combed out by the CALAMISTRUM and mixed with ordinary silk from the SPINNERETS to make a bluish, lace-like composite strand.

Crop   an enlargement of the foregut in insects, in which food is stored.

Crustacean   pertaining to the phylum Crustacea, which includes the crabs, lobsters, barnacles, shrimps and woodlice.

Cryptic (noun crypsis)   pertaining to anti-predator adaptations in animals which take up resting positions on backgrounds or among objects to which they have a resemblance – eg moths with a color pattern resembling lichen-covered bark, grasshoppers resembling stones.

Ctenidium   a row of stiff spines on the rear of the PRONOTUM in fleas.

Cuckoo   see KLEPTOPARASITE.

Cuckoo spit   a frothy secretion produced by the NYMPHS of certain soft-bodied plant bugs in which they live and which protects them from desiccation and some, but not all, predators.

Cuticle   in arthropods, the external layer formed in CHITIN, which is secreted by the EPIDERMIS; acts as an EXOSKELETON, and as a barrier limiting water loss and preventing entry of microorganisms.

Cytoplasm   all the living matter of a cell excluding the nucleus.

Dendrite   one of the finest and highly branched ends of a nerve fiber (AXON) which are specialized for the reception of stimuli which initiate nerve impulses.

Dermecos   the habitat limited to the spaces between the hairs of a mammal's skin in which ectoparasites such as lice and fleas live.

Diploidy   (adj. diploid) the presence within the nucleus of two homologous sets of CHROMOSOMES.

Division of labor   the condition in SOCIAL insect colonies where different tasks are allocated to morphological CASTES specialized for carrying them out – eg egg-laying in queens, foraging and colony defense by workers.

Dorsal   situated at, or related to, the back of the body, ie the side that is generally directed upward.

Drone   a male honeybee (*Apis* species).

Ecribellate   of spiders without a CRIBELLUM.

Ectognathous   the primitive condition in insects where the mouthparts are exposed (cf ENTOGNATHOUS).

Ectoparasite   parasite living on the outside of its host.

Endocrine gland   gland whose secretions pass directly into the blood stream (eg the CORPUS ALLATUM of insects).

Endocuticle   inner layer of the CUTICLE that is recycled at each molt but remains unhardened, by contrast with the hard EXOCUTICLE.

Endopterygote   pertaining to (or one of) those insects in which the wings develop internally, and in which METAMORPHOSIS is complete, there being a PUPAL STAGE (holometaboly).

Endoskeleton   an internal skeleton, as in vertebrates, or elements of the arthropod EXOSKELETON which, as in larger insects, serve as an internal skeleton (eg sites for muscle attachment, also APODEMES).

Entognathous   the condition found in the Collembola, Protura and Diplura in which the pre-oral cavity is enclosed by pleural folds which grow down from the sides of the head (cf ECTOGNATHOUS).

Entomology   the branch of zoology devoted to the study of insects.

Enzyme   a chemical, usually a protein, which acts as a catalyst in chemical processes such as digestion and tissue respiration.

Eocene   the geological epoch which began about 54 and lasted until 38 million years ago: a time of widespread tropical and temperate forests, with an essentially modern flora (except for absence of grasses) and archaic mammals. All modern arthropod groups were well established.

Epicuticle   thin outermost layer of the CUTICLE made of proteins and lipids, which in terrestrial arthropods includes a waterproofing waxy layer and usually a tough protective cement layer.

Epidermis   or hypodermis, the single layer of living cells which underlies and secretes the arthropod CUTICLE.

Epithelium   sheet of cells lining cavities and vessels and covering exposed body surfaces.

Eruciform   of insect larvae such as caterpillars and beetle larvae with well-defined segmentation, abdominal legs or PROLEGS and nine pairs of respiratory SPIRACLES.

Eusocial (eusociality)   pertaining to SOCIAL insect colonies with the highest level of social behavior, cooperative brood care, a reproductive division of labor, with sterile workers and an egg-laying queen or queens and the overlap of at least two worker generations.

Exarate pupa   pupa in which the APPENDAGES are free from the body.

Exocrine gland   gland which produces secretions that are ducted directly to the outside of an animal's body (eg salivary gland, scent gland).

Exocuticle   the hardened outer layers of the CUTICLE, as compared with the unhardened ENDOCUTICLE.

Exopterygote   pertaining to (or one of) those insects in which the wings develop externally, ie with an incomplete METAMORPHOSIS (hemimetaboly).

Exoskeleton   the external skeleton of an arthropod, made of CUTICLE.

Facultative parasite   parasite capable of a particular type of parasitic behavior or life-style, but not obliged to adopt it for survival.

False legs   or prolegs, fleshy outgrowths in insect larvae which function as legs, but are not true articulated limbs.

Femur   the 3rd and most muscular of the four components that together comprise an insect's leg (coxa, trochanter, femur, tarsus).

Flagellum   in insects, the outer (distal) series of segments of antennae which are elbowed, ie have a long basal segment (scape).

Flash coloration   brightly colored parts of an animal's body which are normally hidden but which can be exposed suddenly to frighten away a predator.

Food chain   an hierarchical array of organisms which feed on the next lowest organism(s) or trophic level, eg leaf←weevil←robberfly←bird←hawk.

Foraging pattern   of bees, the pattern of food-gathering behavior which is determined by the local abundance and structure of flowers.

Fundatrix   a female member of a generation of plant-feeding bugs, especially aphids, which produce eggs by PARTHENOGENESIS.

Fungus comb   a mass of fungus cultivated by macrotermitine termites and leaf-cutter ants, on which the insects feed.

Furca   a Y-shaped APODEME of the thoracic sternum in insects.

Fusion   the process, in sexually reproducing organisms, in which sperm and egg unite to complete fertilization and initiate the development of a new individual.

Gall   a tumorous growth of plant tissues stimulated by the presence of a specific virus, fungus or insect egg. In the case of the latter, the gall increases in size as the insect larva inside it feeds on special "grazing" tissue lining the larval chamber.

Gill   in insects, thin-skinned outgrowths of the bodies of aquatic larvae across which the gaseous exchanges of respiration take place.

Gland   a distinct tissue or group of tissues which secretes a specific substance, eg scent or hormones.

Gonopore   the ultimate genital opening in male arthropods through which semen containing sperm is ejaculated during copulation.

Gregarious   of animals which live or nest in groups, but which do not cooperate, ie are not truly SOCIAL.

Hamuli   the hooks on the leading edge of the hindwings of wasps and bees, which engage a fold on the hind margin of the forewings, so coupling the wings together to make a functional whole.

Haplodiploidy   the method of sex determination in Hymenoptera (wasps, ants and bees), where males are derived from unfertilized HAPLOID eggs and females are derived from fertilized DIPLOID eggs, with the normal, diploid, complement of CHROMOSOMES.

Haploidy (adj haploid)   the state of having only one half of the normal complement of CHROMOSOMES and which is found in gametes (sperm and egg) and in male Hymenoptera.

Head capsule   the part of an arthropod's EXOSKELETON which encloses the head and associated structures.

Hemimetaboly (adj. hemimetabolous) see INCOMPLETE METAMORPHOSIS.

Hemolymph   the blood of arthropods.

Hexapod   a member of the superclass Hexapoda, a large group of six-legged arthropods comprising the classes Collembola, Diplura, Protura and Insecta.

Holarctic   found in both temperate North America and temperate Eurasia.

Holometabolous   SEE COMPLETE METAMORPHOSIS.

Honeydew   the sugary fluid, derived from plant sap, excreted by aphids, leafhoppers and treehoppers.

Hormone   a chemical produced in small quantities by a gland in one part of an animal's body, which enters the blood stream and has a physiological effect on other glands or parts of the body. See, eg JUVENILE HORMONE.

Hypermetamorphosis   a series of developmental stages beyond the usual larva, pupa and adult stages in COMPLETE METAMORPHOSIS.

Hyperparasitoid   a PARASITOID of another parasitoid.

Hypodermis   or epidermis, the single layer of cells in arthropods which secretes the CUTICLE.

Hypognathous   of those insects with mouthparts and oral cavity on the ventral surface of the head.

Imago   an adult, sexually mature insect.

Immature   of insects, as a noun, an alternative to "NYMPH" or "larva."

Incomplete metamorphosis   or hemimetaboly, the process of development in the more primitive insects (exopterygotes) which do not have a PUPAL STAGE. Instead, the egg hatches to produce a larva (sometimes called a NYMPH) which resembles a small adult in structure, diet and habitat. Wings develop externally and there is a number of molts before the gonads develop and the final adult stage is achieved.

Inquiline   an insect which spends its entire life cycle as a SOCIAL parasite in the nest of another species. Inquiline workers are rare, absent or degenerate in behavior.

Instar   the stage between two molts in immature arthropods.

Juvenile hormone (JH)   a "hormone" secreted by the corpus allatum of the insect brain which controls METAMORPHOSIS in the young stages and yolk formation in the eggs of females.

Kin selection   the selection of genes in one or more individuals favoring the reproduction and survival of close relatives (apart from offspring) which possess identical genes by common descent. Kin selection is believed to have played an important role in the evolution of SOCIAL behavior in wasps, ants and bees.

Kleptoparasitism   a form of parasitism where a female wasp or bee (kleptoparasite) seeks out the prey or food store of a different species and uses it to rear her own offspring.

Labellum   a pair of soft expansions at the lower end of the LABIUM in flies.

Labium   the lower lip in insects comprising the paired mouthparts of one segment fused in the midline.

Labrum   a cuticular flap forming the upper lip in insects and hinged to the head above the mouth.

Lamellate   any structure comprising a serially repeated array of plate-like elements (lamellae). Often used in connection with the antennae of scarabaeid beetles.

Leaf miner   the minute larva of an insect which tunnels between the upper and lower surfaces of a leaf. Found in beetles, moths, flies and wasps.

Lek   an assembly of sexually displaying males which occupies an area containing no resources of interest to females except a choice of males willing and able to mate.

Mass provisioning   the habit in solitary wasps and bees and some SOCIAL bees, of supplying and storing all the food required for larval development in a brood cell at the time of egg-laying.

Mechanoreceptors   broadly speaking, structures which perceive forces which distort any part of the body. These forces may be air-borne vibrations (sound), water- or substrate-borne vibrations, gravity, and the postural effects of the animal's position. Cf CHEMORECEPTOR.

Metamorphosis   see COMPLETE METAMORPHOSIS, INCOMPLETE METAMORPHOSIS.

Metatarsus   the enlarged basal segment of the TARSUS in aculeate Hymenoptera.

Mimicry   the condition where individuals of one species (the mimic) achieve an increase of protection from predators by resembling the appearance of another species (the model). Cases where an innocuous mimic resembles a poisonous or venomous species are called **Batesian mimicry. Müllerian mimicry**, by contrast, involves the shared resemblance of an assemblage of unrelated species, all of which are poisonous or armed with a sting.

Monophyletic group   a group of species which includes an ancestral species (known or hypothesized) and all its descendents.

Müllerian bodies   leaf glands of *Cecropia* trees which provide food for symbiotic ants.

Myiasis   disease of man and other animals due to infestation by larvae of flies (Diptera) which are not necessarily parasitic. Most human myiases involve the infestation by larvae of already infected wounds. Others are due to the accidental swallowing of larvae with food, and involve the intestine.

Myriapod   member of the UNIRAMIAN superclass Myriapoda, which includes the millipedes and centipedes.

Myrmecophile   an organism, usually another insect, which must spend at least part of its life cycle in the nest of ants.

Neotropical   pertaining to the tropics of the New World, ie Central and northern South America, West Indies.

Neurone   a nerve cell.

Nuptial gift   a "gift", usually prey, offered to females by some male spiders and insects during courtship.

Nymph   an old term for the larva of an EXOPTERYGOTE insect (though in France it refers to the pupal stage of ENDOPTERYGOTES).

Obligate parasite   an animal that must spend at least part of its life cycle as a parasite of another animal.

Ocellus   (a) a simple eye consisting of a single cuticular lens and a few sensory cells; (b) an eye-like spot or pattern on the hindwing of a butterfly or moth. Cf COMPOUND EYE.

Oligolectic (noun oligolecty)   pertaining to species of bees in which the females collect pollen from only one or a group of related plant species.

Ommatidium   a single, optical unit of the COMPOUND EYE of an arthropod.

Öotheca   an egg-case or capsule made of a horny substance derived from the collecterial glands of female ORTHOPTEROID insects.

Opisthosoma   the abdomen of a chelicerate.

Orthopteroid   one of, or pertaining to, a group (Orthopteroidea) of insects with a shared ancestry, and including the orders Opthoptera (crickets and grasshoppers), Phasmatoidea (stick and leaf insects) and Dermaptera (earwigs).

Ovipositor   the egg-laying tube in insects, in most groups being derived from elements of the 8th and 9th segments.

Ovoviviparous   pertaining to those arthropods in which females retain eggs within the genital tract until the larvae are ready to hatch. Hatching occurs just before or as the eggs are laid.

Palaearctic   the biogeographical zone which includes temperate Eurasia and Africa north of the Sahara.

Panorpoid complex   the scorpion flies (Mecoptera), true flies (Diptera), butterflies and moths (Lepidoptera) and caddis flies (Trichoptera), which together form a MONOPHYLETIC group with a shared common ancestor.

Pantropical   pertaining to organisms or groups found throughout the tropics.

Parasite   an animal which feeds on the tissues of another animal, the host, without killing it. The host receives no benefit from the association.

Parasitoid   pertaining to those specialized insects whose larvae live as either external or internal parasites of other insects, eventually killing the host.

Parthenogenesis   development of a new individual from an unfertilized egg. Occurs in conditions where rapid colonization is important and/or there is an absence or only a small number of males in the population.

Pectinate   comb-like, usually pertaining to the much branched antennae of male moths, such as in the Saturniidae.

Pectine   paired, comb-like sensory APPENDAGE unique to scorpions, situated on the ventral side of the 2nd abdominal segment.

Pedipalp   appendage on 3rd segment of the CEPHALOTHORAX of chelicerates, variously modified, eg for seizing prey in scorpions, sensory or used by the male in reproduction in spiders.

Phloem sap   sap found in the main conducting vessels (phloem) in plants.

Phoresy, phoretic copulation   phoresy is the process by which one, usually smaller, animal hitches a ride on the body of another animal; in phoretic copulation, a male insect flies bearing a female with the genitalia of both insects engaged.

Planidium larva   the mobile first INSTAR larva of certain PARASITOID Diptera and Hymenoptera, which actively seeks out its host, using long bristles in locomotion.

Pleuron (pl. pleura)   lateral part of a THORACIC segment of an insect.

Pollen grains   the male sex cells of flowering plants produced in structures called anthers.

Pollination   the process by which pollen grains are transported by various agencies such as wind, water, birds, bats, but mainly insects, to the stigma or receptive female parts of the flower.

Polymorphism   the occurrence within a population of several discontinuous genes or phenotypes where even the rarest type has a frequency higher than could be maintained by recurrent mutation and is therefore the direct result of NATURAL SELECTION.

Polyphyletic   of a taxonomic group in which the most common ancestor is not assigned to the group, that is, a taxon which is based on characters which are not uniquely derived. In other words, a group which is not natural.

Predacious (noun predator) of an animal which preys on other animals for food.

Prepupa the larval phase of an holometabolous insect after feeding has ceased and in which larval CUTICLE becomes separated from its EPIDERMIS (hypodermis) and the developing pupa lies within the persistent larval cuticle. Sometimes called the pharate pupa.

Primary host host in or on which the sexually reproductive forms of a parasite, or a plant-eating insect such as an aphid, are to be found; cf SECONDARY HOST.

Primary parasitoid a PARASITOID which feeds directly on its host's tissues rather than (as in a HYPERPARASITOID) on those of another parasitoid.

Primitive ancestral.

Progressive feeding the habit in EUSOCIAL insects where larvae are provided with food on a regular basis during the development, as opposed to MASS PROVISIONING.

Prolegs see FALSE LEGS.

Pronotum the dorsal cuticular SCLERITE covering the first segment of the THORAX in insects, sometimes enlarged to cover the rest of the thorax, as in most cockroaches.

Propodeum the true first abdominal SEGMENT in apocritan Hymenoptera which is incorporated into the rear of the THORAX and separated from the ABDOMEN by a narrow waist.

Proprioceptor a sense organ which receives information about parts of the body, especially relating to their position. See RECEPTOR.

Prosoma see CEPHALOTHORAX.

Prothorax the first of the three SEGMENTS of the THORAX of an insect.

Proventriculus the "stomach" or gizzard of arthropods, with thick, muscular walls lined with chitinous teeth.

Pupa, pupal stage the non-feeding and relatively inactive stage between the larva and adult in holometabolous insects, during which most larval tissues are broken down and reformed into adult structures. See COMPLETE METAMORPHOSIS.

Puparium the hardened, persistent larval CUTICLE in higher flies (suborder Cyclorrhapha), which encloses the PUPA.

Pygidium the rearmost TERGITE of an insect's ABDOMEN.

Queen substance, Queen pheromone a chemical emitted by the mandibular glands of queen honeybees, which inhibits the building of queen cells by workers and the development of the workers' ovaries. Substances with the same function have been found in the queens of SOCIAL wasps (Vespidae).

Quinones a group of chemicals called cyclic diketones emitted as poisonous, repellent secretions by a wide range of insects, including cockroaches, earwigs and beetles, such as the Bombardier beetle.

Radiation, adaptive the invasion, through time, of a wide diversity of adaptive zones and niches by a group of organisms undergoing evolutionary diversification.

Receptor any sense organ which receives input from environmental or internal stimuli. See CHEMORECEPTOR, PROPRIOCEPTOR.

Reflex bleeding the sudden bleeding of brightly colored, noxious blood from special bleed points in limb articulations by insects in response to attack; found, eg, in larvae and adults of ladybirds (Coccinellidae).

Reproductive a member of a SOCIAL insect colony (males, queens) whose role in the society is reproductive.

Resilin an elastic, rubber-like protein found in the CUTICLE of insects in elastic hinge joints and also involved in the jumping mechanism of fleas. Like rubber, resilin can be stretched under tension, storing the energy involved, and returns to its original length and shape when the tension is released.

Rhabdome sometimes called the retinal rod, this is a structure formed from the united sensory borders of the retinal cells in the COMPOUND EYE.

Rostrum the beak-like piercing and sucking mouthparts of true bugs (Hemiptera).

Royal jelly sometimes called bee milk, a complex mixture of nutrients secreted by the hypopharyngeal glands of worker honeybees and fed to the larvae. Larvae destined to be queens are fed entirely on royal jelly; those destined to be workers receive it only for the first 3 or 4 days of larval life.

Saprophagous feeding on decaying plant or animal material.

Savanna dry scrub-dominated grasslands with *Acacia* trees and patches of bare earth.

Scale a modified hair, arising from a socket, which has become broad and flattened.

Sclerites thick chitinous plates forming units separated by thinner membranes in the EXOSKELETON of an arthropod.

Scutum the middle and largest of three SCLERITES which form the dorsal cuticular covering or notum of each thoracic SEGMENT of an insect.

Secondary genitalia of male insects, copulatory apparatus remote from the genital opening to which sperm or SPERMATOPHORE is transported before copulation. Found in spiders, and in dragonflies and damselflies (Odonata).

Secondary host host in or on which the larval, resting or asexually reproductive stages of a parasite, or of a plant-eating insect such as an aphid, may be present; cf PRIMARY HOST.

Segment repeating unit of a body (or of an APPENDAGE) with a structure basically similar to that of other segments; segments may be grouped into TAGMATA, as in the head, THORAX and ABDOMEN.

Semisocial of insect colonies in which females of the same generation cooperate in brood care, with some reproductive division of labor in that some individuals are mainly egg-layers and others are mainly workers.

Simple eye see OCELLUS.

Siphuncle a fleshy outgrowth of an aphid's body through which defensive, waxy secretions are emitted.

Slit organ widespread in the arachnids, slit organs are sense organs comprising a slit-like pit in the CUTICLE covered by a thin membrane which bulges inward, making contact with a hairlike process connected to the nervous system.

Social living together in colonies. There are, however, different grades of sociality; see EUSOCIAL, SUBSOCIAL, SEMISOCIAL.

Soldier a member of a worker sub-caste in termites and ants adapted in structure and behavior for a defensive role.

Spinneret a small tubular structure from which silk is extruded by spiders and many larval insects.

Spiracle external opening of a TRACHEA or breathing tube in arthropods.

Sternite a plate of CUTICLE covering the underside of an insect body SEGMENT.

Sting the modified OVIPOSITOR of aculeate Hymenoptera (wasps, ants and bees) which has lost its egg-laying function and is used to inject venom into insect prey or attacking predators.

Stridulation the making of a sound by rubbing two specialized body surfaces together, as in, eg, crickets and grasshoppers (Orthoptera).

Style a short antennal APPENDAGE found in some flies (Diptera).

Stylet any sharp, piercing, needle-like organ such as those that form the mouthparts of bugs, fleas and mosquitoes.

Subimago a stage in mayflies immediately before the adult (IMAGO) which is winged, capable of flight and resembles the adult except that it has a thin, dull skin covering the whole of the body and wings.

Subsocial of insect colonies in which adults share care for their larvae for at least some of the time.

"Superorganism" any highly social (EUSOCIAL) insect colony which has organizational features analogous to those of single organisms, eg workers corresponding to body tissue, exchange of food by TROPHALLAXIS corresponding to the circulatory system, and reproductive CASTES corresponding to the GONADS.

Superparasitism the parasitization of an already-parasitized host by an insect PARASITOID.

Symbiosis (adj. symbiotic) relationship between two organisms (eg an insect and a plant) whereby both derive benefit.

Tagmata (sing. tagma) body regions comprising a number of SEGMENTS, eg THORAX, ABDOMEN.

Tapetum a reflective layer of tracheae behind the retina of the eye.

Tarsus the series of small segments making up the last and 5th region of the leg of insects, the end bearing a pair of claws.

Temperate region the zones outside the subtropics and tropics which do not as a rule, have marked climatic extremes.

Teneral of adult insects immediately after emergence from PUPAL or final NYPHAL stage, when the CUTICLE is incompletely hardened and lacks final pigmentation.

Tergite a cuticular plate covering the dorsal surface of an insect body SEGMENT.

Thermoregulation the control of internal body temperature.

Thigmotaxis a locomotory response to being touched. In some insects this results in death-feigning.

Thorax (adj. thoracic) body region of an arthropod behind the head and in front of the ABDOMEN, in insects comprising three SEGMENTS; bears the locomotory APPENDAGES (legs, wings).

Tibia the 4th SEGMENT of an insect's leg, between FEMUR and TARSUS.

Trachea (adj. tracheal) a CUTICLE-lined tubule in uniramians and some arachnids, involved in gas exchange; tracheae open to the exterior via SPIRACLES, and end internally in blind-ending TRACHEOLES.

Triungulin minute, long-legged parasitic larvae of oil beetles (Meloidae) which hatch

from eggs laid in flowers and attach themselves to the bodies of visiting bees. The bees carry them to their nests, when the larvae feed on the egg before eating the stored pollen. Triungulin larvae are also found in Strepsiptera.

Trochanter a short segment of an insect's leg between the COXA and the FEMUR.

Trophallaxis the mouth-to mouth exchange of liquid food between members of a SOCIAL insect colony.

Tropics the hot climatic zones centered on the Equator and lying between the tropics of Cancer and Capricorn.

Tubercle a small raised area of the CUTICLE.

Tymbal the sound-producing membrane of a cicada.

Uniramian concerning, or a member of, the phylum Uniramia, arthropods comprising the superclasses HEXAPODA and MYRIAPODA.

Urticating hairs detachable hairs containing irritant substances produced by some spiders and caterpillars and which penetrate a predator's skin causing local irritation.

Vector an insect which transmits a disease organism from one host to another.

Venation the pattern of veins in an insect's wing.

Venom a poison produced by arthropods such as spiders and Hymenoptera, which is injected into prey or enemies.

Ventral situated at, or related to, the lower side or surface.

Viviparous giving birth to live young.

Warning coloration conspicuous color patterns found in animals protected by foul-tasting, -smelling or poisonous chemicals, or a sting, which predators learn to associate with an unpleasant experience and so avoid.

Worker a sterile, non-reproductive member of a SOCIAL insect colony responsible for brood care, nest construction and maintenance, defense and foraging. Termite workers can be male or female, but Hymenopteran workers are always female.

Xylem sap the watery sap found in the woody, xylem-conducting vessels which transport water to the leaves.

Zöonosis a phenomenon where an insect-transmitted disease of an animal species enters a human population.

INDEX

Picture Acknowledgments

Key *t* top, *b* bottom, *c* center, *l* left, *r* right.

Abbreviations ANT Australasian Nature Transparencies. CAH C. A. Henley. NHPA Natural History Photographic Agency. NSP Natural Science Photos. OSF Oxford Scientific Films. P Premaphotos Wildlife/K. Preston Mafham. PEP Planet Earth Pictures/Seaphot.

Cover Bruce Coleman Ltd/Anthony Healy. 1 P. 2–3 P. 4–5 Bruce Coleman Ltd/Frans Lanting. 6–7 P. 8–9 P. 10t P. 10b OSF/J. Cooke. 11 CAH. 12, 13, 16–17, 18 P. 19 CAH. 21 NHPA/S. Dalton. 22, 23 CAH. 24. 24–25 P. 25t CAH. 26–27 NHPA/S. Dalton. 28–29 NHPA/A. Bannister. 29 Dr. J. C. Dickens. 30 P. 31 OSF/G. Bernard. 32 P. 33, 34 OSF/G. Bernard. 35, 36–37, 41 P. 42–43 Mark Collins. 44–45, 45b, 46–47 P. 48 OSF/J. Cooke. 48–49, 51 P. 54 ANT. 55t NHPA/S. Dalton. 55b CAH. 56 OSF/G. Bernard. 57, 59 P. 61t Biophoto Associates. 61b R. Robinson. 64, 64–65 CAH. 67, 68–69 P. 70–71 OSF/R. Packwood. 71t P. 74b T. Eisner & D. Aneshansley. 77, 78–79, 80, 81, 82–83 P. 83t OSF/G. Thompson. 83b OSF/G. Bernard. 84, 85 P. 87 OSF/G. Bernard. 89, 90–91, 91t 94, 95 P. 97t CAH. 97b P. 98 NHPA/G. Bernard. 98–99 OSF/T. Shepherd. 99b OSF/J. Cooke. 100b P. 100–101 OSF/G. Bernard. 102 NHPA/S. Dalton. 103, 104 P. 105 NHPA/A. Bannister. 108, 108–109, 110, 111, 112–113, 114, 114–115, 115, 116–117, 116, 117, 118, 119, 120, 120–121, 122, 122–123, 128–129, 131, 132 P. 134–135 OSF/S. Dalton. 135t PEP/J. M. King. 136–137, 138, 138–139, 141l P. 141r NSP/J. A. Grant. 143 CAH. 146, 147, 148 P. 149 NHPA/A. Bannister. 150, 150–151 P. Hillyard.

Artwork

Abbreviations SD Simon Driver. RL Richard Lewington.

13, 14, 15, 17 SD. 18, 19, 20 RL. 23, 27, 29 SD. 30, 32, 33, 34, 38, 39, 40, 42 RL. 44 SD. 46, 48 RL. 49 SD. 50, 52, 53, 56, 58, 60, 62, 63, 65, 66 RL. 67 SD. 70, 72, 73, 74, 75, 80, 84, 86 RL. 87 SD. 88 RL. 91 SD. 92, 93, 98, 100, 102, 106, 107, 118, 124, 125, 126, 127, 130, 138, 140, 142, 144, 145, 151 RL.